KEEPERS OF THE LIGHTS

LIGHTHOUSE KEEPERS & THEIR FAMILIES
DOOR COUNTY, WISCONSIN — 1837–1939

by

Steven Karges

Wm Caxton Ltd
Ellison Bay, Wisconsin
2000

Published by:

Wm Caxton Ltd
12037 Highway 42, Box 220
Ellison Bay, WI 54210

(920) 854-2955

Printed in the United States of America.

10 9 8 7 6 5 4 3 2 1

ISBN# 0-940473-39-9 (paperback original)

This book is set in a version of Palatino type chosen for its readability and attractiveness; it is printed on acid-neutral paper bound in sewn signatures and is intended to provide a very long useful life.

COVER PHOTO — The Dunlap Reef rear range light, 1914. The view is looking south toward the old Sturgeon Bay railroad bridge. This structure, without the light tower, still exists as a private home located at 411 South 4th Avenue in Sturgeon Bay. Dunlap reef is now marked only by buoys. Photo courtesy of the Milwaukee Public Library/Wisconsin Historical Society.

Table of Contents

List of Illustrations

Preface

Door County is the northern end of Wisconsin's thumb peninsula. It separates the waters of Green Bay from those of Lake Michigan, and with its rocky headlands on the west coast and sandy beaches on the east, it is well known as one of Wisconsin's most picturesque and beautiful areas. Each year, the visits of thousands of tourists testify to the area's attractiveness.

As a boy I often made trips to Door County from Oshkosh, where my dad was chairman of the geology department at what is now UW-Oshkosh. Among the reasons we went was to visit our neighbors the Jameses; he was chairman of the English department, and they had a cottage which probably originally had been the barn at the Eagle Bluff Lighthouse. I wish I could say my interest in Door County lighthouses stems from seeing the Eagle Bluff Light on these visits, but all I can remember is being with the Jameses, though I could hardly have missed seeing the lighthouse. On our visits, we often took the ferry from Gills Rock to Washington Island, and I remember being intrigued by the Coast Guard station on the east side of Plum Island and the lighthouse and dwelling on the west. How I longed to be able to actually visit these buildings.

After graduating from Wisconsin State University Oshkosh and receiving my Ph.D. in history from the University of Wisconsin, I began my teaching career at WSU Whitewater. I continued to visit Door County, and I met and married a fellow graduate student who shared my love for Door County. After buying property near Baileys Harbor, we subscribed to the *Door County Advocate* to help us keep track of what was going on in the county. One day I noticed an article reporting that the Door County Historical Society was soliciting proposals for a history of Door County lighthouses. I was looking for a research topic, and the request seemed like serendipity — it might allow me to combine my love of Door County, my training as a historian, and my nascent interest in lighthouses — and it might even give me a chance to visit those intriguing buildings on Plum Island. Fortunately the society liked my proposal and gave me a small grant to get started. I warned them that the job I wanted to do would take several years, but I did not envision it taking as long as it has.

Door County originally had thirteen separate light stations, though the Sturgeon Bay Canal Light and North Pierhead Light eventually were combined, and several were abandoned. In discussing the lights, I have organized them into four geographic groups, rather than treating them chronologically.

The northern group includes: Pottowatomie Light on Rock Island, the first and oldest light located on the northernmost point of Door County; the Plum Island Lights; the original Porte des Morts Light (on Plum Island); the Plum Island Range Lights; and the Pilot Island Light.

To the south, the old Baileys Harbor Lighthouse; the Baileys Harbor Range Lights; and Cana Island Light form a second group.

Across the peninsula the Eagle Bluff Light and Chambers Island Light form a third group.

The lights in the Sturgeon Bay area make a fourth group. They include: the North Pierhead Light, Sturgeon Bay Canal Light, Dunlap Reef Range Lights, and the Sherwood Point Light.

The historical society wanted to emphasize the human elements of Door County lighthouses — the keepers and their families and what life was like at the lighthouses — and that is the primary focus of this book. The life of lighthouse keepers and their families changed a good deal over the years from 1838 when Pottowatomie Light first went into service until 1939 when the Coast Guard absorbed the Lighthouse Bureau and gradually replaced the civilian keepers. I have continued the story until the present, but I have only written about civilian keepers and their families, since the Coast Guardsmen were usually at the lights for short periods of time, and, by 1983, all the stations had been automated. Also, vast social and economic changes overtook Door County during the 145 years of civilian operation, but the elemental forces of wind and wave remained, and the lights continued to shine out across the waters to guide mariners plying the waters around Door County.

Today all the civilian lighthouse keepers of Door County are long dead. Only their children, nieces, nephews, and grandchildren still remember when keepers climbed the stairs to light the lamps or lit the fires under the steam-powered fog signals. The surviving relatives all agree that while there was danger and hardship, more for some than others, life at the lighthouses was good. Much of the history of that way of life already has been lost, but, even at this late date, a good deal can still be preserved. It is to that end — the telling of the lives of the Door County lighthouse keepers — that this book is directed.

Besides getting to know the keepers and their families, I also met and was befriended by many people who were interested in the project. Many helped me in my research and writing, and I would especially like to mention and thank Marge Anderson, Marion Augustine, Peg Foster, Louie and Rosie Janda, Ruth Scholz, Orv Schopf, Dick and Lucile Kostka, Charlie Voight and his family, Dan Larson, George Evenson, and the Door County Historical Society. I also want especially to thank my wonderfully supportive and professional editor, Caroll Heideman. Thanks also to Bruce and Barb and Mike and Janet who helped me more than they know. Lastly I want to thank my wife, Lynn, and daughter, Kimberly, who put up with me, went with me, and encouraged me, especially when the going was rough.

The Lighthouses & Range Lights of Door County Wisconsin

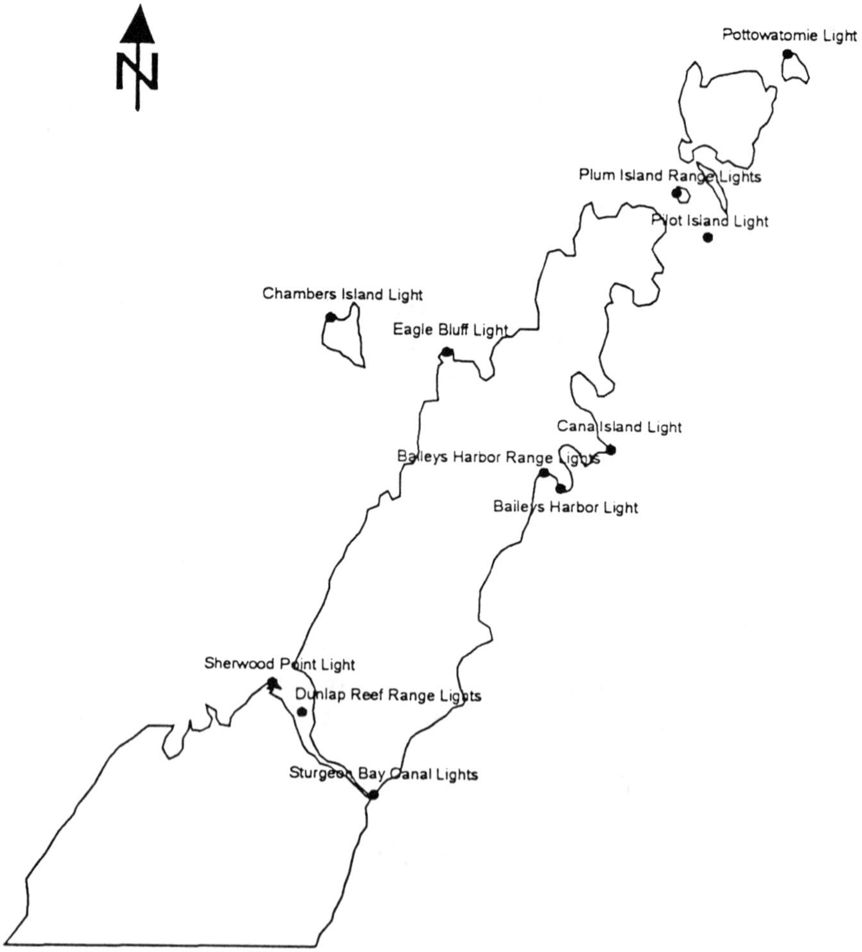

Chapter 1
Door County Lighthouse Keepers

Lighthouses have existed as long as sailors have put out to sea and needed assistance in returning to port. History chronicles the existence of lighthouses from the time of ancient Egyptians. Early in our country's history, the colonists erected lighthouses. One of the first bills passed by the new United States Congress in 1789 made the existing colonial lighthouses the responsibility of the national government. Since that time lighthouse keepers have been government employees. The Secretary of the Treasury and the Commissioner of Revenue supervised lighthouse operations until 1820, when the responsibilities were delegated to the Fifth Auditor of the Treasury, Stephen Pleasanton. In addition to being responsible for the books of several federal agencies, he became "General Superintendent of Lights." His auditing skills may have been superb, but most agree that his lack of engineering or maritime experience was a serious handicap to his administration of the country's lighthouses. Pleasanton's greatest failure was his refusal to adopt the Fresnel lens during his thirty-two year tenure.

As is often the case in situations like this, Pleasanton's resistance to the Fresnel lens was based on less than objective grounds. It had long been understood that the light at a lighthouse should be elevated, but the source of light was a problem. Many arrangements were tried, but the first important modern advance was a lamp that had a hollow wick, invented by a Frenchman named Ami Argand in 1781. The hollow wick allowed oxygen to pass through the wick as well as around it, and produced a light of seven candlepower with little or no smoke. In the United States, Captain Winslow Lewis combined the Argand lamp with multiple parabolic reflectors to produce a stronger, more visible light; he patented the system in 1810 and sold it to the government in 1812. Pleasanton became friends with Lewis and relied heavily on him for technical advice.

Since Lewis already owned the equipment necessary to manufacture his lighting system, he became the supplier of lighting equipment for virtually all American lighthouses after 1812. In 1836 the contract for the lighting apparatus at Pottowatomie Light, Door County's first light, called specifically for a light of this design containing eleven lamps and reflectors. The original Porte des Morts Light on Plum Island had a similar light source. However, the system had major defects — the parabolic mirrors rarely were truly parabolic even when new, and the silver coating on the reflectors lasted only a few months because of the abrasive cleanser the keepers were instructed to use.

In 1822, a French physicist named Augustin Jean Fresnel developed an entirely new and vastly superior lighthouse lens. Shaped like a hollow beehive, a Fresnel lens has a series of glass prisms held in a brass frame. A central prism surrounds the light source and refracts or magnifies the light. Prisms above and below the central prism, reflect and refract the light to produce a single beam of light. This allowed a single lamp to produce a much more powerful light while using much less fuel than other lighthouse lens arrangements. Fresnel lens are classified into seven orders depending on the focal length, the distance from the center of the light to the inner surface of the central prism. Since there was just one lamp in the lens, keepers had a much easier time with their operation and maintenance. Another advantage to the system is that it easily can be altered to create different light patterns that can serve to identify a particular lighthouse — a light's characteristic. However, while the Fresnel lens was quickly adopted in Europe, Pleasanton stubbornly refused to admit that it was superior to his friend's device.

Complaints about Pleasanton's lighthouse administration caused Congress to investigate the situation. The investigators reported that the Fresnel lens should be introduced as soon as possible and that the administration should be reorganized completely, with technically qualified inspectors rather than private contractors placed in charge of the previously established lighthouse districts. They also recommended creation of a nine-member Lighthouse Board to manage the entire system. Congress approved the investigators' recommendations and created the Lighthouse Board in 1852.

The Lighthouse Board was distinctly military in nature, having two high-ranking naval officers, one officer from the Army Corps of Engineers, one officer of the Army Corps of Topographical Engineers, two distinguished civilian scientists, and the Secretary of the Treasury, as well as a naval officer and an army officer to serve as secretaries. By the 1860s the usual practice was to have a navy officer in the post of inspector and an army officer as engineer in each lighthouse district. At least once a year (and often more frequently) the inspector made an official inspection of each lighthouse station.

Congress eliminated the nine-member Lighthouse Board in 1910 and replaced it with the Bureau of Lighthouses, which became part of the Department of Commerce, and military control of the system was replaced by a civilian Commissioner of Lighthouses. George R. Putnam, a civil engineer and civil servant with a distinguished record, was commissioner for twenty-five years. Shortly after he left the commissioner's position, President Franklin D. Roosevelt's Presidential Reorganization Act of 1939 abolished the Bureau of Lighthouses and the Lighthouse Service was transferred to the U.S. Coast Guard in the Treasury Department, where it has remained, except during wartime, to the present.

One of the first tasks the Lighthouse Board undertook was to refit existing lights with Fresnel lenses and to install the lenses in all new lighthouses. The Pottowatomie and Port des Morts Lights soon had the new lenses and, where appropriate, all the rest of the Door County lights received Fresnel lenses as original equipment. New lamps replacing the Argand type also went into service with the new lenses. Although having various names, all the lamps had concentric wicks of various sizes.

Until the later 1850s they burned sperm whale oil, but its cost increased dramatically as sperm whales became nearly extinct. Several types of replacement oil were tried, and by the late 1860s lard oil had become the most common fuel. Finally, in 1877, the Board began to convert the lamps to mineral oil or kerosene which ignited at a lower temperature and burned cleaner than lard oil. At the same time, the authorities called for the building of brick oil houses at all lights as money became available. In the 1880s the incandescent oil vapor light — which generated a brighter light with no increase in fuel consumption — began to replace the older lamps. In the 1920s acetylene gas lamps began to be installed in lights that were being converted to unmanned operation.

Only two of the Door County lights were built during Pleasanton's reign; all the others were built during the Lighthouse Board era. The Board brought not only the Fresnel lens, but orderliness, stability, and professionalism to the lighthouse service during the course of its existence. Because so many of the Board members were engineers or scientists, the standards, research, and organization of the lighthouse service improved significantly. Lighthouse keepers were federal employees and the Pendleton Act creating the federal civil service became law in 1883, but lighthouse keepers were not placed in the Classified Civil Service until 1896, when President Cleveland's executive order included them.

Before this time, lighthouse appointments were highly political. The local congressman made a recommendation to the port collector in the area, who forwarded it to Washington for approval. The port collector's position also was a political appointment, and so he very rarely opposed a Congressman's recommendation, and Pleasanton and the Lighthouse Board almost always supported a collector's recommendation. Despite the political nature of the process, it worked very well in Door County, and there were no instances of scandal such as occurred in other parts of the country. Examination of the appointments indicates that there were two prime requisites for getting a lighthouse keeper's position: Being a veteran of the Revolutionary War, the War of 1812, the Mexican War, or the Civil War was almost always a requirement before 1896; and, since Door County was a GOP stronghold, membership in the Republican party apparently was also necessary. Having influential friends in the party certainly also helped. An exception to these generalizations sometimes occurred at stations having steam-powered fog signals where steam engineering experience might be crucial in the recommendation.

After receiving their initial appointments, Door County keepers usually remained as keepers for the rest of their working lives, often spending years at the same station. During the Lighthouse Board era an increasing number of men rose through the ranks from assistant to keeper which tended to create a career service. When transfers occurred, almost all the assistants and keepers moved around within Door County or the immediate area.

Beyond political affiliation and veteran status, the qualifications for appointment seem to have been minimal. Being able to read, write, and keep simple accounts and being handy enough to make minor repairs seem to have been the major factors. Under Pleasanton it appears that keepers received no training and virtually no written instructions detailing their duties. Each lighthouse was supposed to have an instruction sheet on the operation of the lighting system, but this often was missing. Not surprisingly, the Board was appalled by this situation and began developing written instructions for the keepers, sometimes down to the smallest detail. Soon there was a spate of publications including such titles as *United States Light-House Establishment Instructions to Light-Keepers and Masters of Light-House Vessels;*

Instructions and Directions for Management of Lenses, Lights and Beacons; and *Management of Lens Apparatus and Lamps* that spelled out the duties and responsibilities of keepers in great detail. Even if a person had no idea of how to polish lenses, trim wicks, or replace mantles, if he could read, there were step-by-step detailed instructions and ample illustrations in a publication to guide him successfully through the process. Little was left to chance and there were few opportunities for flexibility in the primary duty of the keeper — tending the light. For example, by 10 AM each day the lamp and lens had to be cleaned, polished, refueled, and everything put in readiness for the light to be lit at sunset. Keepers were expected to train their assistants to perform the various duties of the keeper, especially that of tending the light itself, so if something went wrong during the assistant's watch, he would not have to disturb the keeper.

During the day, after readying the lighting apparatus, there were a number of other duties as well. Keepers were required to keep a log book in which they recorded weather observations, repairs, visitors, personnel issues, inspector's visits, and hours or minutes of fog signal operation and fuel consumption. While they were cautioned to keep personal comments out of the log, this was very hard for some of them to do. Keepers also had to prepare and send in monthly, quarterly, and annual reports, submit supply requisitions, and prepare lists of damaged or worn out equipment that needed replacement. Lighthouse Board inspectors were meticulous in their examination of the books and logs.

In addition to the daily routine governed by the tending of the light itself, keepers also followed a seasonal rhythm that varied little from station to station. Ordinarily, lights in Door County opened when the ice went out from the harbors, bays, and passages and lake and navigation resumed. Conversely, the keepers closed their lights in winter when the formation of ice ended navigation. This meant that the weather rather than arbitrary dates on a calendar determined when the keepers exhibited their lights, though this changed with the advent of more powerful, steel-hulled ships, and today the Coast Guard determines the navigational season.

Keepers usually arrived at their posts before navigation opened, spending their time cleaning and preparing to exhibit their lights. At stations with steam fog signals, they had to make sure the machinery was reassembled, painted, polished, and lubricated and the pipes and boilers filled with water. They cleaned the grounds and collected any driftwood from the beaches; the larger pieces were cut up for fuel and the smaller ones burned. Most keepers planted vegetable gardens, and many landscaped their grounds with flowers and shrubs. They took down storm windows and put up screens, repaired winter damage to docks and buildings, and got their boats ready for the season ahead.

For most keepers summer was a time to paint the station's buildings inside and out, including the inside of the lantern house and the brick oil houses. The Board supplied in paint in seemingly endless quantity. Fences received a coat of whitewash, and floors and woodwork were sanded and varnished. Some keepers even painted the roofs of the buildings. Cutting, splitting, and piling wood for fuel was an ongoing chore, and cutting the grass was another regular job.

Autumn and the approach of winter meant the final harvest from their gardens, replacing screens with storm windows, making sure there was enough wood piled near the dwelling, and generally preparing for the cold weather to come. As the days got shorter and ice began to form on the water, they began preparations for actually closing the station. After shuttering their dwellings, many keepers and their families went on trips or moved to Washington Island or Sturgeon Bay. They returned to their stations in spring to begin the cycle again.

Obviously the keepers lived very close to nature and in harmony with it. Just as fishermen could tell from the winds and clouds whether to go fishing, keepers were expert judges of the weather. They were also skillful boatmen who confidently set sail in conditions that today would keep most sailors in port.

Keepers were a close-knit group who knew from experience that they could count on one another. Many were brothers or related through marriage; most keepers were married, and their wives often served as official or unofficial assistants. Wives and children were expected to help to keep the station spotless, for before the arrival of telephones, the inspector might show up without notice.

Inspectors often had fearsome reputations. The wife of one assistant on Pilot Island reportedly always ran off and hid among the rocks at the north end of the island whenever an inspector visited. One inspector told a keeper that given the choice between having a tidy keeper with an untidy wife or a less-than-orderly keeper with an orderly wife, he would choose the latter couple because she would nag her husband into keeping the station spotless. There was friendly but earnest competition among the keepers to have the best-appearing station, especially in later years when inspectors awarded flags, stars, certificates, or other symbols to the top-rated keepers.

Fortunately most of the keepers were friendly, social individuals. This was especially crucial at stations where several families might share a dwelling. Friends from the area or keepers from other lighthouses often stopped for a visit. Then as now, lighthouses seemed to attract visitors. Well before the turn of the 20th century, Door County had already become a popular tourist destination. Most keepers faithfully recorded in their logs the names and home towns of visitors from near and far. During the day, the keepers always seemed able to find time to show their visitors around the station, often taking them up in the towers and sometimes, under close supervision, even into the lantern rooms. Keepers' wives more often than not provided refreshments for visitors.

At stations with fixed lights and no fog signals, keepers generally had no assistants. This meant that several times during the night the keeper would have to wake up to check that the lamp was operating properly. If the wind changed direction or speed, the ventilators in the lantern might have to be adjusted; impurities in the fuel might cause problems, or (in rare instances) the fuel reservoir might run dry. Any of these incidents would require immediate action by the keepers. Some keepers had alarm clocks to awaken them, but many were so attuned to the operation of their lights that they would wake from a sound sleep if something happened and their light needed attention. Except for Sherwood Point (at least at first), stations with steam-powered fog signals or lights with flashing characteristics and clockwork mechanisms had one or more assistants. At those stations the keepers kept watches of four or six hours when the light was operating. However, if it got foggy in the night and they had to operate the fog signal, all the keepers might be awake.

During the day, once their general lighthouse duties were fulfilled, keepers were free to do whatever they wanted. At island stations, keepers often went ashore or to Washington Island several times a week for groceries, supplies, mail, or simply to visit friends and relatives. At land-based stations keepers went to the nearby towns for the same reasons. Keepers could have other jobs as long as they did not interfere with tending their light. Several keepers were fishermen in their spare time; one was a well-known boat builder; another raised horses; and one owned and operated a dance hall.

Lighthouse duty is sometimes described as lonely or monotonous, but while these words may have applied to some stations, they do not adequately describe the life of the Door County keepers. Even the stations on islands were close to settlements, and there was a good deal of visiting and being visited. Indeed, the keepers were probably a good deal less lonely than many of the pioneer farmers in the county who had to travel for miles on poor roads to get to town. For many years, travel by boat (or by sleigh in the winter) was much easier for the keepers than travel by road, and there was always enough activity at the stations to keep life from becoming monotonous.

For the most part, lighthouse keepers in Door County enjoyed a good life. They lived in sturdy, multistoried homes, while many farmers and some villagers lived in small log cabins or shanties. Fish and game were plentiful, and many keepers cultivated vegetable gardens and fruit trees and kept cows, pigs, and chickens for the family table. As long as they performed their responsibilities, keepers enjoyed secure federal government positions that were largely unaffected by changes in the economy, though as time went on, their pay did not keep up with pay in the private sector. Since they were not at first part of any government pension system, many of the early keepers worked until they could no longer manage their duties, and one of the problems the Lighthouse Board faced (mostly without success) was what to do with its aging work force. In 1918, Congress finally established a program under which keepers could retire at age 65 with thirty years of service, and with compulsory retirement at 70. Retirees could receive up to three-quarters of their annual salary.

All of the lighthouse keepers of Door County are dead, but beams of light still shine out from the stations that they so faithfully tended.

Chapter 2
Pottowatomie Light — Rock Island

Virtually all visitors to Rock Island land at the dock in front of Chester Thordarson's great hall and boathouse. As they spread out to explore the island, those interested in seeing the lighthouse strike off to the north, following a trail that well may have been cut by the first keeper. The path climbs and descends gradually, rising from lake level to some 150 feet above the lake when the hikers emerge from the forest into the clearing around the lighthouse. Today the painstakingly cleared opening is only a fraction of its original size, and the gardens, hay field and barn have been replaced by trees. While the lantern is gone from the tower, the visitors can look out across the Rock Island Passage to St. Martin Island to the north just as the keepers did as they tended the light. The history of the area, however, begins long before the history of this lighthouse that stands high atop the bluff overlooking the passage.

Four hundred years ago this part of Wisconsin was a land of forests, islands, lakes, bays, and inlets populated by various Native American nations, including the Pottowatomie, Chippewa, Menominee, Fox, and Winnebago. In 1634–35, the Frenchman Jean Nicolet visited the area, and historians surmise from his journals that he found members of the Pottowatomie nation living on Rock Island and the mainland to the south, the area we know today as the Door County peninsula. Nicolet apparently spent some time with the Pottowatomie, but whether he actually set foot on Rock Island as he coasted along the east shore of Green Bay cannot be determined with certainty. Other Frenchmen followed Nicolet including Radisson, Grosseillier, Marquette and Joliet, and La Salle.

The French were interested both in the Native Americans' furs and in their souls. In 1669, Jesuits established the St. Francois Xavier mission upstream from the mouth of the Fox River near the present city of De Pere. In 1717, the French erected Fort La Baye closer to the mouth of the Fox. The route from Mackinac Island to Green Bay, up the Fox, and down the Wisconsin to the Mississippi gave the French fur traders access to a vast, valuable furbearing region, though Rock Island itself played a passive role in the development of this trade. Individual parties may have camped on Rock Island, but no missions, forts, or trading posts were established there.

French control of the region ended in 1763 at the conclusion of the French and Indian War; as part of the settlement, England took control of France's North American empire. Thus, under the 1783 Peace of Paris, the United States not only gained her independence, but also acquired the territory east of the Mississippi and south of the Great Lakes. However, the British withdrew from the area only after the conclusion of the War of 1812. To control access to the Northwest Territory, the Army Department built a series of forts at strategic locations, including one named Fort Howard near the mouth of the Fox River and on its west bank. The village of Green Bay soon developed on the river's east bank and quickly grew into a thriving community. Green Bay became the county seat and was also the site of the district land office; it was across the river from a military post and an Indian agency; it was the only Lake Michigan port in the region; and it was the starting point of various military and civilian roads and trails that led off into the interior. In 1820, Green Bay and Prairie du Chien were Wisconsin's only important population centers, and already a pioneer steamship had visited Green Bay.

With the completion of the Erie Canal in 1825, commerce on the Great Lakes grew rapidly. As the fur trade declined in the face of advancing settlement, the fishing industry in the upper Great Lakes began to expand. Sailing vessels soon were making regular trips carrying lake trout and whitefish to Buffalo, New York. If Rock Island had played a passive role in the fur trade, she played

Pottowatomie Light, Rock Island, 1940. Photo courtesy of US Coast Guard.

an active role in the fishing industry. In 1831, the Menominee Indians ceded to the United States a large part of eastern Wisconsin, including all of what would become Door County. In the spring of 1834, surveyors marked township lines on the mainland. The following year, they completed their survey of Washington Island and Rock Island, and settlers could begin buying the land.

The dangers involved in navigating the entrance to Green Bay from Lake Michigan were clearly indicated in early 1832 when thirty Detroit merchants, masters, and owners of vessels petitioned Congress to build a lighthouse on Rock Island, then the entrance to Green Bay:

> . . . the interests of their commerce and navigation on these waters require the erection of a light house on 'Isle Pou' or 'Pottowatomie,' situated at the entrance of Green Bay in Lake Michigan. The ship channel in entering the Bay is on the North side of this island and is about one mile in breadth, the approach to which is rendered hazardous in dark nights in consequence of two extensive shoals, . . . There is no point on the Northern Lakes, where in the opinion of your Memorialists, a light house is more imperiously required than at this. The Island is a high rocky Bluff at least Sixty feet above the surface of the lake, where a tower of forty feet in height would give the light sufficient elevation.
>
> Your Memorialists feel that the increasing commerce on the Northern Lakes will justify them in an earnest appeal to the liberality of Congress of an appropriation.[1]

The petition was referred to the House Committee on Commerce, and the committee chair subsequently introduced a bill providing for construction of a lighthouse on Pottowatomie Island, but the House failed to approve the bill. Two years later on 30 June 1834, however, a similar bill became law and $5,000 was appropriated for building the lighthouse. In May 1836, Congress appropriated another $3,000, and in March 1837, Congress provided an additional $5,000. Why the 1837 appropriation was necessary is not clear, since the actual cost of the project was only $5,789, and the remaining $7,211 was returned to the surplus fund.[2]

In the 1830s, fishermen working west from Mackinac began setting their nets in the waters around Rock Island. In the middle of the decade, the first of these fishermen actually took up residence there, rather than just camping on the east side of the island; by 1840 there were at least seven people residing at the south end of the island. During the next few years, Rock Island's population grew. These residents were primarily interested in fishing rather than farming, though they planted small garden plots and a few fruit trees. However, a number of circumstances — among them the lack of a good harbor, an increase in the size of the fishing boats, and a change from sail to steam engines — caused the population to dwindle. By 1870 Rock Island had declined into a relatively unimportant, largely deserted island with only the lighthouse keepers remaining.

In August 1834, Reverend Jackson Kemper, an Episcopal minister who was making a trip to inspect church missions in the Northwest, boarded a boat in Green Bay. Also on board was Abraham Wendell, collector of customs at Mackinac. Two people with prominent positions in Wisconsin history — Judge James Doty and Hercules Dousman, son of the wealthy Michael Dousman of Mackinac — were among the group that saw Kemper off. Kemper recorded in his journal that the captain sailed along the Door

County shore line, passed north of Washington Island, and then anchored off the northwest corner of Rock Island.

> When at Pottowatomie or Louse island the Capt. took the Collector [Abraham Wendell] ashore to fix upon a site for a light house the Gov. has ordered built.

When the party landed they found that there was a shelf only two or three feet wide at the foot of a perpendicular cliff. There were occasional ravines, but they were too steep to climb according to Kemper. The group then coasted along the west shore in their small boat, but they concluded that further exploration would take too much time and so returned to their vessel and continued on their journey.[3] Wendell apparently never actually set foot on the site he selected for Pottowatomie Light.

Having selected the location for the proposed lighthouse, Abraham Wendell next signed a contract with Michael Dousman on 2 April 1836, setting forth the details for the construction of a lighthouse tower and dwelling house on Rock Island. The tower was to be built from stone or hard brick laid in good lime mortar with a foundation three or more feet deep as necessary. The plans called for the tower to be thirty feet tall and eighteen feet in diameter at the base with walls three foot thick. At the top, it was supposed to taper to nine feet in diameter with walls twenty inches thick. On top of the tower a soapstone platform eleven feet in diameter and four inches thick with a scuttle door was to be placed. The tower was to have three windows and a circular stairway from the ground floor to within six feet of the platform. The last six feet were to have an iron ladder. On the platform was to be erected an eight-sided cast iron lantern surrounded by an iron railing and topped by a ventilated copper dome. When completed, the tower was to be plastered with roman cement and given two coats of whitewash. The lantern and tower woodwork were to receive two coats of white lead paint and the dome was to be painted black.

In addition, the contract called for construction from stone or brick of a dwelling house thirty-four feet by twenty feet, with a cellar and two upper chambers built under the sloping, shingled roof. The contract also specified construction of a kitchen fourteen feet by twelve feet to be attached to the house, as well as a brick outhouse four feet by five feet with a shingled roof. All work was to be finished by 1 October 1836, just six months later, and, upon completion of construction and approval by government officials, Dousman was to receive $5,000.[4]

Dousman was responsible only for building the tower, lantern, dwelling, and outhouse, and on 10 August 1836 Wendell contracted with John Scott of Detroit, Michigan, to provide the lighting apparatus. One month after the lighthouse was finished, Scott agreed to install a light of the Winslow Patent design containing eleven lamps and fourteen-inch reflectors, each to contain six ounces of pure silver. The contract also specified various accessory items to be provided, including two spare lamps, double tin oil butts sufficient to hold five hundred gallons of oil, and assorted tools. When Wendell or his agent agreed that the contract had been fulfilled, Scott was to receive $474.[5]

Dousman's crew cleared the lighthouse site and began quarrying rock for the dwelling and tower from a location south of the site. The men brought their supplies through the woods from an easier and more protected landing almost two miles to the south, rather than carrying them up the cliffs in front of the station. Since only the general site for the buildings was specified, the men themselves picked the actual location for the tower, which was located thirty feet north of the dwelling. For unknown reasons, Dousman did not meet his contract completion date. Not until 20

October 1837 did Joseph Hobbs, superintendent of the buildings at Pottowatomie Light, certify to Wendell

> that the material of which the lighthouse and dwelling are made, are of the best quality and that the work is done in a substantive and workmanlike manner.[6]

When Wendell received this statement, he paid Dousman and Scott. However, contrary to Hobbs' report, there were serious problems with the construction; in 1858, the original tower and dwelling were replaced by the present combined tower and dwelling.

The exact date upon which the Pottowatomie Light first shone out over the Rock Island passage to Green Bay is not recorded. On 8 September 1837, Levi Woodbury, Secretary of the Treasury, appointed John Wright of Detroit, Michigan, keeper of the light. However, Wright refused the appointment, and on 19 December 1837 (too late to begin operations in 1837), the secretary appointed David E. Corbin of Saginaw, Michigan as keeper. Corbin served as a sergeant in the regular United States Army during the War of 1812 and was wounded at the Battle of Plattsburg; he came west after the war to serve with the Fort Howard garrison. Upon leaving the army, Corbin worked for the American Fur Company at Green Bay, and he may have met Abraham Wendell while visiting the company's post at Mackinac. As part of his duties as port collector, Wendell was responsible for lighthouse keeper appointments, and presumably, he at least knew of Corbin. In return for tending the light, Corbin received an annual salary of $350, supplies, and a residence.[7]

Despite the survey which had been conducted of Door County, including Rock and Washington Islands, a good deal of confusion prevailed at first in regard to the exact location of the new lighthouse. When the area was opened to settlers eager to buy land, the land office commissioner at Green Bay, acting on his own initiative and on the basis of a verbal report, withdrew the presumed site of Pottowatomie Light from sale. Unfortunately, the land he set aside was on Washington Island, not Rock Island, and this led to claims that the light had been built on the wrong island. Not until 9 June 1840 was the matter straightened out, when President Van Buren reserved for the use of Pottowatomie Light:

> the fractional west half of lots No. 2 and 3 containing 109 acres of fract. Section 14 and the whole of fract. Section 15 containing 20 37/100 acres both situated on the North-West Cape of Rock Island in Township 34 R., 30 East of the 4th Prime Mer.[8]

In 1840, Corbin complained to his superiors that some of the plaster had fallen off in his dwelling and that the lighthouse needed whitewashing. Although less than four years old, there were indications that all was not well with the construction of the station. Two years later, inspector W.D. Wilson reported that the station was

> very badly constructed, the mortar used not having the proper admixture of lime, permitting the water to ooze through it much as to keep the tower generally very damp.

To remedy this situation, Wilson recommended that the buildings be painted with water cement and whitewashed. This suggestion apparently was not followed, since no action was taken. Corbin asked for new lamps for his light, but his lamps were in better shape than most that Wilson had seen on his inspection tour; Wilson only made a few repairs and gave Corbin some hints on burning the lamps. The station's supply of oil was sufficient for at least a year, but, because of his isolated location and the relative difficulty of landing at the station, Wilson left an additional year's oil supply with Corbin.

The keeper had already removed four to five acres of woods around the light, and Wilson suggested removal of an additional two or three acres to improve the light's visibility and usefulness. The inspector also noted that Corbin had opened a road two miles long from the light south to the lake, "the only accessible way to the light and which is highly necessary for public use." The path and stairs down the bluff in front of the station had not yet been built. For doing all this extra work, Corbin thought he should receive a small addition to his salary. Wilson agreed because it would allow Corbin "to place some additional comforts around him in his dreary and lonely home." Clearly the inspector felt this would be a good policy in order to keep Corbin at the station. Wilson felt Corbin was a man of considerable energy, the kind of person particularly well suited for Pottowatomie Light.[9]

John McReynolds, who replaced Wilson as inspector, visited Rock Island in 1845 and found Corbin to be well qualified, if lonely. According to McReynolds, Corbin's only companions were his favorite horse and faithful dog. The inspector granted Corbin a twenty-day leave of absence — the first time Corbin had the opportunity to leave the island for that long in eight years — on the condition that the keeper return with a wife(!) Corbin accepted the terms and left to take his leave. Interestingly, despite his predecessor's recommendations, McReynolds found everything at the station in good order with no repairs necessary. The inspector noted that Corbin had made his own road to the lake, and, since there was no well at the light, Corbin had to bring all his water and supplies over this road. According to McReynolds, given

> that from the isolated and lonely condition of this officer who is required to make his own road, is denied every enjoyment, and has no other food than

> that which he himself produces and who must attend to his duties in sickness or in health, he should have an addition of $50 to his present salary.[10]

But fifth auditor of the treasury Stephen Pleasanton, McReynold's superior, did not accept his inspector's recommendation.

The following year, McReynolds again found everything at the station in almost perfect order, with no repairs necessary. However, he also learned that Corbin had been unsuccessful in his quest for a "helpmate;" twenty days apparently was just too short a period of time to accomplish that goal, so Corbin was once again "doomed to solitude during another dreary winter" with only his pony and dog for companions.[11]

In 1847, the fountains of the old lamps had worn out, and McReynolds had a new set of lamps installed in the light. Once again McReynolds noted,

> He suffers from his solitary and isolated situation, being cut off entirely from his fellow man, except occasionally in summer. His personal supplies did not reach him till first of June 1847. During the winter he had to kill his favorite cow.[12]

The inspector again asked that Corbin's salary be raised to $400 per year due to his situation, but, as in the past, Pleasanton did not accept this recommendation. McReynolds overestimated Corbin's isolation in an effort to convince Pleasanton to grant the raise; in reality, Corbin and the fishermen and their families from the other side of Rock Island often spent time with each other.

It was about this time that Jack Arnold — an old friend and a sergeant and veteran of the War of 1812 — moved in with Corbin as an unpaid assistant. Unfortunately, Arnold fell sick in 1848 and died despite Corbin's devoted care. His body was taken the length of the island and buried in the cemetery near the fishermen's homes on Rock Island's east side.[13]

Corbin had the first and, for a long time, the only horse on Rock Island, an animal named Jock. Corbin often let other settlers use Jock to haul their stove wood, dock timbers, and other loads too heavy for manpower alone. With so many drivers, Jock got quite tricky and (some thought) lazy in his old age. One of his tricks was to make several half-hearted efforts at pulling a load and then finally to pull with all his might. One day a teamster using him to haul logs pretended to hitch Jock to the logs, but actually did not. Slapping the reins, Jock made two or three of his initial preparatory pulls without any progress and then gave an enormous tug. Much to the amusement of the teamster, Jock almost landed on his nose.[14]

Corbin used Jock to haul the island's first cook-stove from the landing to the station in 1850. The stove caused quite a stir, and most of the island's residents trekked up to the lighthouse to see Corbin's marvel. In fact, there may have been a good reason to make improvements in the kitchen. Corbin had been unsuccessful in persuading a woman to come to live with him earlier, but the 1850 US Census reveals that the lighthouse may have been crowded that year, for Catharine Storce and her three children were recorded as living at the station. Catharine was 30 years old, and she and her children were Wisconsin natives. In addition, there was also a 19-year-old laborer named William Kingsley listed at the lighthouse. Whether he was actually living there or just happened to be there when the census taker came was not revealed.[15]

The records show that the winter of 1851–52 was especially cold and long. Corbin's energy seemed to wane, and he asked John Boon, one of Rock Island's pioneer settlers, to care for his horse. When summer came, Corbin failed to revive. The fall was cold and windy, and despite all efforts, Corbin continued to fail. He died in December 1852 at the age of 57 and was buried in a small cemetery a few yards south of the lighthouse he had so faithfully tended.[16]

After Corbin's fifteen-year tenure, the residents must have felt that subsequent keepers were changed with bewildering speed. Mr. Cass served only from 1852 to 1853; Captain Allen was there from 1853 to 1855; and Joseph Le Cuyer kept the light from 1855 to 1857. On the latter's death, Mr. Simon Allaird became keeper.[17]

While Allaird was keeper in 1858, a major change occurred at Pottowatomie Light. That year, a Lighthouse Board crew razed the original tower and dwelling and constructed the lighthouse that still stands on the site. The 1886 Light List noted that the original buildings washed away, but it was hardly possible that waves destroyed them, since the structures were more than a hundred feet above lake level. In fact, some stones from the original buildings remained on the grounds for over thirty years before being thrown over the cliff in front of the light. What more likely happened was that dampness eroded the masonry. Until the 1850s, most lighthouse towers were single-walled and retained heat and cold which allowed moisture to attack the mortar. Inspector Wilson reported that the construction workers had used the wrong mortar mixture originally, one that was not particularly resistant to moisture. Presumably the mortar had deteriorated so badly that it became necessary to abandon the original structures and build a new lighthouse.

The work crew blasted out a basement in the limestone bedrock, and using local stone, built a two-story structure thirty-three feet by thirty-one feet, with the long side oriented approximately north and south. Later, a one-story wood frame addition seventeen feet by ten feet was attached to the southeast corner. The addition had a cistern under it and was used both as a summer kitchen and as a regular kitchen at various times. The main structure had four rooms and two closets on the first floor. A stairway connected the first floor to the second floor, which had four rooms, four small closets, and an upstairs hall and keeper's office. Which of the rooms were used as bedrooms and which as living rooms depended on the wishes of the keepers and their wives. Sometimes the keeper chose to live on the first floor; at other times he chose the second floor. The upstairs office contained stairs leading to the lantern, as well as a window from which the keeper, looking out over the passage, could make a record of the vessels sailing between Rock Island and St. Martin Island to the north. The stairs and office were built within the four corner supports of the square wooden tower in the front gable, which projected through the northern end of the roof. The tower had one landing and one window. A platform twelve feet square covered with sheet copper was placed on top of the tower. The platform held a nine-sided lantern made of cast iron and wood, with a sheet copper roof. It was forty-one feet five inches from the base of the tower to the center of the ventilator ball of the lantern. Inside the lantern, the district lampist installed a newly adopted 4th Order Fresnel lens built by L.S. Sautler and Company, Paris, France. The sperm whale oil lamp in the lens provided a light which was visible for fourteen nautical miles under optimum conditions. The lens had three clear panels and one silvered panel, so the arc of illumination was 270 degrees, and its characteristic was fixed white, since it did not revolve. The focal plane of the lens was 159 feet above lake level.[18]

Allaird had scarcely moved into the new lighthouse structure in February 1859, when Frank Sawyer replaced him. Sawyer, born in New York, was 34 years old and had served at lighthouses in Michigan. He and his wife Sarah and two children, Jane and Frank, lived in the new lighthouse until the Board removed him in August 1861. While the country's attention was occupied by the Civil War, Martin Trobee kept the light on Rock Island illuminated. Upon his resignation in May 1865, Abraham

Capers, a one-legged veteran from Maine, and his family moved into the lighthouse. In March 1866, the Lighthouse Board for the first time appointed an assistant keeper at Pottowatomie Light, and Abram Grover, another Maine veteran who had served in the cavalry, moved into the second floor of the lighthouse with his family. The reason for appointing an assistant keeper was the change in fuel from sperm whale oil to lard oil. The Board found that the decline in sperm whales had increased the cost of sperm oil too much, and they changed most lights to lard oil, which was cheaper but more difficult to burn.

The population of Rock Island had dwindled so much by this time that the island's school closed, but Mrs. Grover gave lessons in the lighthouse cellar. Among her students were the Knudsen boys who lived at the other end of the island; all of them would one day become lighthouse keepers. Capers was known for his gardening skills, especially for raising fine sweet corn and cabbages. He also kept two or three horses at the station. The inspector reported that the station was in good condition, although some plaster in the house needed repair as did the cistern.

At this time the Lighthouse Board increased keepers wages from $350, the original 1837 level, to $560 annually; wages for first assistants rose from $300 to $400. Despite the increase, Grover left his post and turned to fishing for two years before he and his family left Rock Island permanently. Mrs. Paulina Capers became her husband's acting assistant. In March 1870, William C. Betts, a Civil War veteran from New York, replaced Capers as keeper, and in May of that year, James Fuller, also a veteran from New York, replaced Mrs. Capers as assistant keeper.[19]

William Betts was born 22 March 1833 in Tonawanda, New York, the son of a veteran of the War of 1812 and a grandson of a military surgeon in the Revolutionary Army. When he was ten, his parents moved to Michigan, and in 1855 Betts moved to Wisconsin.

When the Civil War broke out, he enlisted in the 4th Wisconsin Volunteers in October 1861, serving first as an infantryman and later in the mounted infantry. He spent most of his career in the west fighting at Baton Rouge, New Orleans, Port Hudson, and Mobile; he reenlisted in 1864, and was discharged at Vicksburg in June 1865. On 22 March 1870, Betts received his appointment as keeper of Pottowatomie Light, a post that he held until he resigned 1 May 1886. In September 1872, seventeen months after he assumed his post, the 38-year-old bachelor keeper married 16-year-old Emily J. Rohn. The new Mrs. Betts was well acquainted with lighthouse activities and operations since her father, Victor Rohn, had been keeper of the Port des Morts Light Station on Pilot Island since 1866, and her mother was the assistant keeper. In 1874, William and Emily had the first of nine children. When James Fuller resigned as assistant in March 1872, Mrs. Betts, like her mother, became her husband's assistant.

The oldest surviving Pottowatomie Light keeper's log does begins on 2 August 1872. The keeper was to make a daily record of important events at the station, bad weather, and similar information, but at first Betts' logs record primarily incidents such as shipwrecks or severe storms with long gaps between events; the accounts are not all storms and ship wrecks, however. On 13 November 1874, Betts wrote:

> A story comes to us today of the loss of two fishermen. Their Boat Capsized yesterday during a snow squall. And sunk about four miles North West from here. One of the men leaves A family his name James Halley A native of Ireland, the other was a single man Born in this Vicinity. Name Henry Root.

Similarly, on 10 January 1876, Betts reported that the day before two men had left Detroit Harbor on Washington Island in a small boat to row to the mainland. Half an hour later a terrible storm came up. A day later the men had not returned home, and Betts felt there was no doubt that they had perished and been carried out into Lake Michigan in the ice. Two log entries later, on 3 May 1876, Betts wrote:

> The two men who were lost last January have been seen several times once from Caney [Cana] Lt. House and once from Jacksonport. The men were apparently frozen stiff and sitting upright in the boat among a mass of ice. . . . At last account they were still adrift. There is not much hope now that they will be found and buried.

In 1875, when the light house tender *Dahlia* made her annual visit to deliver supplies, the crewmen also unloaded materials for constructing a boathouse at the landing south of the light, for making minor repairs to the dwelling, and for building a wooden fence along the edge of the cliff north of the light. On August 1, a repair party arrived to do the work. Eleven days later they left without building the boathouse.

> The foreman thought he could not make one stand. He was drunk when he came here and went to Escanaba once and came back drunk again. When he was not drunk he seemed to spend most of his time finding fault with the men under him.

Betts was very disgusted with the foreman's treatment of his men and disappointed that the boathouse had not been built.

Standing on the platform atop the Pottowatomie Light tower looking northward toward St. Martin Island over the Rock Island passage, it is hard to imagine a storm like the one Betts witnessed on 1 December 1876. After a three-day northerly gale, the wind blew so strong

> that it carried water or spray onto the lantern which is 137 feet perpendicular elevation above the lake. Something that never happened before since I have been here.

Betts never mentioned such an event occurring again during his tenure as keeper. The waves generated by such a storm and the ice moving through the passage in the winter and spring were the major reasons that only a landing, but no boathouse or boatways were built at the foot of the bluff in front of the station.

The year 1876 was a presidential election year, and though Tilden won the popular vote, the situation in the electoral college was confused. Washington DC was a long way from Rock Island, but Betts stayed abreast of events in the capital. He was concerned also on December 13, several days after another serious storm, that no lights were visible in the lighthouses on Poverty Island to the northeast or Point Peninsula to the northwest. He noted in his log,

> It is something like the election returns, one day we hear that Tilden is elected and the next we are positively assured that Gov. Hays is the happy man. Now we do not know who will be our next President or what is the trouble with the Light-Houses at Point Peninsula or Poverty Island.

Betts started to keep a daily log on 26 July 1877; on that day, he reported that for the first time since he had become keeper the new lighthouse inspector had actually come to the station and personally inspected the station rather than sending the lampist to check things and report any problems. Betts was very impressed and pleased that the inspector had come personally. Apparently,

Captain Miller, the district inspector, instructed Betts to keep a daily log of the weather and any significant events rather than just a record of incidental occurrences. The entries from then on faithfully record when the keeper first exhibited the light in the spring, usually in mid-April or early May, and when the light was discontinued in the fall, usually in December. In between, Betts carefully logged his weather observations. During the winter when the light was dark, the Betts family moved from Rock Island back to their farm on Washington Island. Emily was certainly familiar with this routine as her family had made the same annual migration from Pilot Island to Washington Island. Until the stations were kept open year around, most of the Door County keepers either traveled during the winter or relocated to be closer to their family and friends. Usually this meant moving to Washington Island or to Sturgeon Bay. For keepers at isolated stations, the move also meant that the children could attend the local schools, though it was not uncommon for a keeper's wife to act as school teacher. For example, Mrs. Betts, assisted by her husband, taught the children during their months at the light.

The new Pottowatomie Light was much better built than the original one had been. Year after year, the Lighthouse Board's annual reports note that either very minor repairs or no repairs at all had been required. Betts, however, continued without results to send in requests for repairs. Finally, in June 1879, when the *Dahlia* delivered the annual supplies and Inspector Miller made his inspection, Betts got some action. In Betts' words, Miller

> is not well pleased in regard to the way the Engineer treats the repair reports from this station. The stairs up the bluff are in very dangerous condition and have been for some years. The Engineer treats my reports with dignified but silent contempt.

At Miller's direction, Mr. Taylor, the foremen, and four workmen arrived on September 5. They landed during a storm and had difficulty in getting their supplies ashore. Twenty-two days later the working party, who had lived and boarded at the lighthouse, finished their work. They built steps down the bluff and a platform for landing supplies at the base of the bluff, repaired the dwelling, and repainted all the outside work. According to Betts, "The house is now quite comfortable."

The Lighthouse Board ordered a significant change in the lighting apparatus at Pottowatomie Light in 1880. The district lampist removed the old lard-oil lamp and replaced it with a new 4th Order, one-wick lamp which burned mineral oil, more familiarly known as kerosene. Because it was more flammable, kerosene was much easier for the keeper to use than lard oil. No longer would Betts have to warm the lard oil and rush it up the tower to the lamp before it became too cold to burn well on freezing nights. Kerosene was also less prone to smoking the lantern, which meant that far less time had to be spent in the arduous task of cleaning the entire lantern, and Betts felt it provided a more brilliant light. The old lard-oil lamp fixtures were stored in the cellar for three years before being taken back to the lighthouse depot. The Board was well aware of the hazards posed by storing kerosene inside the lighthouse and recommended that separate, flameproof oil houses be built at all stations for oil storage purposes. However, a lack of funds to do such construction was a serious problem. Fortunately, no serious fires occurred, because it was not until 1904 that Pottowatomie Light got a separate, brick oil house.

On 27 June 1880, three days after the new mineral oil lamp was installed, Betts learned of a shocking event that had occurred the week before at Pilot Island:

> The second assistant John Boyce cut his throat with a razor and was found dead in half an hour from

> the time he was last seen alive. No cause for the deed is known and unless he was partly deranged there was no apparent cause.

According to Betts,

> He was a noble hearted man. Kind to all and had many friends in this vicinity. May God forgive him. Grace be to his ashes.

Because Betts went to Washington Island for supplies, mail, and newspapers at least once a week, and often times more, he kept remarkably up to date on national events, despite the isolation of Rock Island. He had some strong opinions, as shown in his log entry for 30 June 1882; after writing that it had rained all night and all day with fog, but not much wind, he wrote:

> I suppose that cowardly Gitteau President Garfield's assassin has payed the penalty of his detestable crime today and it is just the right kind of a day to hang him — dark gloomy and uncomfortable. If we have another President assassinated, I hope the assassin will be crucified.

By 1880, the only people who spent most of the year on Rock Island were members of the Betts family. Washington Island had better harbors, greater opportunities, and more fertile farm land, and the change from sail to powered fishing boats which could travel further and faster, had left Rock Island virtually deserted. However, Betts sailed or rowed to Jackson Harbor or to the busier Washington Harbor once or twice a week for supplies and mail. Thus, while the family was on an island, they were probably no more isolated than many pioneer farm families living in Door County. In addition, there was a great deal of work to do every day at the station. After the light was extinguished in the morning, the apparatus had to be inspected, cleaned, fueled, and got ready to be lighted in the evening before sundown. Water no longer had to be carried from the landing as Corbin had done, but it did have to be brought up 154 steps from the lake. Betts raised horses for sale, and they had to be cared for each day. After the children were born, Betts brought a cow to the island. The garden had to be tended; there was always maintenance to be done on the boats; there was wood to be sawed and split for the kitchen stove and for the fireplaces in cool weather. While Betts was keeper, he was not responsible for painting and other maintenance, though those duties later became the keeper's responsibility as the Board sought ways to economize.

Betts received a nasty shock in September 1882 when the Lighthouse Board notified A.W. Hall, collector of customs and superintendent of lights for the district, that because Congress had made a severe cut in the appropriation for the fiscal year, it was necessary to abolish the position of assistant keeper at stations that could be maintained with a keeper only. Stations included in the reduction were the Pottowatomie and Cana Island lights. Under the headline "Penny Wise and Pound Foolish," the *Door County Advocate* reprinted an article from the *Milwaukee Republican-Sentinel* which ended,

> This is a pretty state of affairs, to say the least. The next thing we know the keepers will be discharged and the lights discontinued altogether. Such contemptible meanness is without a parallel in the annals of this great nation.[20]

Betts received the reduction notice on September 28. Full of anger, he uncharacteristically let his feelings about his employers show in his log:

> We got notice yesterday that Assistant Keepers services were no longer required. Our government is getting careful now. If it had looked after the Star Route thieves as sharp as it does Light Keepers it would be able to pay the Assistant Keepers yet.

And he was still angry the next day:

> I hope the National debt will now be paid. There is no longer any reason why it should not be, since the Govt. paper about assistant Light Keepers.

News of the reduction traveled quickly throughout Door County. On September 29, the day after Betts learned that his wife's job was abolished, Robert Severs, the Washington Island correspondent for the *Door County Advocate,* wrote to the paper blasting the Lighthouse Board's action. The biggest reason for Betts' anger probably was not the impact on his workload, for his wife continued to assist him, title or not, but the impact on the family income which went from $960 a year to $560. There were six members in his family now, so his heated reaction to the news is perhaps not surprising.

It was no longer necessary to carry water from the landing located south of the lighthouse, but a supply of water remained a particular concern for the family. They relied on water channeled from the roof to a cistern, as well as on water carried in buckets up the steps from Lake Michigan. In late October 1881, Lighthouse Foreman Dabson and six men arrived to make repairs at the station, to build a new woodshed, and to construct a new cistern. After sixteen days of work, the repair party left for Washington Harbor and then returned to the lighthouse depot in Detroit, Michigan. The late spring of 1884 was warm and dry, with little or no rain, and owing to a defect in its construction, the cistern ran dry the first week of June. At the end of June, Betts complained that the cistern was still dry and that water for the family and livestock had to be carried up 154 steps from the lakeshore each day. Despite some rain in mid-July, the cistern was still dry at the end of July. Finally Betts exploded in his log:

> If the men who pretend to keep up repairs at light stations do not provide for a water supply here before long, I shall quit this business. They make wells at other stations where water is handy without wells, but neglect this place almost entirely.

The hot, dry weather continued throughout August, and serious forest fires filled the air with smoke while the Betts family continued hauling their water up the steps in front of the station. Finally, on September 1, a party of workmen arrived to fix the cistern and make other minor repairs. Seven days later Betts took the work party in his sailboat to Pilot Island, but it was October before a series of heavy rains broke the drought and filled the cistern. Betts did not carry out his threat to quit over the cistern situation, but the incident revealed his growing unhappiness with his job as keeper of the Pottowatomie Light. He had felt for a long time that his repair requests were ignored, and funds never seemed available for construction of the oil house; furthermore, his wife's position as assistant with its $400 yearly income had been lost, and now there was the whole matter of the leaking cistern and lack of water. On top of all these things, the 300-acre farm the family owned on Washington Island was developing nicely.

It appeared from his log that the 1885 season was a good one for Betts, with no major problems, but in reality matters were coming to a head. In late summer, Emily informed her husband that she was pregnant. In October, Betts sold over 3,000 board feet of pine from their farm to the Sturgeon Bay Lumber Company. In March 1886, a baby boy was born in the family's farm house. Sometime between then and April 17, when he was to begin to exhibit the light at Pottowatomie Light for the season, Betts sent in his resignation to the Lighthouse Board, though he had to remain at his post until a new keeper was appointed. On May 8, he complained that there had not yet been word concerning the new keeper. Finally on May 11, Betts received a letter from Jesse Miner, a Washington Island friend and assistant at Pilot Island, telling of his transfer to Pottowatomie Light. That day, after over sixteen years of service on Rock Island, Betts wrote, "I am glad to get away from here for I am as tired of this business as I can be." Three days later with no further comment or fanfare, Jesse Miner wrote in the log, "New keeper moved in."

William and Emily Betts were very highly regarded by the people of Washington Island, and he was known throughout Door County. The *Door County Advocate*'s Washington Island correspondent viewed Betts' resignation with indignation:

> Capt. Betts was forced to take this step because of the insufficient salary received by him, the pay being less than he can earn at common labor where there is no responsibility. It is a sad commentary upon the methods of our government that competent officials are thus compelled to throw up their positions in consequence of the small compensation allowed them for work that requires the closest attention and also isolation from society. The authorities should be ashamed to deal in this manner with some of the most competent men in the people's service . . . .[21]

After he resigned, Betts and his wife turned to developing and operating their farm at Indian Point on Washington Island. Later, Betts and two of this sons sailed a small schooner hauling freight. When he died in 1930 at the age of 97, he was called Door County's oldest resident. Mrs. Betts became well known as

Washington Island's midwife. She and her husband tended the Pottowatomie Light very faithfully before the turn of the century, and she lived to see it automated and the dwelling closed before she died in March 1950 at the age of 95.[22]

Jesse Miner's appointment as keeper was probationary at first, but the Lighthouse Board made the appointment permanent on 8 September 1886. Miner was born on Rock Island, the son of pioneer settlers Henry and Martha Miner, and he had moved with his parents to Washington Island in 1850, when he was a only a year old. During his lifetime, Jesse served as a mail carrier and a lighthouse keeper, and he became the unofficial historian of Rock and Washington Islands.

Like many new keepers, Miner spent much of his time during his first few weeks at the station cleaning and whitewashing the inside of his dwelling, entertaining visitors, and visiting his parents at Washington Harbor. Shortly after his appointment, thirty people came from Washington Harbor to picnic and spend the afternoon with him. All this in addition to his duties associated with maintaining the light itself.

However, after making his first inspection, Captain Cook praised the new light keeper. Cook requested that Miner, in addition to logging weather conditions and significant events, record each day whether the Poverty Island and Peninsula Point Lights were visible and whether he heard the Port des Morts fog signal.

Miner's life and activities had a certain rhythm and regularity. He spent his winters at Washington Harbor with his parents and friends. Usually in early April, Miner would return to Rock Island to open the station, often having to cross the still-frozen passage between Washington and Rock Islands on the ice. Among his first activities after arrival was the tapping of maple trees in the area to begin the process of making syrup. April, May, and June were devoted to cleaning, whitewashing, sanding, and painting. Though the dwelling was built of stone, the sheds, the privy, the doors and windows, and the fence along the bluff top had to whitewashed or painted each year. The tower and lantern had to be refurbished, and at least once a year, the lens had to be cleaned and polished, and the pedestal, service table, and floor painted. In spring Miner had to prepare the empty oil tins for return to the depot on the *Dahlia*. Spring was also the time to plant the station's vegetable garden. Once a month, Miner put a new wick in the lens lamp, while cleaning both it and the spare lamp. At the end of each month, he prepared a monthly report and mailed it the first or second of the month from Washington Harbor. The mail boat touched there once or twice a week unless there was bad weather, and Miner usually sailed or rowed to Washington Harbor at least once a week. July was taken up with haying on the land around the light, while fall was a time to prepare the station and its equipment for winter. Miner repaired and painted the boats, harvested his garden, and began to secure things for the winter. He also hunted the abundant deer and rabbits on the island, and the Thanksgiving dinner at his parents home was usually venison he had shot rather than turkey. In middle or late December (or, a few times, in early January) ice would begin to form on the lakes and bays as vessels scurried back to lay up in their home ports. When the ice closed navigation, Miner discontinued the light, closed the station, and returned to Washington Harbor wait for spring.

Two situations of great significance for Miner occurred with little or no pattern. Since Pottowatomie Light was a fixed, white light with no moving parts, it was rather simple mechanically. The only major problem Miner had with the light was when the lamp chimney around the flame in the lens broke, but that happened without warning. The lamp would then smoke and coat the lens with soot. This seems to have occurred once or twice each season, and it sometimes took Miner several days to return the lantern to its accustomed sparkling condition. The other situation was the unpredictable nature of the lighthouse inspector's visits. Other, more remote stations could expect yearly or twice yearly inspection, but Pottowatomie Light was on the route to a number of other lighthouses, lightships, and other navigational aids, and the *Dahlia* often stopped at Rock Island as she made her rounds. Given the unpredictability of the almost monthly inspections and the level of Miner's activities, it was surprising that only once during his tenure was Miner absent when the inspector called.

Miner was an interesting and friendly individual. He was 36 years old and a bachelor when he was appointed keeper at Pottowatomie Light, but he had a wide circle of friends and enjoyed having visitors at the station. The visitors seem to have been of three kinds: long-term, short-term, and daily. Until 1895, his mother Martha spent periods of from several weeks to several months at the lighthouse, and Miner referred to one of the rooms, probably upstairs, as "mother's room" when he whitewashed and painted in the dwelling. Miner's special friend Jens Jacobsen stayed for months at a time at the lighthouse, and other visitors came on fishing boats as they delivered the mail. Miner often persuaded visitors to remain for several days either until the mail boat came again, or until he could take them back to Washington Island. The light station was also a popular destination for picnickers. According to the Door *County Advocate*'s Washington Island correspondent:

> . . . some of our young people surprised the keeper of the Rock Island light and a very pleasant time was spent in a beautiful grove near the station. The party had brought baskets which were packed with the choicest vivands, to which all did justice. It was one of the most agreeable days that has ever been spent on the island.

And, in another account:

> Anton B. Gunderson took a party of ladies and gentlemen to Rock recently to visit Jesse Minor the light-keeper. They report having a good time, as everybody does that goes to visit Jesse.[23]

Jesse had so much company that he noted in his log at the end of November 1894: "Mail came at noon. Mother and Ollie went home, I am all alone for the first time for over six months. . . ."

Sometimes, however, visitors were not particularly welcome. On 2 September 1888, Miner recorded that three visitors had arrived asking for help since their boat was leaking so badly that they were compelled to come ashore. They then crossed to Washington Island for several days before returning to the southern part of Rock Island. On September 19, they abandoned their boat and stole the lighthouse yawl. They then sailed to Washington Island, stole a fisherman's boat and fled. The next morning when the theft was discovered, two boats set out looking for them, but no trace of the thieves was found. Fisherman John Jenet came to Rock Island to return the yawl and take possession of the thieves' abandoned boat. Miner commented Mr. Jenet was here. His boat was stole last night by some Tramps who have been here a week." Jenet's boat was later found run ashore near Leathem, Michigan where the thieves left it before fleeing into the woods.[24]

Miners' friend Jens Jacobsen had an intriguing if minor role in the history of Pottowatomie Light. Conan Eaton and Anne Whitney, Washington Island historians, suggest that Jacobsen was Miner's assistant, but friend and unofficial assistant is a better description. Jacobsen's name does not appear in the official list of keepers and assistant keepers. According to Miner's logs, Jacobsen spent long periods of time at the light. Whether Miner paid him or they were just friends cannot be determined. Miner recorded that in September 1887 he spent several days "wheeling away the ruins" of the original tower and dwelling. In an interview in 1950, Jacobsen told Anne Whitney that the task of disposing of all the old rubble and stones fell to him and Miner:

> Yes, yes we threw all the old stone over the hill, down into the lake; but now I think of all the strange markings that were on them and regret my lack of intelligence or appreciation of what they were.

In the intervening sixty-three years, Jacobsen had become very interested in Native American activities in the area. In view of that interest he continued,

> Perhaps I could have added something to the archeological history of the Island. They must have been some sort of hieroglyphics.[25]

Since the construction crew had opened a quarry to secure the stone for the buildings, the passage of time must have clouded Jacobsen's memory.

In 1889 reporter Robert Severs wrote:

> Jesse Miner, the keeper of the Rock Island Lighthouse, has a man cook who is also a literary gentleman, and they seem to take much comfort, and the house is always neat and in good shape.

The description would seem to fit Jacobsen who was very interested in literature and became well known as Washington Island's poet. Jacobsen later married Olive Adeline Garret, Miner's niece. Miner's log has numerous references to "Ollie" coming and staying for various lengths of time at the lighthouse. Since he often spoke of

Ollie arriving or departing with his mother, it may well be that Ollie was Miner's nickname for Olive Garret.

Jacobsen, who died in 1952, built a museum on his property on Washington Island's Little Lake. Handcrafted from native timber, the museum contains a collection both of pioneer and of more modern artifacts and is open to present day visitors.

In August 1891, Miner wrote in his log "Mrs. Cornell went home." When she had come or for how long she had stayed was not recorded. Mrs. Hannah Cornell was the widow of William Cornell, a fisherman. She, like Miners' parents, lived at Washington Harbor with her children. Miner continued to see Mrs. Cornell, although her presence on Rock Island was not recorded. Then on 14 March 1895, Bo L. Anderson, who had replaced Robert Severs as *Door County Advocate* correspondent, wrote to the editor:

> March 19th 1895, Mrs. Wm. Cornell and Jesse Miner, keeper of the Rock Island light, will be united in the bonds of matrimony.

After noting that Reverend Carlson would perform the ceremony, he continued:

> After the ceremony and singing the couple will be greeted at the home of the groom by relatives and friends, also dinner will be served. That they find peace and happiness in each other's company is wished by their many friends.[27]

Two weeks later, on the day after he had come to Rock Island to prepare to open the station, Miner wrote in his log, "My wife came to the station 1 PM" This was Miner's only reference to his wife in his logs, but she lived with her husband at the light; and never again did Miner's mother come for extended periods of time at the station, as she had in the past. On 4 July 1895, Reverend Carlson also performed the marriage ceremony for Jens Jacobsen and Olive Garrett.

Finally, in 1894, nineteen years after the drunken foreman had failed to build the station's boathouse for William Betts, a Board crew constructed a boathouse at Corbin's old landing north of the place where Chester Thordarson would later build his great stone boathouse and hall. Boatways sixty-eight feet long were built out into the lake so that boats could be hauled out of the water and into the boathouse. A new, larger landing crib was built on the site of the old crib, and the old crib was removed. The new crib was built of cedar and pine logs with cedar cross-ties, and the men filled it with large rocks and boulders from the surrounding area.

In October 1898, Jesse Miner resigned as keeper of the Pottowatomie Light, ending a twelve-year tenure at that station and a fifteen-year career as a keeper. He apparently resigned because of ill health. He and his wife spent most of the rest of their lives living in his parents' old home at Washington Harbor. Mrs. Miner passed away in 1914, and Jesse Miner died 26 December 1915.[28]

Louis Hutzler, Miner's replacement, arrived on Rock Island in October 1898. A Michigan native, Hutzler entered the lighthouse service in 1892 as first assistant keeper at the South Manitou Light across Lake Michigan. At the time of his appointment as keeper of Pottowatomie Light, the Lighthouse Board authorized Hutzler to hire a laborer for five months each year during the navigation season. Laborers were hired by the keeper, not appointed by the Board as were assistants. They also received less pay than did assistants. The action recognized that the Pottowatomie Light keeper needed help, and hiring a laborer was less expensive than appointing an assistant.

Hutzler was a bachelor, but he had a girl friend, Miss Jessie Haus, back in Michigan. On 8 June 1899, he sailed down to the Plum Island Light in a friend's boat. Three days later the Plum Island crew put him aboard the Ann Arbor Car Ferry bound for Frankfort, Michigan. Five days later, on June 16, Hutzler and his new bride arrived at Plum Island via the same car ferry. The next day, Hans Hanson and George Cornell, assistants at Plum Island, took the Hutzlers to Detroit Harbor, and the couple then made their way to Rock Island. The newlyweds stayed at Pottowatomie Light for only a very short time. In mid-July, the Lighthouse Board transferred Hutzler to Long Tail Point Light in Green Bay to replace Captain Gaylord who had died at his post. Hutzler remained there for four years before being transferred to Grasse Island Light, also in Green Bay. He retired from this post in 1933 and died in 1947.[29]

The Lighthouse Board transferred Frederick Raether to Rock Island, but canceled the transfer before it became effective. Instead, the Board promoted Lawrence Brown, who was then twenty-three years old and had been his father's assistant at Cana Island since March 1893, to keeper and transferred him to Pottowatomie Light.

The assistant keeper's position at Pottowatomie Light was abolished in 1882, during Betts' tenure, but there were periodic requests to reinstate the position. In March 1901, the Board honored the requests and appointed John Meikle, Jr., a bachelor from Sturgeon Bay, as assistant to Brown. However, in June, the Board transferred Meikle to the light at the entrance to Green Bay, replacing Joseph Kilgore who then came to Rock Island as Brown's assistant.

Kilgore was the son of Moses Kilgore, one of the pioneers of Door County. He welcomed the move to Rock Island, since the Green Bay light was built on a crib, and the dwelling had room only for the keeper, his family, and an assistant. Thus, if the assistant had a family, he could not bring them to the light because of the lack of room and the danger of children falling overboard and drowning. Kilgore and his wife Alice were Baileys Harbor natives and were very glad to move with their family to the more spacious Rock Island location.[30]

In 1901, there was discussion of building a lifesaving station on or near Rock Island; when ships had difficulty in the area, there was no means of notifying the Plum Island lifesavers to provide help. There were also suggestions that the federal government should lay the first man-made, all-weather connection across Deaths Door, a submarine telephone cable from Northport to Plum Island and then on to Lobdell's Point at the southwest point of Washington Island.

After three years, in June 1802, Charles Boshka replaced Lawrence Brown as keeper. Boshka who was born in Racine, Wisconsin in 1869 and entered the lighthouse service in his hometown in 1895. Two years later, the Board transferred Boshka to Pilot Island as first assistant; in 1902, he was promoted to keeper and transferred to Pottowatomie Light. Boshka's wife Mollie and their three-year-old daughter Ella moved into the lighthouse with Joseph and Alice Kilgore. The Boshka's son Lucien was born the following year.

In 1903, Congressman E.S. Minor of Sturgeon Bay secured an $8,000 appropriation for laying a submarine telephone cable from Northport to Washington Island via Plum Island, as earlier planned. In addition, the cable was to be extended from the northeastern end of Washington Island to Rock Island near the boathouse and from there overland to the lighthouse itself. There never was an electrical power line to the lighthouse and the keepers therefore continued to burn kerosene for light in the dwelling and in the lens, but the arrival of the telephone line in 1904 ended the isolation of Pottowatomie Light. The telephone was only for official business to allow help to be summoned quickly in an emergency, and the telephone link to the Plum Island Life Saving Station effectively ended the talk of building another lifesaving station in the vicinity.

In 1904, twenty-four years after the conversion from lard oil to the more flammable and dangerous kerosene, a crew finally built the oil house at Pottowatomie Light. After laying a concrete foundation seventy-five feet east of the dwelling, the men built a brick structure approximately six feet by eight feet, with a metal roof and metal door. As many as ninety five-gallon cans of kerosene could have been stored in the building, but because it lacked shelving the actual amount stored was probably less. Only kerosene was kept there, since there was another storeroom in the entrance to the attic of the dwelling. The crew not only repaired the station's boathouse, they also extended the boat landing to fifty feet from shore, and built new boatways and replaced the log landing crib below the lighthouse. This landing was only sixteen feet long and the water depth at the end was three feet, two feet less than at the boathouse landing.[31] Because of the shallow depth at this landing, in stormy weather the keepers hauled their boats out of the water over the rocks using a heavy-duty winch.

Personnel changed at the lighthouse in 1905. In September, first assistant Joseph Kilgore was transferred to the Kenosha Light, exchanging places with Walter Ottosen. When Kilgore arrived at Kenosha, he looked the situation over and decided to resign his position. He then telephoned his wife, who had not yet left Rock Island for Kenosha, telling her to move to Baileys Harbor where he would join her. However, instead of resigning, Kilgore transferred to the Plum Island Range Lights as second assistant.

Ottosen, who replaced Kilgore, had the distinction of being the only Washington Islander to fight in the Spanish-American War, serving in both Cuba and the Philippines.[32] In August 1907, he was transferred to Pilot Island, and Mollie Boshka became her husband's assistant. By this time, however, the Board was no longer appointing keeper's wives as assistants except as a temporary measure. Mrs. Boshka held her position for only one month, before the Board appointed John Fitzgerald first assistant keeper. He remained in that position until the lighthouse Bureau promoted him to keeper in 1928 when Cornell left.

The arrival of the telephone made communication easier, but the problem of a reliable, convenient water supply continued to plague the station's residents. In the 1909 description of buildings, premises, equipment, and facilities at Pottowatomie Light, the water supply, procured by pail from Lake Michigan, was described as ample but of poor quality at times. Keepers still made the same climb up the steps on the bluff from the lake to the dwelling that William Betts had complained about years before. This time however, the report sparked action on the water supply situation; within a short time, a well-drilling crew arrived at the station and put in the present well, a few yards to the southwest of the dwelling. This was the last major construction project that occurred while Pottowatomie Light was still a manned station.

In 1910 Chester Hjortur Thordarson paid $5,735 for 661 acres of Rock Island owned by Rasmus Hanson of Jackson Harbor. He bought four smaller tracts from other owners at the same time, and two years later bought several acres near the island's southeast corner. Except for the Pottowatomie Light reservation, Thordarson in 1912 became the sole owner of Rock Island. Born in Iceland in 1867, Thordarson immigrated with his parents to Milwaukee in 1873. He went into business for himself in 1894, making electrical equipment; ten years later he won a gold medal at the St. Louis World's Fair for designing and building the first half-million volt transformer. The success of the Thordarson Electric Company and his more than one hundred inventions made him rich and famous.

Around the turn of the century, he and his wife began vacationing on Washington Island. When the property they wanted on Washington Island was not for sale, they turned to the purchase of Rock Island. Over a period of time, Thordarson developed a huge and magnificent estate on the southern part of the island.[33]

The Lighthouse Bureau transferred Charles Boshka in 1911 from Rock Island to the Plum Island Range Lights. Edward H. Cornell replaced Boshka as keeper, while Fitzgerald remained as assistant. Cornell had begun his career at North Manitou Light in Michigan, becoming second assistant keeper at Pilot Island in March 1900. Four years later he was promoted to first assistant. His next assignment was South Fox Island Light in Michigan, which began in March 1910 and lasted until November 1911. Cornell was born 20 March 1861 of native parents in Elgin, Illinois, and thus was 50 years old when he became keeper at Pottowatomie Light. His wife Johanna, age 43, had become a citizen in 1884 after her family immigrated to Wisconsin from Norway. At the time of his appointment to Pottowatomie Light, they had two daughters, and, during his assignment, six other children were born.

Johanna and the children probably never actually made their home at the light, since housing eight children in the lighthouse seems unlikely, and the 1920 US Census listed Johanna's occupation as hotel keeper of one of Washington Island's resort hotels. Edward Cornell remained as keeper at Pottowatomie Light until 1928 when he was transferred to Green Island Light, replacing Alfred C. Cornell (no relation). Only two years later, in 1930, Edward retired. Johanna Cornell died in 1939, and Edward Cornell died in October 1953 at the age of 92.[34]

When Cornell left, John Fitzgerald, who had been the first assistant keeper at Pottowatomie since 1907, was promoted to keeper. Born in 1877 in Michigan, Fitzgerald was the bachelor son of Irish immigrants. He lived on the second floor of the dwelling, using the large room on the southeast corner for his canopied bed. He was an avid reader, and the first floor entry was lined with bookcases. Earl Malloch was transferred from Chicago to be first assistant, but his wife and three sons lived on Washington Island during the school year. During their summers at the light Mrs. Malloch cooked for her family and for Fitzgerald.

In 1928 Chester Thordarson had his workmen begin construction of the most impressive of the structures he was to build on Rock Island, the magnificent stone boathouse and great hall that still welcomes visitors to the island. Once it was completed, he apparently regarded the station's wooden boathouse and landing which lay north of his boathouse and south of one of his cabins on the shore as eyesores. In reality, he probably had better title to the property than did the Lighthouse Bureau, since it was located far outside the lighthouse reservation. Thordarson offered to let the keepers store their boats in his own boathouse if he could tear down the lighthouse boathouse. This was agreeable to the Lighthouse Bureau, and all evidence of the boathouse and landing has disappeared. The keepers kept a small boat at the station which they could haul up onto the rocks if necessary, but their larger boats were kept in Thordarson's boathouse.

While construction and activity continued on Thordarson's estate at the south end of the island, lighthouse activities continued in a routine akin to practices of the 19th century. As mentioned previously, electricity never came to Pottowatomie Light. Even the visits by the inspector became routinized. No longer was his arrival a surprise; keepers knew of the date and time of inspections, although they were no less rigorous than in the past. On one such visit on a hot humid July day, Fitzgerald and Malloch went down the stairs dressed in their heavy, woolen keeper's uniforms to meet the inspector at the landing as he came ashore from the tender. The group then climbed back up the 154 steps, sweating profusely.

At the top, having completed this ritual, the inspector announced they were to remove their coats before going inside the dwelling for cool drinks.[35]

John Fitzgerald retired in 1942 and Malloch was transferred to Manistique Light. Ernest Lockhart became the last civilian keeper of Pottowatomie Light, only to help with its decommission in 1946 before his transfer to St. Martin Light. Wet-cell batteries were installed to power the automated light, and the dwelling was closed. In later years the lantern was removed and a beacon was placed atop the lantern deck. Finally, in 1986, the Coast Guard replaced the wet-cell batteries with solar panels. Two years later a crew from the Coast Guard cutter *Buckthorn* assisted by a helicopter erected the present skeleton steel tower to the west of the dwelling and transferred the beacon to the new tower.[36]

Chester Thordarson died in 1945, and the forces of nature began to reclaim his estate and its man-made structures. Despite offers to buy the island for private development, Thordarson's heirs sold the island to the State of Wisconsin in 1964, and it became Rock Island State Park. Accessible only by boat and ferry, Rock Island will remain only minimally developed with its hiking trails, picnicking facilities, and primitive camping sites, leaving the bulk of the island in its natural state. Visitors can make their way from the site of Thordarson's boathouse, as Corbin and other keepers did, north through the woods to the lighthouse. The voices of the visitors die away though in the late afternoon as they make their way back to the landing. At night, the silent lighthouse stands alone at the north end of Rock Island, but, as it has since 1858, the light still shines out across the Rock Island Passage.

Chapter 3
Plum Island Lights

Plum Island has been the site of two different light stations at different times; it lies about midway between Northport, at the end of the Door County mainland, and Washington Island. Thus, the island lies "plumb" in the middle of Deaths Door or *Porte des Morts* Passage, and hence its name, according to some. However, others suggest that the island gets its name from being shaped like a plum. The island is elliptical, a bit more than half a mile wide and something over a mile long, with its long axis oriented northwest to southeast. Approximately 325 acres in area, Plum Island has a dolomite core mantled with glacial and lacustrine sand and gravel. Except on the south and southeast sides, where the dolomite cliffs are exposed, the island has a narrow gravel beach rising five to ten feet above lake level. Inland from the beach, Plum Island is heavily wooded except for cleared areas around the abandoned Coast Guard Station on the northeasterly side and the Plum Island Range Lights on the west side.[1]

Though located close to the busy ferry route from Northport to Washington Island, today Plum Island is quiet. Human visitors rarely disturb the deer, birds, and other animals that live on the island. Some of the buildings are gone, but it is still easy to look out from the lantern room atop the rear range light tower and imagine the Deaths Door Passage full of shipping and the grounds of the station alive with activity. Though now unmanned, the station is automated and continues to function as an aid to navigation. Former keepers might be aghast to see the unmowed range and open areas around the dwelling and fog signal house, but trees have not yet begun to replace the grass, and the long concrete sidewalks have few gaps. As evening approaches it takes little effort to imagine a keeper walking down the concrete walk to light the lower range light.

Finding the remains of the original Porte des Morts Passage Light on Plum Island is much more difficult, and there is no known picture of it when it was still intact. The original Plum Island light is the most elusive of the Door County Lights, and several Door County writers have even questioned whether it ever existed. The confusion arises from the fact that the station was referred to in official documents simply as the Porte des Morts Passage Light, with no other reference to its location. Then, when the new lighthouse was built on Pilot Island in 1858, it was also called the Porte des Morts Passage Light, with no indication or recognition that the lighthouse had been relocated from Plum Island to Pilot Island. Not until the 1870s do the records make a distinction between the two Porte des Morts lights; at first they call the replacement light the Porte des Morts Light on Pilot Island, but later they refer to it simply as the Pilot Island Light. To add futher confusion, the Porte des Morts Passage itself gradually has became known by its English name — Deaths Door Passage or simply Deaths Door.

Even today, finding the site of the original Plum Island lighthouse is almost as difficult as it was at the turn of the century. It is located several hundred feet east of the lower range light tower and back off the beach in the woods; the tumbled-down walls of the lighthouse still exist, though they are overgrown with thick vegetation. Those ruins are of the original Porte des Morts Passage Light, and they are the only ruins that fit the description of the light's location.

In 1837 the US Navy sent Lieutenant Pendergast to examine the need for lighthouses in the western Great Lakes. He reported that there was a lighthouse on Rock Island, and that another light was needed in the Porte des Morts Passage to the south, but that there was a even greater need for a light near the city of Green Bay. The Navy Commissioners accepted Lieutenant Pendergast's recommendation.[2] The reason for his recommendation was that, in 1837, there were more vessels going to and from Green Bay by way of the Rock Island passage and then proceeding east to Mackinac and beyond than than there were vessels passing through Deaths Door and then south to Milwaukee and Chicago. However, by the mid-1840s, traffic through the Deaths Door passage had increased sufficiently to merit construction of a lighthouse to guide ship captains into and out of Green Bay through Deaths Door.

On 8 August 1848, Congress appropriated $3,500 to build a lighthouse on the Porte des Morts Passage from Lake Michigan to Green Bay. On 11 December 1848, President James K. Polk reserved from the public domain all of Plum Island for lighthouse purposes. During 1849, a government crew built the light at a cost of $3,125, and it began operation the same year. The dwelling was square and apparently was attached to a round lighthouse tower. In the 1925 boundary dispute between Wisconsin and Michigan (which went all the way to the US Supreme Court), a key factor in the case was whether the boundary between the two states (which was supposed to be along the "usual navigation channel") was through Deaths Door and then east of Chambers Island as claimed by Michigan, or through the Rock Island passage and west of Chambers Island, as argued by Wisconsin. Since lighthouses were customarily built on the "usual navigation channel," a critical factor in the Supreme Court's decision in favor of Wisconsin was the fact that Pottowatomie Light on Rock Island had been built before the Porte des Morts Passage Light on Plum Island. Both Martin Knudsen, who had served as keeper at Pilot Island and at the Plum Island Range Lights, and William Betts, former Pottowatomie Light keeper, gave sworn statements testifying to the existence of the original Porte des Morts Passage Light on Plum Island. However, by 1923, the light was in ruins and had been largely forgotten.[3]

William Riggins, a native Virginian, received the first appointment as keeper of the newly constructed Plum Island light on 23 August 1849. Riggins, aged 31, moved into the dwelling with his wife Phebe, a 27-year-old native of Ohio, and their three children. In 1855, Royal Riggins, then 16, received his appointment as assistant keeper and began working with his father. In July 1857, the Lighthouse Board replaced the elder Riggins with William Shurtteffy, but Royal Riggins remained on as assistant keeper until both he and Shurtteffy were removed in May 1859, one year after the new Porte des Morts Passage Light had been built on Pilot Island.[4]

Beyond the official records, little is known about William Riggins. In the spring of 1855, after a particularly cold and snowy winter, the editor of the *Green Bay Advocate* (Door County had no newspaper at the time) wrote that he had received a complaint from Riggins that "if we don't send him the *Advocate* he will shut Death's Door upon us the first time we pass through . . . thus forever barring our return." The editor responded that "Mr. Riggin[s] shall have the paper."[5] In a 1928 article entitled "The Forgotten Lighthouse," historian H.R. Holand told of a Mrs. R.M. Harris of Sturgeon Bay who had lived at Rowleys Bay with her parents in the 1850s and who claimed to have been in the Plum Island lighthouse many times. She recalled that "an old man by the name of Riggin" was the keeper. Mrs. Harris went on to say that

> Old man Riggin was a terrible old savage who frequently used to drink up the alcohol delivered for lighting purposes. When in his cups, he is said to have boasted of piracy and other strange and unconventional acts.[6]

Unfortunately Holand gave his readers no information about who Mrs. Harris was or how old she was, but she must have been at least 80 at the time he wrote about her. Since Riggins was only 39 when he was replaced, he was hardly an old man. Another problem with her description is that alcohol was not used in the lamps, and a keeper who drank on duty was subject to immediate dismissal; perhaps the passage of more than 75 years had clouded Mrs. Harris' memory.

The light that Riggins kept was built just east of the present Plum Island lower range light. Experience proved (just as it did at the Baileys Harbor Lighthouse) that the original Porte des Morts Passage Light was poorly located. According to an engineer's report of 30 June 1891, when consideration was being given to the construction of the range lights on Plum Island,

> The original Port des Morts Light was on the S.W. side of Plum Island, adjacent to the main channel, but too far west to mark the entrance. This light was abandoned when the Pilot Island light was established and is now in ruins.[7]

It would certainly appear that the quality of the lighthouse's construction left a great deal to be desired, for the station rapidly deteriorated after it was abandoned in 1858. By 1864, the lighthouse had fallen into ruins.

One of the famous stories of an adventure in crossing "the Door" involved Robert Noble and the abandoned lighthouse. After spending the holidays visiting his girl friend on Washington Island, Robert Noble, a young man of 25 in excellent physical condition, set out on 30 December 1863 in a flat-bottomed boat to return to the mainland. The winter up to that time had been relatively warm, and there was enough open water to enable Nobel to expect to make it across Deaths Door without too much difficulty. Everything went smoothly until he encountered a thick field of floating ice which forced him to land on Plum Island. While he waited for the wind to shift to open a passage, the sun set, the temperature began to fall, and it began to snow.

Looking for shelter, Noble first found the remains of an abandoned fisherman's hut. Unable to keep a fire going, he explored the island in the morning hoping to find another shelter because, while the freezing temperatures made it impossible for him to use his boat, the ice was not solid enough for him to walk on. After walking around the island, all he could find were the tumbledown walls and chimney of the abandoned lighthouse. Using the last of his matches, Noble managed to get a fire going in the fireplace. Unfortunately, the fire melted some snow in the chimney, which fell down and put out the fire. Though unable to restart the fire, Noble somehow managed to stay alive in the freezing temperatures without food, heat, or sleep until New Year's Day 1864. He then finally made his way through the ice and snow back to Detroit Island, arriving there late in the day almost completely encased in ice and with badly frozen hands and feet. Noble survived, but he lost his legs below the knees and parts of his fingers. After being fitted with artificial legs, Noble returned to his well-drilling business, and he later operated a ferry across the bay in Sturgeon Bay before the first bridge was built.[8]

Plum Island remained reserved from the public domain, and was unavailable for sale to individuals after the abandonment of the lighthouse in 1858. The island was largely undisturbed and remained uninhabited until 1895 when, after much discussion, the US Life Saving Service built its Plum Island Station on the north-eastern side of island, facing Washington Island. Captain Inger Olsen and some of his eight-man crew built small homes around the station and brought their wives and children to live with them on Plum Island. Olsen and his men cut a road through the trees around the perimeter of the island so they could conduct regular foot patrols in search of vessels in distress. The road also allowed them to haul their lifesaving equipment in wagons to any point on the island where it might be used to rescue sailors from grounded ships. The lifesavers made regular boat trips year around to Washington Island, since this passage usually remained open, in contrast to the passage to the mainland which froze over in all but the mildest winters.

In 1858, by order of the Lighthouse Board, the Porte des Morts Passage Light was moved to Pilot Island because mariners complained the light was too far west in the passage to be of assistance. Yet even with the change, sailors still had a difficult job sailing into Green Bay through Deaths Door. Shifting currents and winds in Deaths Door caused many accidents. Years later, in June 1889, Captain William Nicholson of the Peshtigo Barge Line, who had been sailing from Green Bay to Chicago twice a week for many years, suggested a way to make the passage safer. According to him, placing range lights as well as a fog signal on Plum Island would prevent captains from mistaking the safe route through the passage.

Range lights are a pair of lights, usually including a front light located near the shoreline and a rear light located some distance inland. They are situated so that when they line up with one directly above the other as seen from the water, they mark a particular compass heading or indicate the alignment of a channel. When the lights are aligned one above the other, one is said to be "on the range," which at Plum Island is a bearing of 330 degrees. During the day, the range light towers themselves can be aligned to mark the range. The "range" may also refer to the cleared or open area on the ground between the lights.

In Nicholson's view, captains going into Green Bay from Lake Michigan were afraid of grounding on Nine Foot Shoal (also called Waverly Shoal) which lay west of Pilot Island and thus often went too far to the north and sometimes ran aground on Pilot or Plum Island. With range lights on Plum Island, mariners would be able to determine when they were enough toward Pilot Island and could safely make the passage into Green Bay. Nicholson also favored changing the characteristic of the Pilot Island Light from flashing to fixed, because flashing lights tend to appear closer to the observer than they actually are. Captain Clark, the district inspector, presented Nicholson's ideas to the Lighthouse Board.[9]

On 7 January 1890, the Board recommended that range lights and a fog signal on the southwest side of Plum Island would be an invaluable addition to navigation aids in the area and should be constructed. The Board asked Congress for an appropriation of $21,000 to finance the construction of the station.[10] The Board made the same recommendation in 1891 and again in 1892, but without success. The project was finally approved 15 February 1893, but no money was appropriated for construction until March 1895, when Congress made the money available. Lighthouse Board engineers set to work at once preparing specifications and plans for the range light towers, a fog signal house, duplicate fog signal boilers and machinery, a keeper's dwelling, an oil house, a boathouse, landings, and outbuildings. Contractors submitted their bids to the Board and contracts were let, but, despite the hopes of people in the area, these activities all took too much time for construction to begin in 1895. However, as early as September 1895, there were rumors that Pilot Island keeper Martin Knudsen would be appointed keeper of the new station.[11]

Finally on 28 July 1896, the tender *Amaranth* anchored off the west side of Plum Island, and the crew began transferring the men and materials needed for the construction of the new station to shore. Under the superintendence of R.I. Hurst, a crew of thirty men was soon at work. They first cleared about an acre and a half for a camp and for the range light tower sites; they then opened a strip twenty feet wide and sixteen hundred feet long from the site of the front range light on the shore along the southwest side of the island back to the clearing for the rear range light. During August, the crew (now enlarged to forty men in an effort to complete the station before it became too cold to work) built a landing dock in front of the dwelling site; the dock was ninety-six

Plum Island station, rear range light tower, dwelling and docks abut 1914. Note the keepers near the boat on the right and the tramway leading to the dwelling. Photo courtesy of the Milwaukee Public Library/Wisconsin Marine Historical Society.

feet long and extended into three feet of water at its outer end. They also constructed boatways ready to set in the water and laid 367 feet of tramway track running from the dwelling to the end of the dock. The Plum Island station was the only light station in Door County that had tramways and, in fact, originally had two.

The *S.B. Paige* captained by Sturgeon Bay's Alexander Lurie made five trips from Kewaunee to deliver 164,000 cream-colored bricks, along with cement and thirty-six cubic yards of sand from Sturgeon Bay and Menominee, Michigan. Captain Lurie also delivered lumber and mill work from Green Bay, and hardware from the Schofield Company of Sturgeon Bay. A hoisting engine was set up to move construction materials from the dock to the tower and to the dwelling sites, which were several hundred feet back from the shore line. Part of the forty-man crew dug out the sand and gravel for the dwelling's cellar; masons then built the brick cellar walls to grade. A hundred feet north northwest of the dwelling other crew members dug out holes and laid the concrete for the center pier of the tower and four piers for the tower's legs; still others prepared the site for the front range light tower and poured its concrete pad. After clearing a roadway from the upper range light to the fog signal house at the western end of the island, part of the crew cleared the space for the fog signal house and built a dock that extended 210 feet into water that was four feet deep at the far end. Pipes were laid from the end of the dock to the fog signal house to supply water for the signal boilers. There were two complete sets of fog signals which were ordinarily operated on an alternating monthly basis. One also served as a backup to the other so sailors weren't left in the fog without assistance if one broke down.

During September work went ahead on the dwelling and the ironwork of the rear tower. The front tower was a two-story wooden building with a square first floor and an octagonal second floor capped by a black metal roof; it was finished and given its

Plum Island front (lower) range light tower, 1940. Plum Island station is located to the left. Photo courtesy of the US Coast Guard.

first coat of white paint. The front range light tower at Plum Island was almost identical to the front range light tower of the Baileys Harbor Range Lights. The crew also cleared another three acres of trees from around the dwelling site.

In October the *Amaranth's* crew delivered the fog signal's two boilers for installation in the forty-foot by twenty-two foot one-story brick fog signal house. They also constructed a brick oil house southwest of the dwelling and completed the brickwork on the fifty foot by thirty-two foot two-story keeper's dwelling. Carpenters than added the roof with its ornate wooden eaves before turning to completion of the dwelling's interior. The station's keeper would occupy the south half of the dwelling; the first assistant would live on the north side's first floor, and the second assistant would live above him. Other members of the crew finished erecting and bolting together the rear tower, which consisted of a four-legged square, pyramidal, iron skeleton with a hollow central cylinder containing a circular staircase. At the top, the men assembled a cast-iron watch room eight feet in diameter, and then erected the black, cast-iron lantern room. The tower measured sixty-five feet from the base to the top of the ventilator ball.

The carpenters finished the inside of the dwelling during November, while some of the men cleared and graded an area two hundred feet square around the dwelling. Many of the crew worked to lay 350 feet of tramway track from the dock to the fog signal house. The boilers, pumps, injectors, tanks, sirens, and related machinery were moved ashore, installed, and piped. Connecting the dwelling to various buildings, workmen laid 300 feet of wooden sidewalk. In addition they laid 1277 feet of sidewalk connecting the rear range light with the fog signal and 1650 feet of sidewalk between the range light towers. Board officials declared the station finished on 4 December 1896, a few days more than four months after the first workmen had come ashore and begun clearing the site, a remarkable feat considering the size and complexity of the project.

When Carl Richter brought the mail out from Washington Island to Martin Knudsen on Pilot Island on 7 December 1896, he delivered an envelope containing the keys to the various buildings at the Plum Island Range Lights, along with instructions to keep an eye on the station during the coming winter. Knudsen officially transferred to his new assignment on 17 March 1897; he went back to Pilot Island five days later and formally transferred the property to Godtfred M.S. Hansen, his former first assistant. The Board also appointed Hans J. Hanson, who had been second assistant at Pilot Island, to be first assistant at Plum Island.[12]

Knudsen had been at the station earlier to help the lampist install the lenses in the front and rear range lights, but he officially began his log at the Plum Island Light on 1 April 1897, a month before the lights and fog signal became operational. As with any new construction, there was a great deal of work to be done before the station was actually in operating condition, even though it was officially declared completed. Knudsen and his son Edward brought several loads of household goods from Washington Island and more from Pilot Island. The station was intended to have two assistants, though the second had yet to be appointed, and the inspector instructed Knudsen to hire a laborer of his choice; Knudsen hired his friend and fellow Washington Islander, George Cornell.

As soon as Theresa Knudsen joined her husband, they began putting their living quarters in order. The crew of the *Dahlia* landed supplies for operating and maintaining the lights, including kerosene to be stored in the oil house. The keepers spent several days cleaning and polishing the lenses, lamps, service boxes, and tools. The lantern rooms and pedestals were given a fresh coat of paint, as were the watch rooms in both towers. Then the equipment at the fog signal, which had been disconnected, drained, and stored for the winter, was reconnected, polished, painted, filled, and tested. In addition to these activities, there were frequent trips ashore, to the lifesaving station, and to Pilot Island to borrow and return tools and other incidentals.

On 1 May 1897, after a month of preparation, Knudsen exhibited the range lights for the first time. The front range light was a 6th Order fixed red light, with a focal plane thirty-two feet above mean lake level. Located in its two-story tower, the light was designed to be visible to a mariner approaching from the south for 8½ miles (in clear weather) in a small arc on either side of the range line. As at Baileys Harbor, the light shown out through a small, second-story window overlooking the water, while a smaller window on the opposite side allowed the keepers to see if the lamp was burning without actually having to go to the light.

The rear range light was 1650 feet to the north northwest on the westerly shore of Plum Island in the white skeletal tower. The lens in this tower was a 4th Order Fresnel lens made by Sautter, Lemonnier, & Co of Paris, France in 1889. Its fixed red light, with a focal plane of 69⅔ feet above mean lake level, was designed to be seen for 13 miles in clear weather. It illuminated an arc of 231 degrees from slightly west of due north, allowing vessels passing out of Green Bay to sight the light as soon as they cleared the bluffs at the northwest side of the Deaths Door passage. After sailing through the passage and aligning the two range lights, captains could make their way safely into Lake Michigan. Thus sailors were able to use the rear range light as a lighthouse and the front and rear lights as range lights. This was a most difficult navigational feat in a passage beset with conflicting winds and currents. Though the rear range light was only 2⅜ miles from the Pilot Island Light, it was not visible to persons at ground level on Pilot Island.

Knudsen and his assistants had also prepared the fog signal for operation, though they did not have to sound it until 9 May 1897. The steam siren sounded a blast of three seconds followed by a seventeen-second interval of silence before sounding again. This pattern was sufficiently different from that of the fog signal on Pilot Island that mariners could distinguish between the two.[13]

Although the keepers had their normal lighthouse and fog signal duties to perform, they continued making adjustments and changes at the station much as sailors do when they take a vessel for its first voyage. The men put additional shelves in the oil house, adjusted the ventilators in the lanterns, leveled the bank near the boathouse so it was not so steep, built a mast derrick, and got ready to hoist a flagpole in front of the dwelling. They also worked at clearing and burning brush around the dwelling. The four-foot pieces of cord wood had to be cut into shorter lengths, and kindling was split at the fog signal house. When sparks from one of the boilers set fire to the wood, the crew from the lifesaving station helped the keepers put out the fire and move the remaining wood. In mid-May, the Board changed George Cornell's status from laborer to probationary second assistant, and he began his career in the lighthouse service.

As with many, new and complicated pieces of equipment, not everything at the station worked perfectly. The lamps in the front range light refused to operate properly, and, after a month, so did siren No. 1; Knudsen sent the broken parts back to the Lighthouse Board engineers. When the *Amaranth* returned to Plum Island in June to remove the builders' camp and extra building materials, she brought the repaired siren and lamps. However, siren No. 1 continued to cause problems. Like most keepers, Knudsen was very handy and was usually able to get the siren operating, but he became increasingly frustrated that the repair work took so much of his time and attention. Finally, when fog siren No. 1 broke down completely, he sent it back to the lighthouse depot.

Pleasant weather stimulated a steady stream of people eager to visit the new station, and the keepers made numerous trips to Washington Island, Pilot Island, and the mainland. In June, Knudsen put screens on the dwelling, planted a garden, and built a storeroom and darkroom in the station's barn. During July, he and his assistants spent much of their time painting, varnishing, and refitting their boats. In the marshy area northeast of the fog signal, Knudsen harvested hay for the family cow.

The keepers continued clearing the area south of the dwelling and burning the brush. One day the fire got out of control, and they spent most of the day fighting it. They had contained it by dusk, but smouldering embers remained a problem for several days thereafter. During September, Knudsen, acting under orders from the inspector, hired Gustof Swenson to help build additional cribs to extend both the dock and the boatways at the dock. Using logs picked off the beach, the men built four cribs, placed them in the water, and decked them over after filling them with rocks.

As the leaves on the trees turned color, Knudsen and his assistants began preparing for the coming winter, one job being to transport the Knudsen family cow to the mainland. The *Dahlia* delivered three tons of stove coal onto the landing, and the keepers wheeled the fifty-pound sacks of coal to the dwelling, using the tramway and wheel barrows borrowed from the lifesaving station. Not only did the keeper occupy the south half of the dwelling, while the assistants shared the north half, but the keeper got half of the three tons of coal, while each assistant got a quarter. The *Dahlia* also delivered a reinforced winter boat for use in thin ice.

In late November and December there was a great deal of fog in the passage; for several weeks the keepers kept steam up in the boilers so the fog sirens could be sounded without delay. This required constant attendance in the fog signal house and also required continual cutting and splitting of wood to replenish what had been burned. Fortunately the range lights functioned in that interval with only normal attention, so that, despite the increased activity at the fog signal, the keepers found time to make almost daily trips to Washington Island or the mainland.

Once trees were cut down, the men, like pioneer farmers, spent a good deal of time removing the stumps and leveling the grounds, a process that went on for years. Knudsen had skillfully blasted rocks out of the landings on Pilot Island, and he now turned his attention to blasting the numerous stumps on the grounds which were too large to pull out. He also spent time building storm doors and windows for the dwelling and fog signal house. On 17 December 1897, Knudsen received orders to continue operating the lights and fog signal until further notice; since this quite possibly meant all winter, the men made a number of hasty trips for supplies. The Knudsens spent Christmas Day at home at the station, with an afternoon skate on the little lake east of the fog signal.

A few days after Christmas, ice began to form in the waters around Plum Island, and, by early January, the Washington Island mail carriers crossed to and from the mainland on foot. There was enough current flowing between Plum Island and Washington Island that the keepers could use their winter boat to go from the lifesaving station to Detroit Harbor at the same time they could go across the ice to Northport or Newport. Freezing temperatures also meant that the water pipes from the lake to the fog signal house froze periodically and had to be thawed. When Theresa went to the family farm on Washington Island, their daughter Agnes came from the farm to the station to help with the cleaning and cooking for her father and his assistants.

In mid-February the ice around the station began to break up. One day the ice might be safe, but the next day the keepers had to use their boats. They continued to make frequent trips to Washington Island and the mainland. Just before the ice finally went out in early March, there was a heavy ice shove against the fog signal landing that knocked it slightly out of alignment. It was a harbinger of things to come; during the next several years the landing was severely damaged by ice action.

The arrival of spring saw the usual routine at the station of cleaning, polishing, painting, and varnishing. In addition, Knudsen seeded the area around the dwelling, put in a garden, and brought the family cow from the farm. The men built more walks to connect various buildings, cut brush and thistles, removed more stumps, and leveled the grounds around the dwelling and rear tower. Once again there was a steady stream of visitors to the station during the summer. Mrs. Hanson joined her assistant-keeper husband in June, providing welcome companionship for Theresa. Knudsen and Cornell were members of the Macabees, a fraternal lodge; they made regular trips to Washington Island to attend meetings and often returned late at night.

Martin Knudsen's son Edward began acting as a substitute when his father or one of the assistants was gone from the station. Having grown up at the various lighthouses where his father had served, he was well aware of the duties and responsibilities of a keeper. He usually served for only a few days at a time, but when first assistant Hanson went on a twenty-one day leave later in the summer, Edward served as his substitute.

Once the Lighthouse Board had built the station on Plum Island, it began using the island as a source of wood, timbers, and spars. In July, Knudsen received orders to solicit bids to cut wood for lighthouses in the area. During August, a tug and barge took twenty-six cords of wood to Pilot Island from the supply of wood that remained from the clearing of the station's site. Despite availability of wood on the island, the keepers rarely cut down trees there for either the fog signal or the dwelling; contractors supplied cordwood to the station under contract. The keepers would then saw the wood into usable sizes and split their own kindling.

On August 8, William and Julius Fischer, Egg Harbor well-drillers, arrived to install a well at the fog signal. They decided to drill on the north side of the fog signal house; after setting up their rig, the Fischers began operations two days later. They drilled the twenty-seven foot well in five days — twenty-two feet of the drilling was through dolomite bedrock. To their great satisfaction, water rose to eight feet below the surface, and thirty minutes of hand pumping followed by thirty minutes of using the fog signal's steam pump did not lower the water level. The keepers connected the pipes from the well to the pumps and boilers and filled in around the well casing. Knudsen and his assistants helped the Fischers load their equipment to take it to Pilot Island where they were to drill a well for the fog signal water supply. Knudsen asked his superiors to permit the Fischers to return from Pilot Island to drill a second well to supply water for the dwelling, but he received word that no second well would be drilled at Plum Island, and the keepers continued to use water from the cistern and the lake.

In October, the crew of the *Dahlia* delivered the annual three-ton shipment of stove coal, fifty gallons of kerosene, and a quantity of paint and paint oil. At the same time, the inspector came ashore to inspect the station. He ordered Knudsen to secure bids for cutting wood on the island as well as for transporting a portion of it to the South Fox Island Station and to select and cut fifty cedars for buoys. Knudsen was also instructed to teach the assistants how to level the lamps and lens, how to keep the station's books, and how to make out monthly, quarterly, and yearly reports.

Life as a keeper was busy. In addition to their daily duties, the men cleaned up the beach in front of the dwelling, burned what logs and rubbish had come ashore, repaired the shingles on the barn roof, and built a chicken coop. During November, when they went to Washington Island, the keepers brought back supplies and provisions for the coming winter, including feed for the cow and chickens. Storm windows and doors came out of storage and were put on the dwelling and fog signal house. At the end of November, the lifesaving station closed for the season, though many of the crew continued living in their homes built around the station.

The keepers spent much of December cutting and splitting wood for the fog signal and dwelling. While on their way to visit their friends at the lifesaving station on 11 December 1898, the Knudsens learned that second assistant Peter H. Peterson from Pilot Island had drowned near the southeast end of Detroit Island. Knudsen, Captain Olson, and two of his lifesaving crewmen spent five hours the next day searching for Peterson's body, but there was too much drift ice for a thorough search, and the body was not found until the following April (see Pilot Island Light chapter). On Christmas Day 1898, the entire Knudsen family gathered at the station to celebrate the holiday; the next day, the Knudsens hosted a social in their quarters for the assistants and their families and for the lifesavers and their families. On 29 December 1898, former keeper Peter Knudsen, who had received the contract to cut wood on the island, arrived by boat with two woodcutters and their equipment to begin cutting wood. Conditions changed quickly, however; by New Year's Eve Day, the mail carriers crossed on ice four to six inches thick between Washington Island and the mainland.

In the afternoon of New Year's Day, Martin and Peter went to Peter's home at Newport, and Martin returned alone over the ice. It was customary for the keepers and the lifesavers to take turns getting the mail in order to give each crew some extra spare time and also to provide a reason for a visit to each others' station. On 16 January 1899, George Cornell received notification that the Lighthouse Board had changed his status from probationary to permanent, and two days later he made a journey to Hedgehog Harbor to get his keeper's uniform. The keepers spent much of their time on their usual lighthouse duties including sounding the fog signal when the wind shifted and blew the ice far enough out of the passage for navigation to take place. The men continued to build shelves and closets in the various buildings. Knudsen and his son also began looking for suitable poles to cut for buoys.

On 1 February 1899 the Knudsens went to Washington Island to attend the funeral of their doctor and close friend, Dr. Theodore Gudmundson. (Martin and Theresa later adopted Dr. Gudmundson's son, Haldor.) Several days later, Martin became very sick with "la grippe" (influenza), and within two days the entire Knudsen family was ill. Cornell also was not feeling well. Fortunately, they all recovered quickly and were able to resume their duties.

As at other lights, spring meant the beginning of the annual routine of cleaning, painting, polishing, and varnishing the dwelling, range lights, and fog signal. It also meant more outdoor work. During March, Peter Knudsen and his crew hauled 150 cords of wood they had cut out of the woods and piled it on the beach in front of the station. Martin and his son cut 45 cedar buoy poles on the east side of the island — they were to be used to mark buoy locations — and transported them to the station, where Edward set to work peeling off the bark. He also cut and peeled thirteen fence posts for the garden his father had laid out northeast of the dwelling. At the same time, the assistants spent their time repairing and painting the station's boats. In early April, the lifesaving station reopened for the season, the surfmen resumed foot patrols around the island, and the ice went out for the last time.

Once warm weather returned and navigation opened, life for the keepers slipped back into the familiar routine. First, there were the general lighthouse duties revolving around the operation of the range lights and fog signal. Second, since Plum Island was still not completely cleared of stumps and graded into the nearly park-like lawns it eventually would have, the men devoted time to the grounds and garden. Third, there were the frequent trips for mail, supplies, family, and friends to Detroit Harbor and the mainland ports. Mrs. Knudsen and Agnes cooked the meals for the men and did other household chores. Days at the station were busy, and there was always an element of uncertainty; if at any time visibility was reduced, all other work was immediately abandoned to get the fog signal operating as quickly as possible. The fog might lift in minutes or remain for days, adding yet more uncertainty.

While preparing to paint the rear range light tower, Knudsen discovered a crack in the north column near the base, despite the fact that the tower was only two years old. After he received permission to repair it, he drilled holes in the column, attached a copper plate, and wound two layers of copper wire over the plate to hold it in place to prevent further cracking. In 1997, Knudsen's repair job was still clearly in place.

In May, Knudsen's sister Mrs. Charles E. Young, visited the Knudsens for several weeks before going to Algoma where her husband, formerly keeper at Chambers Island, had been transferred.

The month of June 1899 got off to an unusual and romantic start. On June 8, Louis Hutzler, keeper at Pottowatomie Light, arrived at Plum Island. Two days later, Knudsen signalled the *Ann*

Arbor Car Ferry No.3 bound for Frankfort, Michigan to stop, and he put Hutzler aboard. A week later the ferry hove to off Plum Island and landed Hutzler and his new bride at the station. The next day, Knudsen's assistants took the newlyweds to Detroit Harbor as they made their way back to the station at Rock Island. Edward Knudsen, who had often substituted at the station and worked for his father, became the Washington Island mail carrier.

In July the *Dahlia*'s crew loaded the buoy poles the Knudsens had cut, and a schooner came to pick up a load of wood from the 150 cords Peter Knudsen and his crew had cut; the district inspector also ordered Knudsen to secure bids for the cutting of 400 cords of wood during the coming winter.

However, the most important event of the month was a telegram on July 25 announcing Knudsen's transfer to the Racine Pierhead Light to replace George Larson, who had resigned. Knudsen and his family were well known and well liked in the area, and people were very sorry to hear of his transfer.

> Everybody is heartily sorry to have Mr. Knudsen leave this section where has long been a resident and is well and favorably known. He is withal a royal good fellow.[14]

Martin and Theresa Knudsen left for Racine on August 1 where they lived until 1917, when the Lighthouse Bureau transferred Knudsen to the North Point Lighthouse in Milwaukee. Most people expected that the couple eventually would return to Washington Island. However, when Knudsen retired in 1924 at age 70, the couple elected to remain living in Milwaukee. Martin Knudsen lived an active retirement with occasional visits to Washington Island until he died on 26 July 1943 of complications from a broken hip. Door County's most widely honored lighthouse keeper was buried in Racine, Wisconsin.[15]

On 1 August 1899, Martin Knudsen turned over the station to his former first assistant Hans J. Hanson, whom the Board promoted to keeper. George Cornell was promoted to first assistant from second assistant, and C.W. Baer received a probationary appointment as second assistant. Hans J. Hanson was born in February 1866 in Sevastopol, Wisconsin, to Norwegian parents. His wife Anna was ten years younger, and when her husband received his keeper's appointment, she was pregnant with their first child. Hanson had begun his lighthouse career at Pilot Island with Knudsen in September 1892 before coming to Plum Island when the station opened. Once the Knudsen's furniture and household goods had been shipped to Racine, Hanson began cleaning, painting, and varnishing the keeper's quarters.

Since Hanson had been at the station since it opened, he easily made the transition to keeper and maintained established routines. He and his assistants spent much of the fall working on the grounds, painting the outside and inside of the rear tower, and helping load wood onto schooners to be shipped to Pilot Island and South Fox Island stations. In early September, while the assistants were working on the grounds, they discovered the fog signal dock was on fire. Before it could be put out, fire had severely burned several planks, though fortunately the dock was quickly repaired. Since they had not sounded the fog signal for two days, the men were at a loss as to the cause of the fire.

Important events in the personal lives of the keepers also occurred. On 14 September 1899, first assistant George J. Cornell left for Detroit Harbor at 10 AM to get married; he returned with his wife at 2 PM the next day. Also in September, the Lighthouse Board appointed Edward Knudsen assistant to his father at the Racine Pierhead Light. This left only one Knudsen a resident of Washington Island, Edward's sister Agnes. On 26 November 1899, a messenger came from Detroit Harbor to tell Hanson that his wife was in labor. He left at once, but by the time he got to his wife, she had already given birth to a daughter. Hanson returned to his post, but his wife and daughter Harriett did not return to Plum Island for several months.

That year when the *Dahlia*'s crew attempted to land the usual three tons of coal at the station's dock, the waves were too rough, and the crew was forced to put the coal ashore on the dock at the lifesaving station. The keepers then had to move the fifty-pound bags of coal in wheelbarrows about a half-mile through the woods to the light station. This represented a great deal of extra work for the men, since at the station they would have had to move the coal less than a hundred feet. Preparing for winter also meant taking down the screens and putting up the storm windows, raking the lawn, putting more stones in the landing cribs, burning more brush and stumps, and working on the boats — all of these activities, as always, in addition to tending the all-important lights in the towers and the boilers and sirens in the fog signal.

The new century dawned clear and cold. To celebrate, the keepers and lifesavers went skating on the pond east of the fog signal. The men kept at their duties until January 26 when Hanson received notice of Baer's discharge at the end of his six-month probationary period; the inspector apparently did not have to give reasons for such an action. Hanson hired a laborer temporarily until the Board's replacement for Baer, Jonathan B. Young, arrived at the station on February 19. A week later he brought his wife and child to Plum Island to join the Cornells and Hanson in the dwelling. While the continued cold caused the pipes from the well to the fog signal to freeze, it made easy work of trips over the ice to Washington Island and the mainland. However, when the weather warmed, a strong northwest wind caused the ice to shove against the fog signal dock, moving the two outer cribs some eight feet to the south. Later in April, another ice shove overturned several of the cribs, completely ruining the dock, though the keepers salvaged the tramway tracks, an unused pump house, and most of the heavy planks that had decked the cribs.

With the arrival of spring, the keepers once again began their routine of cleaning, polishing, painting, and varnishing, as well as tending the grounds and putting in their gardens. The steamer *Havanna* ran ashore on the southwest point of Plum Island near the lower range light at 2:30 AM on 30 May 1900. Fortunately, she was going slowly because of foggy conditions and did not go hard aground. By 5 AM her crew had, by their own efforts, gotten the vessel afloat and underway without damage. In early June, lighthouse engineer Wredge arrived for a two-week stay during which he and the keepers completely overhauled the equipment in the fog signal. After Wredge left, the men spent more than a week cutting grass around the station, raking it up, and putting it in the barn for hay. Hanson celebrated the Fourth of July by sounding the fog signal, not because of the holiday, but because it was foggy during the day. Early in August, first assistant Cornell went on a fifteen-day leave of absence, and his brother Alvin Cornell substituted for him. Since the range lights had remained open all winter, when many of the other lights were closed, this was the first time in over a year that Cornell had been away from his post for an extended period. When he returned, Hanson took leave for eighteen days, hiring Alvin Cornell as his substitute. During August, most of the 400 cords of wood cut during the winter were transported to the Poverty Island and the Pilot Island stations.

On September 10, Hanson returned to his assignment. The next day he and George Cornell took one of the station's boats to Detroit Harbor to get provisions, send mail, and return Alvin Cornell to his home. On their way back a fierce squall capsized the boat. Hanson and Cornell clung to the boat until it was washed ashore near the lifesaving station. The boat was undamaged, but Hanson lost his trunk and his wallet. He never found the trunk and later found only $30 of the amount he was carrying at the time of the accident.

As fall approached, despite uncertainty about whether the station would remain open during the winter, the keepers began making preparations. They made numerous trips for provisions, cut and piled stove wood near the dwelling, dug potatoes, cleaned the grounds, and placed more stone into the cribs in front of the boathouse. Hanson butchered a hog he had fattened and salted down the meat. In mid-November, Hanson received orders to keep the station open until further notice, to cut 40 buoy poles, and to get bids for the cutting of 200 cords of wood on the island. The Hansons hosted Thanksgiving dinner in their quarters for the Cornells and the Youngs. As the weather got colder and more snow fell, the pace of activities slowed, though there still were frequent trips to Washington Island and the mainland.

Hanson was ordered to extinguish the lights and close the fog signal for the season on the last day of January. They had not sounded it for some time, so the men were able quickly to drain and clean the boiler and other machinery in the fog signal and also to prepare the range lights to be shut down. Both assistants and their families went ashore on February 1; the Hansons remained another week before leaving to visit friends on Washington Island. Hanson's periodic inspection visits found the Plum Island Range Lights wrapped in cold and snow.

The Hansons returned to the station in late February and were soon followed by first assistant Cornell, second assistant Young and their families. After several days of preparation, Hanson officially opened the station for the season, relighting the range lights and readying the fog signal. This also marked the beginning of the well-established routines of cleaning, polishing, painting, and varnishing. In May, Engineer Wredge spent a week repairing and overhauling the boilers and machinery in the fog signal. Later a Lighthouse Board work party spent several weeks at the station. Two of the crew members were painters, and they painted the entire interior of the dwelling — ordinarily the responsiblity of the keepers. Interestingly, the men left the varnishing to the keepers. Other members of the crew removed the stones from the cribs at the fog signal and floated the four usable ones to the landing in front of the dwelling. They added additional logs to the cribs to raise them to the proper height above the waterline, filled them with stone, and decked the cribs with heavy planks, extending the dock. The boatways were lengthened, and a new boat car was installed to haul the boats out of the water and into the boathouse.

On 29 September 1901, Hanson and his assistants observed the day of President McKinley's funeral by flying the flag at half-mast and doing no work except that required by lighthouse duties. While digging potatoes in his garden, Hanson found a twelve-inch Indian hunting knife made of pure copper. In fall the crew of the *Dahlia* delivered three new, improved 5th Order lamps for the front range light. However, since the lens needed modification, the keepers did not install them.

Hanson's wife and daughter and Mrs. Young and her children went ashore on 31 October 1901. This was in compliance with orders from the inspector that all women and small children were to be sent ashore by November 1 from island light stations which would be closed for the winter. Cornell's wife and child remained at Plum Island because Cornell was going to winter at the closed station and look after it. Hanson and Young went ashore to get groceries and household utensils so they could board together until the station closed.

Then in mid-November, Hanson was ordered to keep the station open all winter, but the families decided to stay on Washington Island since Hanson and Young were able to visit them regularly (usually at least once a week). Hanson was allowed to employ a laborer for the winter months, and he hired Peter K. Christianson of Ellison Bay, who had won the bid to cut cordwood on the island during the past several winters. This practice stopped in 1901, when the keeper was ordereds not to seek bids for cutting cordwood or to cut down any more trees. For domestic use, the men were to cut fallen trees or logs taken from the beach. Nothing special happened on Thanksgiving, but on Christmas day Hanson and Young ate both dinner and supper with Cornell and his wife.

Once again as winter deepened, the pace of activities slowed at the range lights. Hanson and Cornell even had enough time to go icefishing in January. Whether it was the cold or being away from his family or another opportunity, Jonathan Young decided in February to resign as second assistant; on 4 February 1902 he borrowed Bo Anderson's team to move his household goods to Detroit Harbor. Young's resignation took effect at the end of February, and he left the station then for the final time. However the position did not stay empty for long. The Lighthouse Board transferred Edward Knudsen from being his father's assistant in Racine back to Plum Island to replace Young. Since he had spent a great deal of time at the range lights while his father was the keeper, Knudsen easily slipped into the routine of operations. An additional benefit of the transfer was that it made it much easier for Knudsen to visit his girl friend on Washington Island. Hanson himself went on a seventeen-day leave of absence, taking his family to Sturgeon Bay to visit family and friends.

The fog sirens continued to be a problem. In April, the steamer *Alexander McDougal* ran onto the reef on the southwest point of Plum Island in fog and rain. The captain told Hanson that, although he had heard the for siren while outside of Pilot Island, he could not hear the signal when he was close to Plum Island. After about two hours grounded on the reef, the vessel's crew freed her, and she proceeded on her voyage.

The fog signal had been operating the entire time, but mechanical failures made it increasingly difficult to keep the sirens working. Finally in late May, Hanson notified the inspector that Siren No. 2 could not be fixed and received orders to crate up the siren and ship it back to the district depot for repair. On June 1, a foggy Sunday during which the men sounded the remaining siren all day, the steamer *Iron Chief* went on the beach in front of the front range light tower with a barge in tow; fortunately, the steamer backed off after a short time and continued into Green Bay. Only a week later, a new siren arrived at the station, but, unfortunately, siren No. 1 soon broke down and had to be replaced.

In July a working party arrived for a three-week stay to replace the boatways and to install cribs for a second landing just south of the boatways so they would be protected from waves from the south. Engineer Wredge also stopped at the station to overhaul the boilers in the fog signal and to install the new 5th Order lamps which had arrived the previous year. He had to remove part of the lens in the front tower to make the lamps fit in the lens. Another visitor was Edward Knudsen's uncle, Charles E. Young, who had been transferred from Algoma to the Menominee Pierhead Lightin Michigan. He would return to Plum Island three years later as keeper.

Despite their best efforts, the keepers continued to have difficulties with the fog sirens. Finally, the engineers decided to make a change. In mid-November, they notified Hanson that less complicated ten-inch steam whistles were being sent to the station to replace the sirens without a change in the existing characteristic. Since he had orders to start using the whistles on December 10, Hanson installed them on December 5 in order to check them first. He was very embarrassed and concerned to report to the inspector that, despite orders, shortly after he had set up the whistles on December 5, it had started to snow, and he could not wait until

December 10 to begin using them. The inspector assured him that he had acted properly.

The day after Christmas, Hanson developed a disabling carbuncle on his right hand. In the days before penicillin, such an infection was a very serious matter, and Knudsen quickly took Hanson to the doctor in Detroit Harbor. Mrs. Hanson soon followed when the doctor estimated that her husband would be confined for two or three weeks.

Although Hanson was absent, the new year began routinely for Cornell and Knudsen. Not until 19 January 1903 did the Hansons return to Plum Island, and it was another three days before the keeper officially returned to duty. The year proceeded uneventfully, as the keepers went about their usual tasks. On June 29, second assistant Knudsen left on a twenty-five-day leave of absence. He married Miss Anne Symmonds the next day in the Baptist Church on Washington Island.

The Hansons, expecting the range lights to remain open all winter, spent most of October on vacation, visiting friends and family in the Sturgeon Bay area. Aa crew of government plasterers arrived in mid-November to replaster the interior of the dwelling, a job that took them most of a month.

During the fall, the keepers decided to build an ice house at the station. Surprisingly, they seem to have decided to go ahead on their own without asking or receiving permission. Such activities normally were closely controlled at any station with several thick books of rules, regulations, and procedures. But, though he had not given official approval, the inspector evidently had no objections, since on subsequent visits he did not order them to remove the ice house. It was a temporary structure and probably was built on the shore near the dwelling so that it would be easy to fill in the winter while still providing handy access during the summer. Both January and February of 1904 were particularly cold. Indeed, Lake Michigan froze so far out that year that no open water was visible from the towers on either Plum or Pilot Islands. The men spent several weeks harvesting ice blocks and insulating them in the ice house with sawdust hauled in bags from a sawmill on Washington Island. It was hard, cold work, but the anticipation of having ice to cool food and drink during the warm summer months undoubtedly made it worthwhile.

Probably the most exciting news of the season was that on November 30, the contractor set the poles for a telephone line which was to be connected to the mainland by cable. The next day they also strung wires to the lifesaving station, but it was not until 17 May 1904 that they laid the underwater cable connecting Plum Island with the mainland at Northport. The underwater cable from Washington Island to the Plum Island Life Saving Station had been laid earlier and men from the life saving station connected the cable to the wires running between the two stations. Hanson proudly entered in his log on May 20: "Communication was had by telephone between Main-Land and Plum today for the first time." The sense of isolation on Plum Island, despite the visibility of the mainland, was now lessened, although the telephone was to be used only for official business.

On 30 May 1904, before he could enjoy much of the ice he had helped to store, second assistant Edward Knudsen received notice that the Lighthouse Board had promoted him to first assistant and was transfering him to the Kenosha Light Station. Three days later, after packing their household goods, the Knudsens left by boat for Kenosha. Hanson hired an acting assistant as a substitute until the new second assistant, Alfred C. Erickson, arrived at Plum Island on June 25.

A week later, Peter Brust, an area welldriller, arrived by boat to drill a well south of the dwelling for the keepers' use; up to that time it was still necessary to carry water from the lake. Even though the well at the fog signal — only a short distance to the north — was only twenty-seven feet deep, the new well was drilled down seventy feet before an adequate water supply was reached.

After an uneventful summer and fall, Hanson was ordered to close the station on 5 January 1905 for the winter. After two days of work, first assistant Cornell and his family departed for Washington Island, while second assistant Erickson left for his home in Whitehall, Michigan. Hanson and his family remained at Plum Island. Later, when they left to visit friends on Washington Island and in Sturgeon Bay, Cornell came out to stay at the station.

In April 1905, Hanson and his assistants were all back on duty preparing for the opening of navigation. They were hard at work before the *Ann Arbor Ferry No.3* passed through the Deaths Door passage on her way to Menominee, Michigan on April 17. After a routine spring and summer, Hans J. Hanson, the second keeper at the range lights, received a telegram on 8 August 1905 informing him of his transfer to the Menominee, Michigan Pierhead Light; he left the next day for his new assignment on Peter Knudsen's schooner *Iris*. Hanson himself spent the rest of his career at Menominee, planning to move back with his wife upon retirement to Sturgeon Bay to grow cherries in the orchard they had already planted. However, on 6 October 1923, two years before retirement, he suffered a heart attack while bringing a load of wood to his lighthouse and died.[16]

Charles E. Young from Menominee Pierhead Light was the new keeper was who exchanged assignments with Hanson; Young was returning to Door County where he had begun his career in 1889 on Pilot Island. Like many keepers on a new assignment, Young engaged in a burst of cleaning and painting, even though the station had been thoroughly cleaned and painted that very spring. Young seemed particularly interested in the appearance of the range lights. In addition to painting, he and his assistants pulled stumps, levelled the grounds, cut weeds, and took care of the grass; these activities paid off, for when the chairman of the Lighthouse Board, Rear Admiral Reiter, inspected Plum Island, he wrote in the log, "It is gratifying to find the station in such excellent condition."

After closing the station for the winter on 23 January 1906, Young and Cornell joined their families on Washington Island; Erickson went to Whitehall, Michigan. Young and Cornell returned to their posts on 1 April 1906, but Joseph Kilgore, who had been at Pottowatomie Light on Rock Island, replaced Erickson as second assistant and moved his family into the dwelling a month later. George Cornell received notice on September 17 that he had been promoted to keeper and was being transferred to the Racine Reef Light. He and his wife packed up their furniture and household goods and left for Racine one week later. At the same time, the Board promoted Joseph Kilgore to first assistant, and Nels Jepson of Washington Island became the new acting second assistant.

During September Young moved his family to Washington Island for the winter. A Board work crew arrived in October and built 1,149 feet of fence enclosing the dwelling and outbuildings. The old wooden walks around the dwelling were replaced by 276 feet of concrete walks, and the wooden walks stretching about a half mile from the front range light to the fog signal house were repaired. Later, they too would be replaced with concrete walks. The keeper and his assistants continued working on the grounds, cleaning up and wheeling in dirt to permit more grass to be grown on the sandy soil. Pilot Island station closed in late December, but Plum Island did not close until 17 January 1907.

When Young opened the station 1 April 1907, he once again had a new second assistant. The Board had replaced Jepson with 22-year-old Morris Weiss from Baileys Harbor. Activities at Plum

Island proceeded routinely until July 11 when Young received notice of his own transfer to the Kenosha Station. After two days of packing, Young turned the station over to first assistant Kilgore and left for Kenosha. Young spent the remaining twenty-five years of his lighthouse career at Kenosha, retiring in 1932 because of ill health. He and Mary remained in Kenosha after retirement, where he was a member of the First Methodist Church and a Mason. He died 16 October 1938 following an extended illness and was buried in Kenosha.[17]

Joseph Boshka, a 34-year-old Wisconsin native, replaced Charles Young as keeper at Plum Island, arriving on 17 July 1907. He and his 29-year-old wife, Anna, would have a daughter born to them while at Plum Island. Although attentive to the usual routine of cleaning, polishing, painting, and varnishing, Boshka seems to have been more concerned with the operation of the machinery at the station. He was immediately concerned about several leaking pumps and the poor condition of the No. 1 fog signal. It is also interesting that a decade-long policy of cutting trees and removing their stumps was to be reversed by Boshka; he planted a number of trees around the dwelling and other buildings. As usual, the closing of the range lights depended on when the Ann Arbor ferries discontinued going to Menominee, and, on January 16, Boshka and his assistants laid up the fog signal and extinguished the range lights. He then left for his home in Racine, while Kilgore and Weiss went to Baileys Harbor.

Kilgore was given the responsibility of making periodic inspections of the station while it was closed. During one such visit on 1 April 1908, two ferries attempted to pass into Green Bay earlier in the season than usual. Kilgore lit the lamps in the towers and then called Boshka and Weiss to return to Plum Island. When the ferries turned back because of heavy ice, Boshka extinguished the lights, and not until six days later did he officially open the range lights for the season and begin the usual routine of chores. Boshka received notice in August 1908 that his keeper's pay of $600 per year — the same pay that Martin Knudsen received in 1897 — had been increased $2 per month to an annual total of $624.

The 1908 navigation season passed without incident, and the station closed after the ferries stopped running on 13 January 1908. The assistants left for their homes in Baileys Harbor, but Boshka remained at Plum Island for two more weeks before leaving for Green Bay and Menominee.

That spring, the assistants reported for duty on 5 April 1909, though bad weather delayed Boshka's arrival four days. Boshka's and Kilgore's families joined them a month later. Weiss was a bachelor, but on June 11 he left on a ten-day leave to get married in Baileys Harbor; Weiss brought his wife Agnes back to Plum Island at the end of his leave.

Travel for the keepers was eased considerably during the summer, when the district inspector informed Boshka that he was sending them a gasoline engine to power one of the station's boats. Boshka hired William Jess, justice of the peace on Washington Island, to install the engine. Jess completed the work in late July, but the engine did not work well on its maiden voyage to Detroit Harbor. After several weeks of unsuccessful tinkering with the faulty engine, a Board mechanic arrived and installed a new coil, which solved the problem. The inspector also authorized Boshka to have a cabin constructed on the boat to protect passengers from the elements. A gasoline launch meant having almost the same freedom to travel that a car gave to keepers on the mainland. The end of all ferry operations on 8 January 1910 marked the end of navigation for the season.

Assistant Kilgore reopened the station 31 March 1910, four days before the keeper returned. This would be his final opening at Plum Island; he received a telegram on July 15 instructing him to report immediately to Wind Point Light, Racine, Wisconsin as first assistant. He departed Plum Island later that day, leaving his wife and children to follow later. Kilgore was subsequently promoted to keeper and transferred to the Grand Haven Light on Lake Michigan's eastern shore; he died there 11 February 1920, a few weeks short of his fifty-third birthday.[19] George Merugs arrived as first assistant three days after Kilgore left.

In November Boshka received the now customary notice to close the station after the last ferry left Menominee. Boshka and his assistants extinguished the lights and shut down the fog signal on New Year's Eve 1910. The lights were dark and the fog signal silent until 28 March 1911.

The year began routinely, but 1911 would be a year of change. At the end of May, second assistant Weiss was transferred to Cana Island as first assistant; both he and his wife were from nearby Baileys Harbor, so the transfer was welcome. The district inspector notified Joseph Boshka on 8 November 1911 that he had been appointed keeper at the Holland Michigan Harbor Light. His replacement at Plum Island was to be his brother, Charles Boshka, the keeper at Pottowatomie Light on Rock Island. Charles Boshka officially took charge of the station on 22 November 1911. His wife Mollie, whom he had married in 1898 on Pilot Island, arrived soon after with their daughter and son. His brother had stayed only four years at Plum Island, but Charles Boshka remained there until June 1925 when he retired after thirty years of lighthouse service. Born in Racine, he served at Door County lights for much of his career; he and his wife retired to a home on Washington Island where he died at age 56 on 12 October 1925. Mollie continued to live on Washington Island until her death 5 September 1945.[19] Oscar Johnson replaced Charles Boshka and was followed in turn by Clayton Kinkaid, the last civilian keeper at the Plum Island Range Light.

Among the last assistants serving at Plum Island was Herman Erickson. He had taken a civil service exam for an assistant keeper position and he received an appointment at Michigan's South Fox Island Light Station in June 1937. Erickson left his wife and five children behind in Sister Bay, Wisconsin when he went to his initial assignment. The following year, Erickson was transferred to Plum Island as second assistant. His daughter Helen made the first of many visits to the island in April 1938. She arrived there riding in a Coast Guard boat from Northport to the Plum Island Coast Guard Station (formerly the Plum Island Life Saving Station) and then walked through the woods with her father to the range lights.

Her father lived in the upstairs quarters of the second assistant, which had a kitchen, bedroom, and pantry, and living room (that they used as a second bedroom). A Kohler generator provided power for lighting during the summer, but kerosene lamps were used in the winter. There was no refrigeration, and water for cooking and drinking had to be carried in from the pump outside. For several years, Mrs. Erickson and her three daughters spent the summer months at the station. The girls enjoyed hiking, picking berries, playing games, and going fishing with their father. As often as possible they went with the Coast Guardsmen as they made their daily trips to Washington Island for mail and supplies, and their father would sometimes row them over to Pilot Island or to Northport for a visit. More often, however, the girls rode to and from Northport in the larger Coast Guard boat. There was a telephone on a pole at Northport that the Coast Guardsmen used to call their station to get a ride back to their station. When the Erickson girls wanted to talk to their father, they would use the phone to call the Coast Guard station, and someone there would connect them to the phone at the range lights. After the Coast Guard absorbed the Lighthouse Service in 1939, Erickson joined that service. In March 1942 he was transferred to the Wind Point Light in Racine, Wisconsin. Before retiring in 1958 after a 20-year career, Erickson served for several years at the Manitowoc Breakwater Light.[20]

The range lights were manned by Coast Guard personnel after Kinkaid left Plum Island. Following World War II, the Coast Guard consolidated all operations on Plum Island at the Plum Island Coast Guard Station. The range lights were electrified and automated, and the dwelling was closed. A wooden watch room was added to the west end of the brick fog signal building, overlooking Deaths Door passage. It was manned by personnel from the Coast Guard station, who also maintained and operated the diesel-powered compressed-air fog signal. Without keepers at the range lights to maintain them, the wooden front range light tower deteriorated. It was replaced in 1964 with the present steel skeletal tower. The lamp and lens were removed and an electric beacon placed on top of the tower. The barn, privy, oil house, boathouse, docks, boatways, and other buildings were removed from the station, leaving only the dwelling, the front and rear range light towers, and the fog signal house on the grounds. In 1975, the Coast Guard discontinued operation of the fog signal, removed the equipment and storage tanks, and boarded up the fog signal house.

Today the Plum Island Range Lights and fog signal house are probably seen by more people than any other station in Door County, since they are visible from the ferries as they make their way to and from Washington Island. However, like the Pilot Island Light, Plum Island is virtually inaccessible. The automated range lights still help to guide mariners through the Deaths Door passage, as they have since 1897, but weeds grow tall on the station's grounds and no keepers tread the concrete walks that still connect the existing buildings and indicate the locations of those that have disappeared.

Pilot Island light looking southwards from near the west landing, 1914. Photo courtesy of the Milwaukee Public Library/Wisconsin Marine Historial Society.

Chapter 4
Pilot Island Light

Standing on the ferry dock at Northport, at the northeastern tip of the Door County Peninsula, you are immediately struck by the buildings of the Plum Island Range Lights across the channel in front of you. Much less obvious is a small island to your right, a short distance off the south end of Plum Island. Very small and low-lying, Pilot Island seemingly hovers on the horizon, miles from anywhere. However, it is much closer to Washington and Plum Islands than it appears from Northport, and it takes a keen eye to distinguish the Pilot Island Light. Viewing the station from the water must be done very carefully, so as to avoid the reefs and shallows that surround the southern half of the island.

To set foot on the island itself can be a complicated process — you first must get permission from the Coast Guard authorities to land, next you must wait until the waves are calm before tying your boat up to the large concrete crib about twenty-five feet off the west shore, and finally you must jump off the crib into chest-deep water to make your way over slippery stones to emerge on the site of the ruined marine railway. Once on dry land, you follow the old cement walks through the underbrush from where the boat-ouse was located to the lighthouse. And it is a good idea to keep an eye on the weather, or you may find yourself stranded on Pilot Island.

Pilot Island is a low rocky mass of dolomite approximately 3.7 acres in size. It is elliptical in shape measuring some 775 feet from north to south and about 350 feet from east to west at its maximum. Rocky shallows much more extensive than the island itself extend for several hundred yards from the shore on the east and around to the southwest of the island. The highest spot on the island, where the lighthouse stands, rises only eleven feet above the waters of Lake Michigan. The shallows, while hazardous to vessels, help to dissipate the waves sweeping up the full length of Lake Michigan, and Plum, Detroit, and Washington Islands provide protection from the north; thus, despite its low elevation, there are no accounts of storm waves sweeping over Pilot Island. However, high waves, especially those from the northwest, have often kept people from coming to or leaving the island. In 1858 a few evergreens clung precariously to the island along with low shrubs growing in the meager soil.

When the Board crew arrived at the island in 1858, they faced a major problem simply getting ashore. They built a landing on the shallow reefs on the east side of the island and, on calm days, landed their supplies and construction materials. Having chosen the highest point on the island as the natural site for the light, the crew blasted a hole in the rock for a basement, keeping some of the stone for the basement walls. A 2½-story keepers' dwelling measuring thirty-five feet square was built out of cream-colored brick with a an attached kitchen of one story measuring fifteen feet by seventeen feet and an entrance extending from the dwelling's northeast corner. Projecting from the roof of the dwelling at the western gable was a square tower topped by a ten-sided, cast-iron lantern holding a 4th Order Fresnel lens. The focal plane of the light was forty-six feet above lake level, and the lens cast a flashing white light over the waters.[1]

When William Shurtteffy moved in 1858 from Plum Island to Port des Morts Island as keeper, Royal Riggins came with him as assistant. But, on 27 May 1859, both were removed from their appointments and replaced by William Garey, aged 50, and his 15-year-old son John. Garey apparently was a widower, and his 18-year-old daughter Kate performed the household duties. After only two years, the Lighthouse Board removed Garey and his son. Indeed for the first few years, service at Porte des Morts resembled a revolving door; there were seven keepers in nine years. E.T. Wells served as keeper for two years before being removed. One of his assistants, John Kenard, was promoted to keeper in June 1863, only to be removed six months later, and Joel Westbrook, Kenard's assistant, resigned after Kenard's removal. In January 1864, the Board appointed D.C. Reed as keeper, but he resigned in October 1864. Jacob Stahl replaced Reed, and Joel Westbrook returned as assistant keeper; Stahl resigned in June 1865, but Westbrook remained until March 1867, when the Board removed him. John Kenard, whom the Board had removed in January 1864, was again appointed keeper in June 1865, but fourteen months later Kenard was gone, replaced by Victor E. Rohn on 21 August 1866. Long terms of service were the norm at most Door County lights, and the records give little explanation for this rapid early turnover. The Lighthouse Board removed five of the keepers, presumably for some failure in the performance of their duties, but exactly what the problem was with keepers at this station cannot be explained. Two of the keepers resigned, perhaps seeing greater opportunities elsewhere. Perhaps the isolation bothered them, though later keepers remained for long tours of duty. With Rohn's appointment the revolving door stopped.[2]

Also, while keepers continued to move on and off the island, other changes were occurring at the station. At times fog blanketed the passage, making navigation through the Deaths Door Passage even more difficult and dangerous than usual, and the Lighthouse Board soon decided to install a fog signal. In 1860 the Board received $1500 from Congress to erect a fog bell at the light station, but that proved to be aan inadequate solution. Four years later, a Board crew built a wooden fog signal house south of the dwelling and installed a wood-fired steam boiler to power a fog trumpet. Operation of the fog signal meant added duties for the keeper and his assistant.

As was mentioned above, the Board appointed Victor E. Rohn keeper on August 21, 1866. Rohn, who had been born in Austria, was 35 years old and had been a lieutenant in the Union

Army. His wife, Jannette, was four years younger and a native of Newfoundland. At the time of Rohn's appointment they had seven children, five girls and two boys, all under 13 years of age, with another son to be born two years later. Not wanting to appoint and pay an assistant so close to the end of the navigation season, the Board waited until the following March to appoint Jannette as her husband's assistant. During the summer, Pilot Island was an active place, with seven children playing and helping their parents to operate the light and fog signal. The Rohns had a farm on Washington Island where they lived when navigation was closed for the winter. During the spring and fall, Rohn made regular trips to Detroit Harbor to see the family, for Jannette and the children continued living on the farm while the children were in school.

In 1868 a Board crew replastered and repainted the dwelling and the insides of the tower and fog signal house. Since the fire-clay lining of the fog signal boiler needed to be renewed, Rohn requested and received authorization to have a local mason do the work. Noting that no repairs had been made for several years, in 1874 the Board obtained a $1,200 Congressional appropriation for that purpose. They put a new roof on the dwelling, and they repaired the boats which had been seriously damaged when Rohn saved a shipwrecked crew. Since the time the light was first built in 1858, the station's boats had either been tied up to the small landing built by the construction crew on the east side of the island, or hauled out of the water on the rocks. This made for difficult and sometimes dangerous landings and also took a toll on the station's boats. Thus, the Board ordered construction of a boathouse and marine railway to haul boats at the landing out of the water and into the boathouse.

Despite the improvements, Rohn recorded a comment on 4 July 1874 that many others have cited as evidence of how difficult life on Pilot Island could be:

> Independence day came in fine after a heavy southeast gale. This island affords about as much independence and liberty as Libby Prison, with the difference of guards in favor of this place, and chance of outside communication in favor of the other.[3]

Part of the reason for Rohn's comment was his disgust and disappointment that the heavy southeast gale had prevented him from launching his boat from the east landing and going to Washington Island for the much-anticipated annual Fourth of July festivities. In reality, life at the station must have had its good points since, in September 1871, the Rohn's 16-year-old daughter Emily, who had grown up as a keeper's daughter and was very familiar with life at a lighthouse, married William C. Betts, the Pottowatomie Light keeper from nearby Rock Island.

During the summer of 1875, a Lighthouse Board crew replaced the old trumpet fog signal with a new first-class steam fog siren consisting of a large trumpet with a wide mouth and a narrow throat. In the throat was a fixed disk with twelve radial slits. Behind the fixed disk was another disk with twelve radial slits which revolved 2,400 times a minute. The siren was sounded by driving compressed steam through the two disks producing 28,800 vibrations a minute which projected an intense beam of sound from the mouth of the trumpet.[4] Under ordinary circumstances the siren could be heard for a distance of twenty miles, but fog sometimes distorted the sound, causing zones of silence just where mariners most needed to hear the signal.

Operating the fog signal was time-consuming, since a fire had to be lit to heat the water in the boiler and then maintained to produce steam during the signal's operation. When the weather cleared, the fire was allowed to go out. Once everything had cooled, a fire had to be laid so it could be started quickly and steam produced once more. In addition, the signal's operating parts had to be cleaned and polished, and logs had to be cut and split for fuel, a job which took up a great deal of time. To help with the additional workload, the Board appointed Peter Knudsen as second assistant in May 1875. On 11 November 1875, the new fog signal officially went into service, giving blasts of five seconds duration at intervals of thirty-seven seconds.[5]

For whatever reason, the Board removed Rohn as keeper in September 1876 after ten years of service on Pilot Island. He and his family moved to their farm on Washington Island, although he continued to be a frequent visitor to the station and served as a substitute keeper when needed.

Captain Emmanuel Davidson replaced Rohn as keeper. He was born near Farsund, Norway in 1822 and had left his homeland for the sea as a youth; Davidson served for three years aboard transports carrying soldiers and equipment during the Mexican War. He came to Milwaukee in 1848 and later took command of the schooner *Three Bells,* which carried fish between Whitefish Bay and Detroit. Davidson also sailed schooners between Marinette-Menominee and Milwaukee. He tried farming for three years and ran a Scandinavian boardinghouse in Milwaukee for five years. Davidson apparently received a probationary appointment in October 1876 as keeper at Pilot Island with no previous lighthouse experience. On 4 March 1852, he married Christiana Markasun in Milwaukee. She was born in Fares, Norway on 8 August 1832, immigrating to America in 1850. The couple had four children, two sons and two daughters. Christiana was appointed first assistant at the same time that her husband received his appointment; Peter Knudsen remained as second assistant. However one year after Davidson's appointment, the Lighthouse Board appointed him keeper of the Poverty Island Light, north of St. Martins Island, with Bryon Olson appointed to serve as Knudsen's replacement until his resignation two years later.

Knudsen was one of three brothers who became lighthouse keepers —Martin, Peter, and Nelson. All of them grew up in what might be called a "lighthouse culture," and all would serve on Pilot Island. Their parents, Peder and Maria Knudsen, had emigrated from Denmark in 1858, where Peder was a farmer by trade. In June 1866 the Knudsens sailed from Racine to Washington Island; they lived briefly on the south end of Rock Island in an empty cabin left when its builders moved to Washington Island. During that fall the three Knudsen boys walked to the Pottowatomie Light on the north end of the island to attend school in the basement of the light-ouse, taught by Mrs. Grover, the assistant keeper's wife. Peder had learned the coopering trade in Racine, a skill that was in great demand among the fishermen. In 1867, the Knudsen family, as had many before them, resettled on the larger and more populous Washington Island at Washington Harbor.[6]

Almost immediately after completion of the new fog signal, there were complaints that Davidson was not sounding the signal in thick weather. The main problem appeared to be keeping the signal in operating condition. In October 1879, there was a published report charging that the fog signal was not heard regularly during foggy weather, but two weeks later a knowledgeable government source informed an *Advocate* reporter that the published statements were entirely wrong. The source said he had been on Pilot Island when the alleged dereliction of duty by the keepers was supposed to have occurred. The informant told the reporter in the strongest terms that the keepers had kept the fog signal operating the entire time there was fog in the area. Nonetheless, an official investigation of the matter revealed that the apparatus did in fact often malfunction just when it was most needed. The Board therefore decided to add a second fog signal at the station, though action was not taken immediately.[7]

An eastern newspaperman visiting the Door Peninsula in 1879 recorded his impressions of the Deaths Door area in a letter which made its way to the editor of the *Door County Advocate*. In a portion of the letter written at Cana Island 14 November 1879, the writer described Port de Mort Island as a small island at the entrance to Deaths Door Passage on which there was a lighthouse and fog signal; he noted that the local sailors and fishermen called the island Pilot Island. Containing less than five acres, the island was the home of the lightkeeper, his family and two assistants for nine months of the year. He also commented that nearby Plum Island was uninhabited and covered with a dense growth of pine and cedar.

This forested condition was true of the vicinity in general in 1879, and the area's small number of inhabitants depended almost entirely on fishing for a livelihood. The writer helped foster the idea of the island's isolation when he complained that he had to wait two weeks for good weather before a fisherman could take him to Pilot Island. Once there, he had to wait ten days, he said, before he could get off, and his boat nearly swamped in the breakers near the landing.[8] While late fall weather can be very stormy, the records show that it rarely interfered with the going and coming of the keepers. Perhaps the writer happened to visit during a particularly stormy period.

Martin Knudsen was a man of several talents. While living on Rock Island with his family, he had learned to sail with the fishermen and crewed for Captain Charles Morbeck of Ephriam on his interisland trading schooner. He also learned the coopering trade at his father's side and put his skill to good use when the Knudsen family moved to Washington Harbor. In the 1860s and 1870s Washington Harbor was a bustling port with a number of warehouses, wharfs, and other buildings.

One day while coopering, he received an invitation to attend a party at Mrs. Kalmbach's house in Detroit Harbor, across the island to the south. The Kalmbachs owned one of several docks at Detroit Harbor and were counted among the leading families in the community, so that an invitation to a party of theirs was prized. This was especially true in this particular case since Theresa Koyen, born in Lolland, Denmark on 26 July 1855, had just arrived from Denmark to join her sister and brother-in-law. Petite, cute, and with an attractive Danish accent, Theresa immediately charmed Martin. She was staying at West Harbor, some 2½ miles from Washington Harbor, but Martin was not put off by the distance. The romance blossomed, and the couple were married in April 1875 at Washington Island's Bethel Church.

Not long after their marriage, Martin was elected justice of the peace. Working hard to support himself and his wife, he coopered, fished, cut cordwood, and sold sewing machines. In the winter of 1879-80 an overheated stove set their home afire, destroying it completely. Fortunately, Theresa and their children, two-year-old Edward and baby Agnes, escaped unharmed, and the family moved in with Theresa's parents, who had now also come to Washington Island, on their nearby farm. The islanders took up a collection to help the Knudsens reestablish their home, but money was short, so Theresa knit woolen mittens, socks, and caps to sell.

One of her customers was John Boyce. He had replaced Bryon Olson as second assistant in September 1879. Boyce was a well-known Washington Islander and an excellent carpenter; he was also an eccentric bachelor whose strange habits sometimes surprised residents. According to some, he was a spiritualist who sometimes spent the night sitting on the church steps or in the cemetery. Boyce mentioned to Martin that he thought he would be leaving Pilot Island before too long. When Martin told Theresa about the conversation, she urged him to immediately write to Davidson asking about the job, in case Boyce did leave. Martin hesitated for several days, and then wrote the letter. He was no doubt influenced by a trip he and his father had taken some years before when a neighbor invited them to go along when he returned Victor Rohn to Pilot Island. Martin had been very impressed by Rohn and the work he did. On his way to the Post Office, Martin met Boyce, who offered to deliver the message to Davidson personally. The following Sunday, a mason who was working on the construction of the second fog signal came to the Knudsen's home and asked Martin, as justice of the peace, to come at once to Pilot Island to preside at an inquest into the death of John Boyce.

At the inquest, it was learned that Boyce had helped a farmer to butcher a cow the previous week, and that he had been particularly interested in the location of the jugular vein. Boyce had been found lying with his jugular veins cut, deliberately arranged with his face down on some boards in order to keep the blood from his clothes. Many people believed, both at that time and since, that the loneliness and isolation of his assignment on Pilot Island caused Boyce's depression and subsequent suicide. However, an interview with a resident whose family are long-time residents of Washington Island and are related to Boyce, suggested that his depression was caused by a failed love affair, rather than by his Pilot Island assignment.

Robert Severs, Washington Harbor correspondent for the *Door County Advocate* wrote on Monday, 21 June 1880:

> I wish I could write you a cheerful letter, but alas this time it cannot be. An event has just happened that makes me, and indeed all of us, feel sad. Our young friend John M. Boyce is no more. His place is vacant. Yesterday, at Pilot Island, he terminated his earthly existence by cutting his throat. He has for several weeks past been in quite a low way, and his friends vainly tried to cheer him up. I saw him on Tuesday, the 15th. We all felt sorry to see him looking so sad and careworn. He absolutely looked

> ten years older, but he would not say what the trouble was. Yesterday he complained to Captain and Mrs. Davidson that he felt unwell, and refused to take his dinner. He went out apparently to take a walk on the beach, after dinner. The workmen who are fixing the new fog signal took a stroll in search of duck eggs, and found poor John laid in the bushes, quite dead. His throat had three deep gashes in it, one on the right and two on the left. Any one of the cuts would have been fatal. He had many fine qualitites and a true and generous heart. He was esteemed by all, and had not a single enemy. Peace to his ashes. Would that his departure had been otherwise.[11]

After the inquest, Captain Davidson talked to Knudsen about his letter and asked him to begin work immediately, while he arranged the appointment paperwork. Martin accepted Davidson's offer, although it was some time before he could pass the place where Boyce's body was found without shuddering. Martin Knudsen thus entered the lighthouse service and realized an ambition he had nursed since his boyhood visit to Pilot Island with his father and Keeper Rohn. The appointment assured the Knudsens a steady income, which Theresa managed with care. The only real drawback was that there was no place on Pilot Island for the family to live. However, Martin could and did frequently use the station's boat to sail over to Washington Island to see how Theresa and the children were doing. Also, Theresa could count on relatives and friends for assistance if Martin was unavailable.[12]

Shortly after Knudsen's appointment, the crew finished the duplicate fog signal. After its completion there were no more complaints from sailors about the fog signal on Pilot Island not being sounded, for if one signal were disabled the other was always ready for service. On 15–16 October 1880, Davidson and Knudsen experienced at first hand one of Lake Michigan's most destructive storms, the famous "Alpena Gale." October 15 began as a warm, beautiful, Indian summer day, but the barometer began to fall. The keepers filled the boilers and rekindled their fires ready to sound the fog signals if necessary. By 9 PMthe winds were blowing very hard, and the next morning the storm's waves were tearing away the shoreline and running high on the island. Fortunately no vessels washed ashore on Pilot Island nor were any of the station's facilities damaged. However, several ships went ashore on nearby Plum Island.

After two years as second assistant at Pilot Island, in 1882 the Lighthouse Board transferred Knudsen and promoted him to keeper of the South Manitou Light Station on the Michigan side of the lake. Knudsen's younger brother Nelson became his assistant. Lesander Davidson, Captain Davidson's son, replaced Martin as his father's assistant. Nine months later, in April 1883, the Lighthouse Board transferred the Davidsons to Grand Haven Light Station in Grand Haven, Michigan. That light operated all year, unlike the light on Pilot Island, but the station was located a only short distance from the community of Grand Haven. Lesander later left the lighthouse service and joined his brother as a sailor on the Great Lakes. Unfortunately both of them subsequently drowned. Captain and Mrs. Davidson stayed at Grand Haven for seventeen years until severe rheumatism caused him finally to resign as keeper. The Davidsons then moved to Sturgeon Bay to live with their daughter and her husband, August Rieboldt; they continued living there even after her death in November 1905. On 28 March 1911, Emmanuel Davidson himself died. When Mrs. Christiana Davidson died on 7 January 1922, she was Sturgeon Bay's oldest resident and was buried with her husband at Bayside Cemetery.[13]

When Captain Davidson left for Grand Haven, the Lighthouse Board transferred Peter Knudsen back to Pilot Island.

He had been scheduled to go to the Stannard Rock Light Rock on Lake Superior, but just before leaving, he received new orders to report to Port des Morts Light. Joining Peter was Jesse Miner, another Washington Islander, who in 1883 was beginning his career in the lighthouse service as first assistant. In October 1883, Major A.R. Flint, engineer for the 9th Lighthouse District, arrived at Pilot Island to conduct a survey of the station. He carefully plotted the outline of the island and the location of the station's buildings. In addition to the dwelling, his map showed two separate fog signal houses, a wooden oil storage house, a summer kitchen, a boathouse and landing, a privy, and another small shed. All the buildings were south of the dwelling. To the west and south of the dwelling was a garden measuring fifty feet by seventy-five feet. The north half of the island had no buildings, only rocks, shrubs, trees, and grass. The oil house was simply a wooden shed some fifty feet south of the dwelling, rather than a fireproof metal structure. Paths and wooden plank sidewalks connected the various buildings.[14]

On January 14, 1884, the *Advocate*'s Baileys Harbor correspondent reported that Peter Knudsen had passed through on his way home to Washington Island from Sturgeon Bay.

> It is rumored he went there on business in connection with a certain contract that he is about to enter into. Wonder who the other one is?

Two weeks later the mystery was solved; the *Advocate* reported that Peter Knudsen had married Miss Susan Decker on Washington Island:

> May a long and prosperous voyage through the vale of tears be the worst misfortune encountered by the happy young couple is the unqualified wish of all their friends.[15]

For several years the couple wintered on Washington Island and spent the rest of the year on Pilot Island. During the cold, winter months when the weather closed navigation, their home was the site of numerous parties and get-togethers.

While Peter Knudsen was keeper, there were a number of assistants at the station. After Jesse Miner left for Rock Island, Peter and Martin's younger brother Nelson became first assistant. Others included Jacob Young, who served as acting second assistant from 1884 until he resigned in 1886 to be replaced by Frederick Bertschy. Young was a Washington Island resident who had come to the island from Berlin, Germany at age 14 with his father.

Peter Knudsen and his family spent the winter of 1888 not on Washington Island, but on the mainland at the village of Newport where Nelson also stayed the winter. According to the *Advocate*, this gave Peter

> much needed respite and relaxation from an arduous and irksome duty. Two assistants are provided him, but during the winter months no one is required to live on the inhospitable island, though the keepers are in the habit of making trips as often as circumstances will permit to look after the government property.[16]

Once again an observer far from the scene had a very negative view of life on Pilot Island.

In July 1888, the Lighthouse Board transferred Peter Knudsen to the Peninsula Point Light, south of Escanaba, Michigan. He was shifted to the Chambers Island Light in September 1889, where he remained until he resigned his position in March 1891. At that time Knudsen not only bought a half interest in the schooner *Southside*, but sailed her as well. Spending the winter of

1888 in Newport had caused him to become very interested in the town, so it is not surprising that he purchased a half interest in the Newport property of Hans Hanson in December 1891, uncluding a half interest in Hanson's pier, store, real estate, and all other property.[17]

With Peter's departure from Pilot Island in 1888, Nelson Knudsen became keeper; second assistant Bertschy was promoted to first assistant. Jacob Young, who had resigned as second assistant two years earlier, was now reappointed second assistant; the Board promoted him to first assistant in March 1889 when Bertschy resigned. When Jacob Young was promoted, his son Charles E. Young became second assistant, thus beginning a 45-year career as a keeper. Born on 22 April 1869, Charles spent his life on Washington Island until he entered government service at the age of 18.[18]

On 7 September 1889, the Lighthouse Board transferred Nelson Knudsen and moved Martin Knudsen from South Manitou Light back to Pilot Island. The transfer had many advantages for Martin and his family; when navigation closed, the family could easily winter on Washington Island, which was home for them. There, the children would be able to attend school, and both Martin and Theresa had many friends and relatives on the island. Also, when Theresa's brother Fred had earlier decided to sell his farm and move west, they had purchased the farm, planning eventually to live there.

Knudsen and his son Edward left South Manitou to take over the new station at once, joining father and son, Jacob and Charles Young. Theresa and the remaining children followed a few days later on the *Dahlia,* accompanied by the district inspector. The ship's crew loaded their furniture and belongings and helped to get them settled into the dwelling at Pilot Island, though Inspector Clark refused to bring Nellie, the family's cow, aboard the *Dahlia.*

Martin's friend Captain John Jessen and his son Anton volunteered to take their schooner to South Manitou to pick up Nellie. They brought her safely to Pilot Island, but the waves were too high around the island to land. The Jessens sailed close to Plum Island and unceremoniously pushed Nellie overboard, forcing her to swim ashore onto the gravelly beach on the southwest side of the island. When the waves subsided, Martin sailed over to Plum Island in the station's sailboat, rounded up the cow, got her aboard, and then sailed back to Pilot Island. This was her first trip to Pilot Island, but by no means her last. Every spring she rode in the sailboat out to Pilot Island along with the family's cat, dog, and chickens. Each fall Nellie, the cat, and the dog returned to the family farm on Washington Island. Despite the rocky terrain, there was enough grass for her on the north end of the island.

Shortly after his arrival, Knudsen suggested to his superiors that the station needed a landing on the west side of the island which could be used when it was too rough to land at the original landing on the east side. In late November, Theresa and the children went to Washington Island for the winter, leaving Martin and the Youngs to cook for themselves. It was intended that the light would be extinguished in mid-December, but there were still several steamers operating at that time. The district inspector telegraphed a message to Baileys Harbor which the operator delivered personally to Knudsen, since the telegraph line ended at Baileys Harbor. The message instructed Knudsen to keep the station open, so it was not until New Year's Day that Knudsen and the Youngs could extinguish the light, lay up the fog signals, and return to Washington Island.[19]

Knudsen visited the station in February and March on monthly inspections to see that everything was in good condition. Finally in April, he and Jacob Young returned to Pilot Island for the season. The first jobs were to air out the dwelling, which had become quite damp during the winter, to get the stoves going, and to clean out the privy. Knudsen also took time to write another letter to the Lighthouse Engineers concerning construction of a landing on the west side of the island. As part of their routine duties, the keepers cleaned and polished the glass and brass work of the lens, cleaned and reassembled the fog signals, and tested them. The men made several trips to Washington Island before they officially exhibited the light on 8 April 1890. A week later Knudsen brought his family and household goods out from Detroit Harbor. The keepers' days were full of cleaning, painting and polishing. The *Dahlia* landed a load of coal, but before they wheeled it in wheelbarrows from the landing to bins outside the fog signal houses, Knudsen built a wooden walk connecting the landing and the signal houses. About every other day one of the keepers went ashore, either to Detroit Harbor, to Newport, or to Hedgehog Harbor for mail, supplies, or just to visit. They also went to Plum Island to gather logs for a dock and to get dirt for the station's garden and croquet ground. In May, Knudsen received word that construction of the west landing had been approved. May was also when the keepers whitewashed the station literally from top to bottom, including the garden fence.

In late May 1890, Mr. Moe and his son arrived to build the west landing with the keepers' help. Logs from Plum Island were hewn into massive square timbers. By July they had built a boat landing twelve feet wide and forty-eight feet long out into the water on the west side of the island, north of the dwelling. The men filled the wooden structure with rocks taken from the island. The Moes then decked the landing with heavy timbers. Since westerly winds produced the largest waves, the structure had to be massive to avoid destruction. With completion of the landing, Knudsen turned to solving another problem. If the fog signal were operated for too long, the wells supplying water to them would run dry, so Knudsen pumped out both wells and exploded charges of dynamite at their bottoms to enlarge them.

On 5 July 1890, Jacob Young was promoted and transferred to the Cedar River Light. His son Charles was promoted to first assistant; until a new second assistant could be appointed, Knudsen received orders to employ a laborer. He hired Timothy Coffey from Washington Island.

In late August, Ben Fagg, an employee of a Sturgeon Bay printer, visited the station. He wrote a letter to the *Advocate* that became the basis for many stories about Pilot Island, some of which were apocryphal and usually without attribution. Fagg did his writing while sitting one night in the lighthouse lantern. According to him, Pilot Island consisted of 3¾ acres of rocks and boulders upon which there was an imported croquet ground, a few ornamental trees, a strawberry patch, two fog signals, a frame barn nearing completion, a lighthouse, a boat house and "some blue, bell-shaped flowers and golden rods that grow out of niches in the rocks." Two miles west of Pilot Island was Plum Island, "so-called because it is plum in the center of Death's Door." Fagg had a much different opinion of Pilot Island from that of such earlier observers as keeper Rohn.

> This is truly an isolated spot and some people might call it a very dreary place, but I have now spent five days on Pilot Island and they are among the happiest days of my eventuality.

Every morning at sunrise, Charles Young came and woke Fagg so they could join Knudsen for a swim in Lake Michigan's "almost ice-cold waters." They swam into the breakers around the island, being tossed into the air in a cloud of foam and spray. Fagg had a fine eye and an ability to capture what he saw on paper:

> On moonlight nights it is like being in a dream of ideality to walk alone over the moss-covered rocks and listen to the swish of the breakers that break

> over the breakwater at the boat landing, hear them roaring on all sides of the little island, and to see huge vessels under full sail crossing the moonglade on their way through the Door. One seems to be completely separated from all that is worldly and bad. There is no field for gossip out here. The land is not suitable for general farming purposes, but it is a splendid place to raise an ample crop of good, pure thoughts.

Like so many other visitors, Fagg was fascinated by the fog signals at the station. One was a duplicate of the signal displayed at the Paris World's Fair. According to Fagg:

> The sound is so intense that no chicken can be hatched on the Island, as the vibrations kill them in the egg, it causes milk to curdle in a few minutes. Visitors at the light house on foggy nights sit up in bed when the siren begins its play and look around for their resurrection robes.

Perhaps it was a matter of getting used to the sound, for it seemed not to bother the keepers, their families, or Nellie. The stories of the chickens and milk were copied by numerous later writers.[20]

In October 1890, Mr. Coffey quit his position as laborer, and Knudsen hired another Washington Island resident, 35-year-old Godtfred M.S. Hansen, who thereby began another long lighthouse career. In March 1891, the Lighthouse Board appointed Hansen second assistant, at the same time the promoting Charles Young to keeper and transferring him to the Chambers Island Light. Thomas J. Armstrong from Traverse City, Michigan replaced Young.

In 1891, life for the keepers settled into a familiar routine of cleaning, polishing, painting, and whitewashing. Several times a week there were trips to Detroit Harbor, Newport, or Hedgehog Harbor. Boats needed to be cleaned and repaired, and visitors to the station were always welcome. Knudsen spent several weeks that year blasting rocks out of the east and west landings. The Fourth of July meant blasts of another kind — fireworks. On July 23, the *Dahlia*'s crew delivered twenty tons of coal, all of which had to be moved in wheelbarrows from the landing to the fog signal houses. Five days later the light house tender *Warrington* delivered an iron oil house to the station and brick and cement for a cistern that was to be built in the dwelling's basement to catch rain water. Engineering personnel from the *Warrington* also made some minor repairs to the fog signals. However, Knudsen made needed repairs to Theresa's washing machine by himself.

On September 13, a tug brought district lampist Crump to the station to change the characteristic of the light from flashing white to fixed red, a major task requiring special expertise. Knudsen helped him take down the Fresnel lens, lens pedestal, and the lens revolving apparatus, and together they put up the lens pedestal and lens of the fixed red light. The men also replaced the lens lamp with a new model and increased the size of the ventilators in the lantern, increasing the air flow to the lamp. After helping him pack up the old lens and its various parts, Knudsen took Crump on September 18 by sailboat to the Chambers Island Station.

On the evening of October 28, during a moderate south southwesterly gale, the three-masted schooner *Forest* of Chicago became stranded on the reef at the southwest end of the island. Built in 1868, the *Forest* eventually came to rest with her stern wedged into the rocks on shore and her bow extending into deep water. Efforts to refloat her failed and her masts, spars, and other parts of her rig were brought ashore and stored. During the winter she began to break up. The storms tore loose her cabin and washed it ashore on the island, thus providing a playhouse for the Knudsen children next spring.

Life on Pilot Island during the summer was happy for the children. After helping with their assigned chores, there was plenty of time to see if the waves had brought ashore anything interesting. There were croquet games and fishing trips with their father, and, sometimes they would go over to Plum Island, which was heavily wooded, uninhabited, and a great place to explore. On one of their trips they ran across the ruins of the first Porte des Morts Lighthouse. Late in June or early in July, Martin would take the children to Detroit Island to pick wild strawberries; Theresa stayed home to bake so everyone could enjoy strawberry shortcake when they returned. As the children grew older, they sometimes were allowed to bring friends to stay at the station for several days.[21]

Another welcome visitor was Knudsen's sister Mary, who came to see her brother in early May 1892. She was living in Pomeroy, Iowa with her parents, and it was the first time in a number of years that the two had seen each other. Mary planned to spend about a year with Martin and Peter. Before the family had left South Manitou, Agnes, the oldest daughter, had received a reed organ. Mary was a fine musician, and when she was at the station, the dwelling was filled with the sound of the organ and the voices of the family singing all their favorite songs.[22]

Another pair of frequent visitors and welcome friends were Mr. Bo Anderson and his wife Ida. Anderson was Detroit Harbor's postmaster; he often accompanied Knudsen on his winter inspection trips of Pilot and Plum Islands. He also sometimes substituted for the assistants for short periods of time. In 1894 the Andersons opened the first hotel on Washington Island, the Ida-Bo Inn. It later became the Holiday Inn, and although the old inn burned to the ground in October 1988, Jim and Kathy Findlay kept the name when they rebuilt the present Holiday Inn. Anderson also built a large general store on his property, became Town Chairman, and, with Knudsen, led the drive to have telephone service extended across Death's Door to Washington Island.[23]

In August 1892, the Lighthouse Board promoted first assistant Thomas J. Armstrong to keeper and transferred him to the South Manitou Light. Knudsen's replacement there, Thomas Kitchen, had died of typhoid fever. G.M.S. Hansen was then promoted to first assistant, and Knudsen hired his son Edward Knudsen as a laborer for a month until the Board appointed Hans J. Hanson of Sevastopol as second assistant. Hanson was born in 1867 and had begun his lighthouse career only two years before this appointment. That same month, the crew of the *Amaranth* delivered piping for the cistern and took away the flashing lens and its attachments that had been taken out of the lantern the previous year. Much of the keepers' time during the month had been spent unloading, wheeling, and stacking fifty cords of wood that had been delivered to the station for the fog signals.

During September, Knudsen made arrangements to have a home built on the farm they had purchased from Theresa's brother. Previous to that the Knudsens had either stayed with relatives or rented a dwelling. Theresa and the children went ashore earlier than usual that fall so that she could keep track of the building project. Once their home was built, Theresa and the two youngest children, who were too young to go to school, planned to remain on Pilot Island with the men, while the older children took charge of the house and went to school. Usually, in early to mid-November, Knudsen took his wife, the youngsters, and Nellie ashore, and the men were left responsible for cooking their own meals and housekeeping. When navigation ended, the family would be reunited on the farm.

Martin Knudsen became the only Door County keeper to receive national recognition and fame, and he did so because of his exploits during that fall of 1892. A fierce southwesterly gale struck the area on October 2; it was a harbinger of a very bad storm to come, but the waves calmed sufficiently for Knudsen to take the mail to Detroit Harbor the next day. On October 5, he went to gather sand from Detroit Island for mortar and concrete. That same day the mail carrier brought out lighthouse board mason R.G. Hurst, to build the foundation for the metal oil house, brick the inside of it, and construct a cistern in the dwelling's basement. Using gravel from the west side of the island, the men mixed concrete and laid the foundation. On October 10, they placed the circular metal oil house in position some eighty-two feet southeast of the tower. The men then riveted on the roof, and Hurst began building the brick walls inside the oil house.

On October 17, they finished the concrete floor of the oil house and whitewashed the outside of the foundation. Knudsen noted in his log: "A schooner got on reef about 11 pm. Her name *J.E. Gilmore*." The *Gilmore* had been built in 1867; she was 138 feet long, had a 25-foot beam, and had one deck with two masts. She was sailing through Deaths Door before the wind, without cargo and with shortened sail. Abreast of Pilot Island, the wind shifted, and, before her crew could hoist enough sail to tack clear, the *Gilmore* went ashore on the reef southwest of the island in about three feet of water. She struck the reef very close to the remains of the schooner *Forest*, wrecked the year before, whose deck now barely protruded from the water.

The *Gilmore*'s keel was crushed, but there was hope at first that she could be gotten off the reef. Knudsen and his assistants rigged a breeches buoy to bring the crew ashore in case of an emergency, but the crew remained on board; they were safe there for the time being, and there was a good supply of food on the wrecked vessel. Knudsen went on board to confer with her captain the next day, and the following day, after completing his general lighthouse duties, he sailed to Newport and Detroit Harbor with the *Gilmore*'s captain and also to get the station's mail. On Ocotber 20, after preparing mortar for the cistern, the keeper again went with the captain and the mail to Newport and Detroit Harbor. While the crew remained on the *Gilmore,* the keepers and Hurst began building the cistern, moved the oil cans into the new oil house, and sodded the area around it. On Sunday October 23, Knudsen wrote in his log, "The weather is becoming more like fall." The captain and crew of the *Gilmore* visited the station, although the schooner was virtually on Pilot Island itself. Two days later the *Gilmore*'s captain left the station on a steamer Knudsen hailed. After that, Knudsen and Hanson took the mail ashore. The next day they cleared rubbish from the cellar, finished the cistern walls, and mortared the walls on the inside to make them waterproof.

On the 28th, the men finished the cistern and blasted two rocks in the back cellar under the dwelling. According to the log, the day was cloudy to hazy to rainy, and the wind shifted from south southwesterly to north and became a fierce gale. Knudsen almost casually finished the entry: "The Schr. *A.P. Nichols* stranded on N.W. side here at 8:00 PM" — nothing more than that. Actually the stranding of the *Nichols* and subsequent rescue of her crew was considerably more dramatic than Knudsen's log would lead one to believe. As noted, October 28 was a dull, gray day, and the barometer dropped through the course of the day. The shifting wind increased in velocity and reminded Knudsen of the "Alpena Gale" of 1880. Keeping step with the barometer, the thermometer began to fall and by afternoon it was sleeting and snowing. Four schooners sought shelter in the lee of Plum Island, but were having great difficulty in getting their anchors to hold. Finally two of them slipped their anchors and ran before the wind out into Lake Michigan to avoid stranding on Pilot Island. Before their anchors held, the two others drifted until they were less than a mile from Pilot Island. The crew of the *Gilmore* decided to come ashore from their stranded vessel as the storm increased in intensity. At about 2 PM Knudsen and his assistants saw a three-masted schooner with reefed sails approaching the island from the southeast, apparently intending to sail through the Deaths Door Passage and into Green Bay. By looking through the station's powerful telescope, they discovered that she was the *A.P. Nichols.*

The *Nichols* had been built in 1861; she was 147 feet long with a beam of 30 feet. In 1883 she was sold to Captain David Clow, Sr. and his sons, Oscar, Byron, and David, Jr. Clow was a well-known Door County ship builder and Great Lakes sailor; he had begun his career in Oak Creek, Wisconsin in 1848, moving in 1850 to Chambers Island where he built most of his ships. By 1892, he had retired; Captain David Clow, Jr. was in command of the *Nichols,* while his father was on board as a passenger.

On this fateful trip, Captain David Clow, Jr. made several unsuccessful attempts to pass through Deaths Door before he abandoned the effort and struggled into the lee of Plum Island. Despite dropping a 1400-pound anchor at the end of 600 feet of chain, the *Nichols* began to drag toward Pilot Island as darkness fell. At supper that night, Martin told Theresa that, after watching the *Nichols'* movement, he was afraid they were going to have another wreck on Pilot Island.

About 8 PM, while Theresa was serving her husband and his two assistants a quick cup of coffee, they all heard a terrific crash above the noise of the storm. Rushing outside, they could see the *Nichols* on the reef a short distance offshore, almost touching the bow of the wrecked *Forest* and just north of the stranded *Gilmore.* As the chooner rolled in the surf, the larger waves broke over her decks. Knudsen waded out about forty feet on the slippery stones of the reef, almost to the stricken vessel. Over the noise, he told them to jump overboard and that he would catch them. Captain Clow, Jr., jumped first to see if rescue was possible. As he jumped, a huge wave washed over the *Nichols,* but Knudsen grabbed Clow before he was washed away. This persuaded Clow's aged father, the female cook, and the three other crewmen also to jump overboard into the surf. Knudsen then carefully guided the group along the narrow ridge of the reef and back to shore. Talking later about Knudsen and the trip to shore, Captain Clow, Jr. remarked:

> It is a wonder to me how Martin Knudsen found his way out along that ledge of rocks in the darkness to the *Nichols*. He is about the bravest man I have ever seen. How he managed to keep his bearing after rescuing the crew has been a wonder to me ever since. A single misstep and we would have all fallen off the rocks into deep water and undoubtedly been drowned. He seemed to know the reef as well under water and in the darkness as if it had been above water and in the daytime.[25]

About all this drama, Knudsen's log is silent. His only entry on October 29 was:

> Built a concrete floor in back cellar. I put the Capt. of Schr. *A.P. Nichols* board the Stmr. *J.H. Outwaite.*

Captain Clow made his way to Escanaba to inform his family and the insurance underwriters of the loss of the *Nichols.* Ten days later, the Chicago and Milwaukee newspapers were full of Knudsen's thrilling rescue. In December, the Chicago customs collector sent to his superiors in the Treasury Department a recommendation that Knudsen be awarded a second class medal for bravery for saving the lives of the *Nichols'* crew. In March 1893, Life Saving Benevolent Association of New York presented Knudsen with the association's highest award — a gold medal — in recognition of his courage and humanity in rescuing the crews of the *Gilmore* and *Nichols.* On 29 July 1893, Lighthouse Board Inspector Commander John J. Brice arrived at Pilot Island aboard the *Dahlia.* After inspecting the station, Brice presented Knudsen

Three wrecked schooners on Pilot Island, October 1892. The *A.P. Nichols* is on the right, the *J.E. Gilmore* pointing left, and the *Forest* (in front of the Gilmore) pointing right. Photo taken by Kenneth E. Smith after Knudsen's rescue of Nichols' crew. Photo courtesy of the Marine Historial Collections, U of Detroit Mercy/Edward J. Dowling collection.

Knudsen with a silver medal from the federal government for his actions in saving the crew of the *Nichols*.

There had been a great deal of agitation by residents and mariners in support of building a lifesaving station in the area. Ever since completion of the Sturgeon Bay Life Saving Station, there had been calls for lifesaving stations at Baileys Harbor and in the Deaths Door Passage, but these stations apparently had a low priority in Congress, despite requests from Wisconsin Congressmen. The loss of the *Gilmore* and the *Nichols* on Pilot Island and the subsequent national attention given to Knudsen's heroic efforts brought renewed calls for a lifesaving station there in 1893. Commenting on Knudsen's receipt of the silver medal, his friend Bo Anderson said it would have been even better if the government built the lifesaving station so that Knudsen could stick to being a light keeper rather than being a lifesaver too.[26]

There were attempts to salvage the *Gilmore* and the *Nichols*, but both were too badly damaged to be refloated. The keepers eventually brought ashore and stored in the barn much of their removable equipment. Hurst continued to repair the masonry and chimneys of the buildings. On November 19, Knudsen finally took him to the Poverty Island Light Station to make repairs there. Another Lighthouse Board employee, Thomas Millar, arrived in late November from Detroit to make repairs and adjustments to the fog sirens. After doing their usual cleaning and preparations for winter, Knudsen and his assistants closed the station on December 19, ending a most eventful season.

The lighthouse keepers of Door County generally were a closely knit group, and this was particularly true of the keepers who were from Door County itself. They would visit each other's stations, and most of them wintered either in Sturgeon Bay or on Washington Island. Mary Knudsen had come to Door County in May 1892 to visit her three brothers. After staying with Martin on

Pilot Island, she moved to Newport to live with Peter. Although she originally planned to stay in the area for only a year, she changed her plans. In late March 1893, Martin and Theresa left their home on Washington Island to attend Mary's wedding at Peter Knudsen's Newport home. On 28 March 1893, she married Charles E. Young, who had been first assistant on Pilot Island before becoming keeper of the Chambers Island Light.[27]

After returning to their station on 10 April 1893, the keepers quickly got back to their usual routine of cleaning, fixing, painting, and preparing the light and fog signals for operation. A week later most of the ice was gone, and Knudsen officially lit the lamp for the season. In May, for the first time in his career, Knudsen became so sick with the flu that second assistant Hanson went to Washington Harbor to bring Dr. Gudmundson to Pilot Island to examine him. The doctor stayed until the next afternoon, and Knudsen did not get back to full-time duty for two weeks.

The spring and summer of 1893 were particularly dry, and Knudsen noted every welcome rain in his log. Numerous visitors made their way to the island. Once the general lighthouse work was done each day, the keepers made frequent trips to Newport, Detroit Harbor, and occasionally even to Sturgeon Bay. In August the Knudsens and their youngest daughter sailed to Chambers Island to spend a week with Mary and her husband; the Youngs returned the visit in September. During September the keepers also undertook their only major project for the year, building a new and larger landing crib at the west landing. Using logs from Plum Island and bolts salvaged from various wrecks on the island, they built the crib, filled it with rock, and planked the top. The men also extended the boatways into deeper water. In late October, a two-day southerly gale caused a heavy sea that broke the *Nichols* into pieces, but the new crib and landing were undamaged. On Thanksgiving the Knudsens celebrated with a roast chicken and cake. The weather then turned cold, and the keepers closed the station on December 13, several weeks earlier than usual.

The station did not reopen until 28 March 1894. As usual everything was in good condition when the keepers opened things up and began their routine of cleaning, painting, polishing, and cutting wood for the fog signals. The Lighthouse Board had decided to replace the steam fog sirens with steam fog whistles, which were less complicated and easier to keep repaired. A tug brought a bargeload of materials and equipment to Pilot Island on April 26 along with Thomas Millar, who would do the conversion and make repairs to the fog signals. Two weeks later another man arrived to help Millar. The men put a new cement floor in Fog Signal House No. 2, set up the new whistle, and then moved the equipment from No. 1 into No. 2 so that both whistles and boilers were located in Fog Signal House No. 2. To ensure a more reliable source of water for the boilers, Knudsen and his assistants built a large water supply crib off the west side of the island. It was linked to shore by a footbridge supported by two smaller cribs. On May 18, Knudsen sounded Fog Signal No. 2 with its new whistle for the first time, a five second blast followed by thirty seconds of silence. While the work of converting Fog Signal No. 1 continued, district lampist Crump arrived with a new lens for the station. Knudsen assisted him in removing the old lens and installing the new one, which changed the light's characteristic from a fixed red light to a fixed white light with a white flash every fifteen seconds. On June 8, Knudsen exhibited the new 4th Order Fresnel lens for the first time.

The same day, Millar and his helper, having finished their work, left for Newport. Knudsen repaired the shed that had been Fog Signal House No. 1 and converted part of it into a workshop and fuel house. He also built a darkroom in the former signal house. From then on one of Knudsen's favorite activities was taking pictures, developing the film, and making prints.

Little rain fell during the summer and fall of 1894, and the thin layer of soil on the island quickly became parched. Because of the general dryness, numerous forest fires broke out on the mainland. Knudsen and his assistants spent more time than usual sounding the fog signals due not to fog, but to smoky conditions that obscured visibility. As fall turned to winter, Knudsen began preparing to close the station for the winter. However, on December 15, he received instructions from the inspector's office to keep the light in operation until further notice. The Ann Arbor Railroad car ferries were attempting to remain in service all winter, and Knudsen had to remain at Pilot Island, although all other navigation ceased. As the weather got colder, it was increasingly difficult to keep the fog signals operable, because the water froze in the pipe from the supply crib to the boilers. Finally, rather than extinguishing the fires in the boilers and relighting them when needed, they kept the fires lit all the time in order to keep the boilers from freezing. Knudsen decided to take the schooner *Forest*'s cabin, which had been used by his children as a playhouse after the vessel broke up, to serve as a winter hut on the southeast point of Detroit Island. During the winter, the keepers usually walked from Detroit Harbor to the end of Detroit Island and then either walked on the ice or took a boat to Pilot Island. Christmas was usually a joyous time for the Knudsen family, but this year Martin spent the day at his post rather than with his family. He wrote in his log: "Christmas. Daily routine and a little extra cooking our work."

Although they did not go ashore on Christmas Day, the keepers continued to make regular trips to Detroit Harbor and to Newport. Once again there were calls to build a lifesaving station on Plum Island, and on one of this trips ashore Knudsen sent a letter to the *Advocate*'s editor adding his opinion to the discussion. After reviewing the records of the station while winter winds and cold kept activities to a minimum, Knudsen calculated that since 1863 there had been seventy-two serious accidents such as sinkings, strandings, capsizes, and water-loggings to vessels in the vicinity; twenty-six of them had happened directly on Pilot Island, including eleven strandings in the past two years. Knudsen figured that between 200 and 500 vessels, sail and steam, passed through the Porte des Morts Passage monthly, indicating that a very large amount of valuable property and many lives were exposed to the dangers of the area. While the keepers had frequently rendered valuable assistance, they lacked the necessary means and equipment to function as lifesavers. According to Knudsen, only a fully equipped lifesaving station would meet the needs of the mariners frequenting the passage.[28]

Not until 3 February 1895 did the keepers sight a signal fire burning on Detroit Island, the prearranged signal that word had been received to close the station. It took the men a 1½ days to prepare the light and fog signals for closing. They then departed on the ice, taking their winter row boat with them in case the ice broke. It was a short winter ashore for the keepers, for on 28 March 1895, less than two months after they closed the station, Knudsen and his assistants resumed their duties on Pilot Island. They were joined for the first four days of the season by Charles and Mary Young, who were on their way to their Chambers Island assignment. When they arrived, Martin found a foot of ice in the cistern in the basement of the dwelling, the water supply crib for the fog signals frozen solid, and the landings full of ice that had to be cut out before boats could dock.

During that winter, Knudsen apparently became interested in birds. Despite the icy conditions, he recorded in his log the first birds he saw — titmice, thrushes, and a hawk. Soon they were joined by robins, wrens, sapsuckers, and a sparrow hawk. After an initial burst of enthusiasm, however, his interest seems to have waned, and no further accounts of bird sightings were recorded in his log.

Because of the problem of getting water from the lake in late fall, winter, and early spring, the lighthouse engineers decided to reconnect the abandoned fog signal wells to the new fog signal apparatus, thus giving the keepers an alternative water supply. The *Amaranth* delivered the necessary pipes, valves, and connections. At the same time, the old belts, pulleys, trumpets, and other equipment from the old siren system were taken aboard the tender. In June, the station received its usual fifty cords of wood for the fog signal, and the *Dahlia* also delivered twenty tons of coal which were wheeled from the landing to the fog signal house. Later the tender brought two tons of coal for the stove in the dwelling.

Finally, after years of debate, on 8 August 1895 Knudsen reported that the material for building the Plum Island Life Saving Station had been landed on the northeast side of Plum Island, in plain view of the light station. C.J. Olson of Marinette was awarded a $9,000 contract to build lifesaving stations at Plum Island and Baileys Harbor. A week later Knudsen sailed over to the lifesaving station to see at first hand how construction was proceeding and to take some pictures — photography being a continuing hobby. Building went forth rapidly at the station. The west portion was a single-story boat room, in the middle was a four-story tower topped with a watch room, and on the east side was a two-story wing for crew's quarters. In mid-December, the contractor finished his work and turned the station over to the government officials. Peter Benson, the Washington Island mail carrier, became caretaker while continuing his carrier duties. In March 1896, Inger Olsen, a member of the Milwaukee lifesaving crew was appointed captain at Plum Island and began procuring an eight-man crew for the station, although it was not until July that the station was fully equipped. In 1915, when the US Coast Guard absorbed the Life Saving Service, the Plum Island Station, like those at Baileys Harbor and the Sturgeon Bay Canal, became a Coast Guard installation. It remained manned until 1992, when it was abandoned and the station was moved to Washington Island.

Like many area residents, Knudsen spent the fall preparing for winter. Wood had to be cut and split, buildings painted, and boats repaired. In addition there were preparations specific to the station. He spent a great deal of time making storm windows and doors for the buildings, and there were always minor repairs to be done. The keepers built, disassembled, and reassembled a winter shanty on Detroit Island for boats and equipment; the shanty also served, when necessary, as shelter for the keepers on their trips to Pilot Island during the winter. All these activities, of course, were in addition to their usual lighthouse and fog signal duties and their regular trips to Newport and Washington Island.

On October 16, the 112-foot schooner *Mystic* ran aground on the south end of Pilot Island. The keepers got the crew safely ashore, but the schooner was a total loss. She was stripped of her equipment, and the hull later was burned to recover the iron fittings.

In November, Knudsen sailed the station's sailboat to Sturgeon Bay to have boatbuilder and former keeper Joseph Harris rebuild it in his shop. Knudsen returned to his post on Captain Peter H. Petersen's schooner *Iris,* which Petersen would later sell to Knudsen's brother Peter. In March 1897, Petersen became second assistant at Pilot Island. This winter season came to an end on 10 January 1896, when the keepers fastened the doors and departed for home after their usual maintenance and shutdown routines.

Knudsen made inspection trips to Pilot Island at least once a month each winter, usually accompanied by his son or a friend such as Bo Anderson. On 6 April 1896, he opened the station for what would be his last season as keeper of the Porte des Morts Light. Three days later, after seeing the Cana Island Light at night, the keepers exhibited their light for the first time that season. The next few days were spent reassembling the fog signals and getting them ready for service. Once that was done, the keepers turned to their usual spring chores of cleaning, painting, polishing, and whitewashing, as well as receiving the annual supply of wood and coal. Lake Michigan was particularly low that spring, and the men spent several weeks in May and June blasting and removing rocks from both the east and west landings. Former keeper Victor Rohn came out from Washington Island and spent two weeks in June repairing the station's boats, and Knudsen returned to Sturgeon Bay to get the sailboat back from Harris.

In late June, the Knudsens went to Detroit Island to pick strawberries. On their way back, Martin visited the west side of Plum Island. After several years of Lighthouse Board requests, Congress had appropriated funds in 1895 to build range lights and a fog signal on Plum Island, and rumor had it that Martin would be the first keeper at the new station. Apparently Knudsen was anxious to see if any activity had occurred at the site of the proposed range lights. On 28 July 1896, Knudsen recorded in his log that the crew of the *Amaranth* had landed the first load of materials for the project. After that, Knudsen made numerous trips to the island to observe and take pictures of the progress there. Not all the trips to Plum Island were to the new light, however; on August 19, the Knudsens and first assistant Hansen attended Captain Olsen's wedding at the Plum Island lifesaving station.

The summer and fall passed without incident for the Pilot Island personnel. On November 2, Knudsen received orders to seek bids for cutting more trees on the Plum Island Light site. Within two weeks, Mr. Shelswick from Washington Island was hired to do the clearing. Work progressed so rapidly at Plum Island that in mid-November Knudsen and second assistant Hans Hanson visited the station to test the audible distance of the fog signal blast. While he had not yet been officially appointed keeper of the new facility, on December 7, Carl Richter (Arni Richter's father) brought mail and, more importantly, the keys to the Plum Island Light Station, out to Knudsen from Washington Island.

On 7 January 1897, Knudsen closed the light for the season. On January 19, he visited Plum Island to measure what proved to be 230 cords of wood that Shelswick had cut from the lighthouse site. During January, February, and March, Knudsen made inspection trips to Plum and Pilot Islands. On 17 March 1897, the Lighthouse Board notified Knudsen that he was being transferred as keeper to the Plum Island Light Station. Five days later former keeper Martin Knudsen and G.M.S. Hansen, formerly first assistant and now newly promoted to keeper, visited Pilot Island by boat to make an official transfer of the property to the new keeper.

Godtfred M.S. Hansen had been born in Aarlins, Denmark on 30 May 1855 and came to Washington Island as a young man. He married another islander, Ellen Maria Olsen, on 20 July 1879. When the Scandinavian Evangelical Lutheran Church on the island was organized in 1882, Hansen became Secretary of the Board of Directors. The Hansen's son Frithoff was among the first children baptized and their daughter Anne Marie was one of the first confirmands of the new church. Hansen had worked his way up in the lighthouse service from laborer (1890) to second assistant (1891) to first assistant (1892) and now to keeper of the Pilot Island Light; 28-year-old Charles Boshka replaced him as first assistant. Hans J. Hanson was promoted from second assistant to first assistant at Plum Island with Knudsen. Peter H. Petersen, who had been working as a substitute assistant and laborer after having sold his schooner *Iris* to Peter Knudsen, received the appointment as second assistant at Pilot Island.[30]

The new keeper and crew arrived at Pilot Island on 6 April 1897 to begin preparing the station for operation. Two days later, Hansen exhibited the light for the first time that season. Like all newly appointed keepers, Hansen and his assistants spent an inordinate amount of time the first year cleaning, painting, varnishing, whitewashing, and making minor repairs. They also continued frequent trips ashore to secure supplies, mail, and fresh meat, and to visit friends and family.

Early in June a vessel on its way to Milwaukee picked up Hansen and his wife for a shopping expedition. In light of the promotion, the couple had decided they needed new furniture for the dwelling and had applied for a two-week leave for this purpose. Milwaukee was chosen as the best place to shop. Returning with their purchases at the end of two weeks, they found the waves too rough to dock at either landing and anchored overnight before going ashore on Pilot Island.

The Hansens may have wanted new furniture because they now had more living space and seemed to have a steady stream of visitors. The keeper and his wife became close to Captain Olsen, the head of the lifesaving station, and his wife. The couples enjoyed numerous short visits for dinner or for an afternoon, and they sometimes spent the night at each other's stations. At first Martin Knudsen and his first assistant made numerous short visits to borrow or return tools and equipment that had been overlooked when the new light was equipped. Also Hansen was a notary public, and Knudsen often came to him to notarize official documents. Many Washington Island friends came out to Pilot Island, but there were also visitors from as far away as Chicago and New York. The Hansens had two young daughters who stayed with their parents, and an older son who usually lived with his grandparents but was a frequent visitor. In June 1897, Mollie Friis made her first visit to the island. She came not to see the Hansens, but rather to visit first assistant Charley Boshka. In the following months she became a frequent visitor, and Boshka also found time to see her on his trips to Detroit Harbor for mail and supplies. Many familiar Washington Island names such as Richter, Jessen, Cornell, and Anderson appear in Hansen's log. Another visitor during the first year was the Hansen family cow, though, unlike

Knudsen's Nellie, Hansen's cow was butchered on the island in the fall of 1897.

A visitor of another sort arrived on the southwest reef of Pilot Island at 4:35 AM on Sunday 3 October 1897, when the steel-hulled steamer *Alva* ran aground while running light from Chicago to Escanaba for a cargo of iron ore. Hansen signaled the Plum Island lifesavers for assistance. Delayed by a broken spar, the crew arrived at 6:30 AM. After assessing the situation, part of the crew sailed with the captain to Ellison Bay, where they telegraphed Sturgeon Bay for the wrecking tug *Wright*. However, *Wright*'s coal bunkers were empty, so they sent a telegram to the wrecking tug *Monarch* in Escanaba. *Monarch* arrived at 3 PM, helped pump 1,400 tons of water ballast from the *Alva*, and then, at 5:30 PM, pulled her off the reef without any trouble, only a little more than twelve hours after the $150,000 steamer first went aground.

In early December 1897, Captain Olsen closed the Plum Island lifesaving station for the season. As the number of ships passing Pilot Island dwindled and the temperature dropped, Hansen and his assistants began looking forward to closing the light and returning to their families as well. No steamers or sailing vessels had been seen for a number of days, except for the Ann Arbor ferries, but Hansen received orders on December 20 to keep the station open all winter. The only good news was a leave granted Hansen and Boshka so they could spend Christmas with their families.

The previous navigational season, Knudsen had closed the station as ordered in January and reopened in April, but, with the use of new, more powerful ferries, the Ann Arbor Railroad had continued operations in favorable weather even after the close of ordinary navigation. The company had complained vigorously to the Lighthouse Board that the light on Pilot Island was dark and the fog signal silent. The Board heeded their outcry, ordering Hansen not to close the station.

Since they had not planned to spend the entire winter on Pilot Island, the crew scrambled to bring supplies, especially food, from Washington Island. To avoid running out of kerosene for the light, the Board directed Hansen to go to Rock Island to get fuel from Pottowatomie Light, which was closed for the season. Because of the difficulty of getting back and forth, Hansen was ordered to hire a laborer until April 15. Hansen hired his friend Anton Jessen from Washington Island, though he could work only until March 30; on that date he was ordered to report for duty at the Baileys Harbor lifesaving station as a surfman.

After a long winter, the ice went out for the last time in April, and a new cycle of cleaning, painting, varnishing, and brightening began again as shipping resumed. This would be a special April, however. On 22 April 1898, Hansen reported that after the general lighthouse work was done, the 1st assistant went to Detroit Harbor at 11 AM on private business. Hansen and Petersen spent the day wheeling wood and sounding Fog Signal No. 1. The next day Boshka arrived back at 11 AM with mail, Niels Friis and his daughters, and William Jess, and there were other visitors from Washington Island, Plum Island, and Newport. They came to witness the 4 PM wedding of Charley Boshka and Mollie Friis performed by William Jess, justice of the peace. After the wedding, the couple remained on Pilot Island, and the guests traveled to their homes. The newlyweds got to take a wedding trip only later.

The wedding was just the beginning of a busy season for Hansen and his assistants. In May, the *Amaranth* landed the district engineer, who inspected the station and noted repairs that needed to be done. It was decided to drill a new well, modify the boat landings, and overhaul the fog signal equipment, which was in need of major repairs. It had previously been planned to reshingle the dwelling, so the tender's crew brought 3,000 shingles ashore. The district lampist was also aboard, and he delivered three new lens lamps and took away the old ones. Hansen also received a new kitchen stove. On July 9, the *Amaranth* returned, bringing a scow load of timbers to lengthen the docks. Four days later foreman John Jaffray and a crew of four men arrived to begin work. Six weeks later, they had extended the east boat dock twenty feet, repaired and lengthened the boatways by ten feet, and repaired or replaced all the stone-filled wooden cribs at the east landing. They lengthened the dock on the west side by thirty feet and the boatways by twelve feet, shingled the dwelling and made other minor repairs. On August 16, William and Julius Fischer, local well drillers, finished the well at the fog signal on Plum Island and came to put in a new well for the fog signals. They first dug down to the limestone bedrock, then used their drilling machinery brought from Plum Island.

They finished the well after a week of drilling, and on August 26, Hansen fired up the boiler for Fog Signal No. 1. Pumping the well for three hours lowered the water level just three feet, which left sixteen feet of water in the well. Fischers' contract guaranteed sufficient water for the fog signals for one year; otherwise they would have to return and deepen the well at their own expense. They did not have to return.

In October Hansen once again received orders to keep the station open all winter, and this gave the men time to bring out winter supplies. At first Hansen was given permission to hire a laborer from November 15 until April 15, but a short time later he received orders not to do any hiring until further notice. Because of a deficit in the appropriation for keepers' salaries, the Lighthouse Board had turned down the district inspector's request for a winter laborer at Pilot Island. In mid-November, the crew of the *Dahlia* delivered winter supplies, along with a watchroom stove and new library books. In late November, Hansen again received permission to hire a laborer. Taking no chances, he immediately hired Edward H. Cornell, a friend and fellow Washington Islander.

On Sunday 11 December 1898, tragedy struck the closely knit lighthouse community. After completing their normal morning duties, both assistants left for Detroit Harbor with official mail in the station's sailboat. Second assistant Peter H. Petersen was at the helm. As they approached the eastern point of Detroit Island, Petersen steered across the shoal that extended out from the point, rather than detouring around it, and an unusually large breaker suddenly capsized the boat, throwing both men into the icy waters. Boshka swam into shallow water and waded the half-mile to shore, reaching Martin Jorgenson's home very benumbed. Unfortunately, although the water was shallow, Petersen drowned; despite having sailed for years, he could not swim. He had come to Washington Island twelve years before from Denmark; he was between 30 and 35 years old and was unmarried. At 1:45 PM, Abraham Jessen came out from Washington Island to inform Hansen of the tragedy and to tell him that the station's boat had been hauled up on Detroit Island. Hansen hired Jessen on the spot as a substitute for the drowned second assistant and sent him to retrieve the boat. Efforts to recover Petersen's body were unsuccessful because of ice forming in the area.

Soon, except for the Ann Arbor ferries, navigation ceased. For some weeks, the routine trips between Pilot Island and Washington Island became difficult because of ice fields floating in and out around the island. Not until February 1899 did the ice freeze solidly enough for safe travel. The Lighthouse Board transferred Frank Drew from the Green Island Light in Green Bay to Pilot Island to replace Petersen as second assistant. Drew was able to walk to his new assignment from Detroit Harbor on 6 February 1899, relieving Edward Cornell.

Drew's arrival caused a problem at the station. The dwelling had room for Hansen and his family and the Boshkas. Petersen had been a bachelor, and he had shared a room in the first assistant's quarters. However, Drew had a wife and three young children. While he was at Green Island, his family had lived in Menominee, Michigan, and they remained there for the rest of the winter.

On 24 April 1899, a Detroit Island resident found a body on the beach near the scene of the December 11 capsizing. The lifesaving crew took the body to Detroit Harbor, and, since it was presumed to be Peter Petersen, they signalled Hansen to come to positively identify the body. Petersen's funeral was held the next day, and he was buried on Washington Island. Also in April, Drew went to Detroit Harbor to investigate renting rooms for his family, who planned to leave Menominee now that navigation had opened. Perhaps he could not make satisfactory arrangements, or prhaps his wife, with three young children, wanted to be with her husband; in July Drew built a small structure on the north end of Pilot Island from wood he had salvaged. Fortunately when district inspector Commodore Symonds inspected the station in August, he approved of the house Drew had built and authorized Hansen to give Drew some paint from the station's supply. In his report, the inspector brought the housing situation on Pilot Island to the Board's attention. The inspector also authorized Hansen and his assistants to go to Plum Island to cut timber for a new flag pole and a new mast for their sailboat. Another project that occupied Hansen for most of the fall was the building of a skiff.

That November, Hansen once again received orders to keep the light and fog signal open for the winter. The orders authorized him to hire a laborer, and again Hansen hired Anton Jessen for the winter. To equalize wear on the fog signal, and especially on the boilers, the inspector ordered Hansen to alternate operation of the fog signals on a monthly basis. The keepers began preparing the station for winter, brought out supplies, and in mid-December took their families and household goods ashore to Washington Island. The day after Christmas, the Ann Arbor ferry came in from Lake Michigan, saluted the light house with four blasts of her whistle, hove to, and blew four more short blasts. Hansen sent Jessen out in the station's row boat to pick up Edward H. Cornell. Cornell had formerly worked as a laborer on Pilot Island, but was now second assistant at the South Fox Island Light Station across Lake Michigan. Since his station was closed for the season, Cornell was on his way home to Washington Island; he must not have been in too much of a hurry, because he stayed at Pilot Island for four days before going on to Washington Island.

Hansen had been ordered to keep the station open to assist the Ann Arbor ferries on their voyages, and a note of frustration crept into Hansen's log when he observed on 31 January 1900 that no vessels had been seen in the month since the last ferry had come out of Green Bay and headed across Lake Michigan. Nevertheless, Hansen and his men had to light their light every night and sound the fog signal each time fog or snow obscured the passage. Each of these tasks seemed a waste to Hansen. The winter was mild, and the car ferries were taking the shorter route through the Sturgeon Bay ship canal, rather than through Deaths Door Passage.

While no boats moved, personnel at Pilot Island did. On April 1, Hansen received a message from the inspector's office that Charley Boshka was to report immediately to the Grand Haven Light in Grand Haven, Michigan. Boshka would return two years later from across Lake Michigan to Pottowatomie Light on Rock Island. The board promoted Frank Drew to first assistant and transferred Edward H. Cornell from his position as second assistant at South Fox Island Light to be second assistant at Pilot Island.

On April 18, *Ann Arbor Ferry No.3* passed the station, the first steamer since 31 December 1899; two days later Hansen declared navigation opened for the season. April also meant the beginning of the annual cleaning, polishing, and painting routine, and the return of wives and families to the island. This posed a familiar problem since Cornell also had a family. The Drews moved into the dwelling in recognition of his position as first assistant, and the Cornells moved into the building Drew had built the year before. During the annual inspection, the inspector noted that the station needed a number of repairs and that the housing situation needed to be reviewed.

Life at Pilot Island settled into the familiar routine, though one disturbing feature was the increasing number of repairs that had to be made to the steam boilers of the fog signals. The pattern of heating them up, operating them for a few hours, and then cooling and preparing them for relighting was taking its toll. On July 4 the station presented a cheery sight; Hansen hoisted an American flag to the top of the new flag pole and stretched a set of international code flags he had recently received from the flag pole to the lantern railing. Unfortunately, an early shower prevented the company from shooting off all their fireworks. The keepers and their families continued to make frequent trips ashore, and there were visitors at least once a week during the summer.

There were major changes on Pilot Island during 1901. The dwelling, built in 1858, needed repairs to its brick exterior and chimneys. In addition to the repairs, the work crew enlarged the dwelling to its present size and remodeled it to provide separate quarters for the keeper and the first assistant. Masons built an addition on the southeast side, giving each family a separate entrance and kitchen. Inside there were separate cellars and seven rooms on two floors for the keeper and the first assistant. The room containing the stairs to the third story had a door that connected the separate keeper's quarters. The light tower projected through the roof and contained a watchroom with a ladder to the lantern deck. The rest of the third story was a large finished room with sloping sides on the east side and two unfinished attics adjacent to the tower.

The men added twin two-story brick enclosures for separate stairways on the north and south sides of the dwelling. Each stairway tower also contained a door to the outside at ground level. The crew remodeled the unused fog signal house (which Knudsen had used as a workshop and photo darkroom) into a substantial, single-story, wooden dwelling for the second assistant and his family. The building Drew had built on the north end of the island was then abandoned. The workmen lined the fog signal house that was in use with metal and resurfaced the floor with concrete. They also made repairs to the west landing.

The fog signal house had been renovated, but the fog signal boilers continued to require constant repair. The number of ships passing through Deaths Door continued to decline due to several factors, including increased use of the Sturgeon Bay ship canal, arrival of railroads in the area south of Sturgeon Bay, decline of the pinery, and replacement of sailing vessels with larger, more powerful steamships. However, the Lighthouse Board deemed the Pilot Island fog signal so important that they decided to upgrade rather than abandon the station's fog signals in the last major construction effort on Pilot Island. The engineering department requested bids for a compressed air fog signal plant with an automatic siren rather than a steam-powered signal. Bids were accepted, and the material was delivered to the district office in Milwaukee. The equipment was loaded on a tender for delivery to Pilot Island during the fall of 1903, but it was too late to make the delivery that fall; the tender returned to Milwaukee for the winter.

Before the new fog signal equipment could be delivered, there were major personnel changes at Pilot Island. Godtfred M.S. Hansen was transferred to the Sheboygan Light Station in Sheboygan, Wisconsin on 15 February 1904. He remained there for the rest of his career, which ended in 1914, when he and his wife moved to Racine, Wisconsin. He remained there until his death in December 1931.[31] To replace Hansen, the Board transferred Charles Bavry from his position as first assistant at the Sturgeon Bay Canal Light and promoted him to keeper at Pilot Island. Three months later, the Board transferred first assistant Frank Drew back to Green Island Light. Edward H. Cornell became first assistant and Jesse Denio became the new second assistant.[32]

The *Hyacinth* picked up the new fog signal equipment in Milwaukee and brought it to Pilot Island in the spring of 1904, and, in the latter part of June, a working party arrived at the station. First laying a concrete slab, the masons erected a large rectangular 1½-story brick fog signal building with stone trimmings to take the place of the old wooden fog signal building. They then installed duplicate sixteen-horsepower diesel engines with compressors and an automatic compressed-air siren. The new fog signal went into operation on 12 September 1904. The signal's characteristic was a three-second blast followed by thirty-two seconds of silence. The crew also extended the boat way at the west landing by twenty feet and at the east landing by forty feet, building three new cribs for support. The old fog signal boilers and auxiliary equipment were taken to the Sturgeon Bay Canal Light Station and sold at auction.[33] Two years later, the eighty-seven-foot boatway was replaced at the west landing and the east landing was repaired.

In April 1908, the Board transferred Charles Bavry to the Grand Haven Light Station on the other side of Lake Michigan. Henry Bevry, who had been at Cana Island before being sent to Wind Point Light in Racine, Wisconsin, became the new keeper at Pilot Island. After five years at Pilot Island, he returned to Wind Point Light as keeper. Thirty-one years later, Bevry retired from that post when he reached the age of 70. Although he and his wife chose to live in Racine, for several years after his retirement he was

Lighthouse and adjacent buildings on Pilot Island, seen from the east landing looking west, 1940. Photo courtesy of the Wisconsin Academy of Sciences, Arts, & Letters.

the caretaker of Harold Wilson's Three Springs Game Farm near Sister Bay. He died 9 April 1958 and was buried in Racine.[34]

Shortly before Bavry left, John T. Trucker arrived at Pilot Island. Born 6 October 1881 in Liberty Grove, he had moved as a youth with his parents to Sturgeon Bay. There his father worked for a canning company, and young Trucker worked in the fields for the firm. On 16 October 1902, he married Christina Charney, a Liberty Grove native. For the next five years, Trucker worked in the lumber industry before taking the civil service exam for a lighthouse job. On 27 April 1907, the Lighthouse Board appointed Trucker second assistant at the Suel Choix Point Light, but his stay there was short. He transferred to Pilot Island on 1 August 1907 as second assistant. In March 1910, he received a promotion to first assistant when Edward H. Cornell moved to the South Fox Island Light, and two years later he asked to be transferred to the Sturgeon Bay Canal Light so his son could more conveniently attend school. Trucker accepted a voluntary demotion to third assistant in order to move.[35] Alfred Cornell had been appointed second assistant when Trucker was promoted, and he became first assistant on Trucker's departure. Royal G. Peterson became the new second assistant.

In 1913, the Lighthouse Bureau promoted Walter Otteson to keeper and transferred him from Rock Island to Pilot Island to replace Henry Bevry. Otteson and second assistant Royal G. Peterson received letters of commendation from the Secretary of Commerce for heroism in rescuing three members of a St. Louis family who had been engaged in building a summer home on Detroit Island. Their rowboat became disabled on their way to Detroit Harbor, and they were blown out onto the lake. After an all-night search, the two keepers found the men and returned them safely to Detroit Harbor.[36]

Robert Young and C.I. Haas followed Otteson in 1923 as keepers at Pilot Island. The last civilian keeper at Pilot Island Light was Clarence Anderson, though he joined the Coast Guard in 1940 for the last five years of his career. He was born in Sister Bay 17 December 1895 and served in the army during World War I; he began his lighthouse service in 1921 as an assistant keeper. Two years later, on 14 November 1923, he married Hildegard Boucsein from Washington Island. The couple had two children, Paul and Carolyn (who married Thomas Jessen). Carolyn has many happy memories of the summers she spent with her parents on Pilot Island during the first eleven years of her life. Friends of the keepers often came out in their boats for picnics and potluck suppers. There was a telephone and no electricity, but Aladdin gas lamps provided light by which the family read, played Chinese checkers, or listened to their battery-powered radio. Outside they played croquet using pool balls and mallets her father had made in the station's workshop. They kept chickens in a coop on the north end of the island, and Carolyn had to help care for the family garden. After her father retired in 1945, he lived on Washington Island until his death in March 1959.[37]

Coast Guardsmen manned the light until 1962, when the Coast Guard decided to decommission the station and remove its men from Pilot Island. The station was officially decommissioned 13 June 1962. The Coast Guard took the Fresnel lens out of the lantern and replaced it with a plastic lens, powered first by banks of wet-cell batteries and now by solar panels. The fog signal was no longer considered an essential navigational aid, and so the machinery was removed, leaving the signal house empty. In order to make it difficult for persons to visit and possibly vandalize the buildings, the Coast Guard removed the marine railways from both landings and destroyed the landing cribs at the east landing. A large, concrete crib at the west landing was left, but about twenty-five feet of dock between the crib and shore was removed. Despite the difficulties of landing there after it was decommissioned, Eldron

Ellefson of Washington Island rented Pilot Island from the Coast Guard until 1981, when the Sea Scouts took it over and used it as a camp. Several years later the Coast Guard once again took possession of Pilot Island. Today Coast Guardsmen visit the island about twice a year to check the beacon and solar panels.

Over the years the assistant's frame dwelling, the old wooden fog signal house, the boathouse at the east landing, the frame carpenter shop and wood shed, the summer kitchen, the privy, and the metal oil house have all been torn down or removed. Only the brick dwelling with its tower and lantern and the brick signal house remain on the island. Cormorants, whose wastes have killed the trees, inhabit the north end of the island, and gulls occupy the south end. The once meticulously maintained buildings now have peeling paint, boarded-up windows, leaking roofs, and decaying bricks, and the lawns and gardens are now overgrown with weeds and underbrush. Only the concrete walks, installed after the turn of the century, remain to lead visitors to where structures once stood. As dusk approaches, however, the light atop the tower, once tended by faithful keepers, still comes on automatically to help guide mariners through Deaths Door Passage.

Chapter 5
Baileys Harbor Lights

In Baileys Harbor today, there are still places for travelers to eat and stay for the night, just as there were in the 19th century when it was a busy port. Piers still jut out into the water of the harbor, but sport fishing boats have replaced the great sailing ships that once carried cargoes of lumber, building stone, and farm products from the surrounding area to market. From the piers, however, you can still see the Baileys Harbor lighthouse with its unique bird-cage lantern silhouetted against the eastern sky. A stop at The Ridges Sanctuary allows a close-up look at the front and rear Baileys Harbor Range Lights. You can even stroll down the walk connecting the range lights and imagine walking there in the company of the keepers who tended the lights in the past.

In 1848, Captain Justice Bailey was coasting along the west shore of Lake Michigan in hopes of finding shelter from a storm building in the northeast for his schooner and its load of immigrant passengers. He spotted a small harbor that seemed to be well protected, but his charts had no accurate information about it. Gambling that the water would be deep enough for his vessel, he sailed in and found refuge from a storm which continued to rage for several days. While they waited, he and his crew explored the surrounding area. They found a deep, sheltered harbor surrounded by large stands of pine, cedar, and mixed hardwoods. To the west of the water's edge, there was a ledge of limestone, ideal for building material and making lime. When the storm abated, Bailey loaded samples of stone and timber on his vessel, weighed anchor, and sailed out of the harbor that would henceforth be known as Baileys Harbor and back to his home port of Milwaukee.

Upon docking in Milwaukee, Bailey reported on his voyage to his employer, Alanson Sweet, including an account of the unnamed anchorage south of Deaths Door. Bailey showed his employer the samples he had secured. Sweet owned a fleet of a dozen sailing vessels and was involved in the grain trade and commission business. His ships regularly carried grain to Buffalo, but except for immigrants, return cargoes were often scarce. Since lumber, cordwood, and building stone were in great demand in Milwaukee, Bailey's samples represented potential cargoes for Sweet's ships on their return voyages. Sweet was excited by the potential opportunities and in 1849 bought 125 acres of land around Bailey's Harbor, platted a village, and made plans to develop his holdings.

Alanson Sweet was a frontier entrepreneur. Born 12 March 1804 in Owasco, New York, he was originally a stone mason by trade. He made a trip to Chicago in 1831, and another the following year, and then fought in the Blackhawk War. He helped to plat Chicago and entered the lumber and contracting business there. In 1835, he and his family moved to Milwaukee. He served as a member of the upper house of the Wisconsin Territorial Legislature from 1836–38 and in 1849 was a Milwaukee alderman. Sweet built a number of brick and stone buildings in Milwaukee and also worked on the state capitol in Madison. He was a pioneer in the Milwaukee-Buffalo grain trade, a commission merchant, and was involved in various railroad and plank road schemes designed to improve transportation. Many of his activities depended on close relations with government officials at city, state, and federal levels, and this was particularly true of his Baileys Harbor venture.

After buying the land, Sweet proceeded quickly to develop his holdings. He dispatched a crew of men to build a pier, a sawmill, and several homes, and also to open a stone quarry. That first winter the men finished the pier and then cut cordwood to ship to Milwaukee when the ice cleared out of the bay. Having gotten things underway, Sweet persuaded the state legislature to establish Door County with its present boundaries. He also convinced the legislators that Baileys Harbor was destined to become a great commercial center and pointed out that the village was located approximately halfway between the north and south ends of the new county. Since Baileys Harbor was the only real settlement in the county, Sweet though it should be named the county seat. The legislators were convinced, and so it came to be. Sweet had wanted a more dignified name for the settlement, and he suggested it be called Gibraltar, but he was unsuccessful in his effort to change the name.

Having succeeded at the state level, Sweet next turned to the federal government. To insure the commercial success of Baileys Harbor as Door County's premier port, he argued that a lighthouse was needed. Two earlier lights had already been built in Door County — one on Rock Island and one on Plum Island — to mark the passages between Lake Michigan and Green Bay, and Sweet petitioned Congress to locate a lighthouse at Baileys Harbor for the purpose of guiding mariners into the new port. Once again his entreaties were successful. Not only did Congress decide to build a lighthouse at Baileys Harbor, the federal government actually awarded Sweet the contract to build it.

The bay of Baileys Harbor is U-shaped, surrounded by low ground, and opens almost directly to the south. It is nearly 1¾ miles wide and approximately the same length north and south, and the village of Baileys Harbor lies on the west side of the bay. The plans called for building a lighthouse on an island off the southwest side of the peninsula between the harbor and Moonlight Bay. There is a deep-water channel almost to the head of the bay, but dangerous reefs and shoal waters lurk on either side of the bay's opening to Lake Michigan. Lighthouse Island, as it became known, measured about 1,000 feet north-south and some 250 feet east-west and was surrounded by shallow water and reefs. The island ordinarily is about 1,000 feet off shore, but this distance varies depending on the level of Lake Michigan. The federal government purchased the lighthouse site for $100 from Alexander Mitchell in November 1851.

In 1852 the waters of Lake Michigan were very low. Rather than using boats, Sweet's crew was able to transport building materials to the site using horse-drawn wagons during the 1852 season. The men used limestone from Sweet's local quarry to build a 1½-story stone keeper's dwelling. Attached to the house, they built a conical stone tower that was fifty-two feet from the base to the light's focal plane. At the base, the tower's interior diameter was twelve feet with walls more than three feet thick, tapering to two feet thick at the top. The tower and dwelling were stuccoed and white-washed. The Baileys Harbor Light had (and has) a very distinctive "bird-cage" lantern, named for its resemblance to a giant bird cage. Another unusual design feature was that there was no platform at the top of the tower for the lantern to sit on; instead, the lantern fit inside the exterior walls of the tower. Originally a lamp (fueled by sperm whale oil) and 6th Order Fresnel lens were installed. In 1858 the Lighthouse Board refitted the light with a 5th Order Fresnel lens, but did not change the fixed, white characteristic of the light.[1]

Sweet also received government contracts to build a number of other lighthouses on Lakes Michigan and Superior, but, shortly after he completed building the Baileys Harbor Light, he apparently lost interest in Baileys Harbor. His mill burned, his pier decayed, and many of his buildings deteriorated. In 1857, when energetic settlers in Sturgeon Bay undertook to move the county seat to their village, there was hardly a contest since Baileys Harbor was by that time largely deserted. Later, with its excellent harbor, it re-emerged for a time as an important lumber-shipping port until the nearby forests were cleared. Until completion of the Sturgeon Bay Canal, Baileys Harbor was an important seasonal port; Lake Michigan remains free of ice much longer than Green Bay, so Baileys Harbor was Door County's most important winter port.

The Baileys Harbor lighthouse, now long abandoned, was in use 1852–1869. Note the unusual "birdcage" lantern structure. Photo courtesy of Roy Lukes.

The Lighthouse Board appointed David Ward keeper of the new Baileys Harbor Light on 10 February 1853, and it went into operation with the opening of navigation in 1853. Ward's annual salary was $350, the usual rate for keepers at that time. Michael Green replaced Ward in September 1854, but he served as keeper for only six months before he died in March 1855. His replacement was Newton Bacon, who tended the light from March 1855 to January 1862. The Lighthouse Board removed Bacon at that time and replaced him with William Mitchell; Mitchell was transferred to another station in August 1863, whereupon the Lighthouse Board appointed William Darling keeper at Baileys Harbor.

Darling was born in Virginia in 1820 and had grown up in Michigan. Many of Door County's early keepers were veterans, and Darling was no exception. He enlisted in the Michigan volunteers when the Mexican War broke out and had been among the first of General Scott's troops to enter Mexico City. Upon his discharge, he and his wife moved to a farm near Sherwood, in Calumet County, Wisconsin. But, with the outbreak of the Civil War, he enlisted in the Sixth Regiment Wisconsin Infantry which was part of Wisconsin's famous Iron Brigade. Darling had his foot amputated at the ankle after being wounded at the Battle of Antietam, and he received an honorable discharge in January 1863. He returned home and was appointed Sherwood's postmaster, but moved to Door County upon being appointed keeper of the Baileys Harbor Light. The keeper's salary recently had been increased to $520 a year, a substantial increase over his postmaster's salary and most probably the reason he sought a keeper's appointment.[2]

With the end of the Civil War, both the tonnage and the number of cargoes of wood, building stone, and lime shipped from the piers at Baileys Harbor rose dramatically, and this increased shipping activity created a problem. The lighthouse was almost more of a hazard than a help, for the light was surrounded by reefs and shallows. Moreover, its location at the southeast edge of the harbor rather than at the head of the bay made it difficult, even in good weather, to use the bearing of the light to actually enter the harbor. If captain was only slightly off course, or if wind or waves carried him only slightly off course to the east, the first indication of something wrong was when the vessel went aground. Such groundings were common, and many ships were completely wrecked while trying to make the harbor. Not surprisingly, the harbor was developing a bad reputation among sailors.

In addition, the inspector for the 11th Lighthouse District reported in 1866 that the lighthouse needed to be rebuilt — though probably to accommodate a new lantern rather than because the structure was unsound. The Lighthouse Board requested $15,000 for the project, three times the original cost of the lighthouse. The appropriation was made, and the necessary materials for rebuilding the station were to be landed at the site at the close of navigation so that work could begin in the spring of 1868. However, in 1867, after further review, the inspector recommended erecting range lights on the west shore of the harbor that would enable ships to enter the harbor more easily whether by day or night.

The Lighthouse Board therefore decided that the best course of action would be not to spend the appropriation on the lighthouse, but to abandon the Baileys Harbor Lighthouse and replace it with range lights at the head of the bay, east of the village of Baileys Harbor, and also to build a new lighthouse at Cana Island, north of Baileys Harbor between Moonlight Bay and North Bay. The Board informed Congress of its decision and received authority for the change. On 20 July 1868, the federal government granted $6,000 for the range light project in addition to the earlier appropriation. A part of the funds was used to buy approximately thirty-two acres of land from the State of Wisconsin for the range lights; the purchase took place on 6 October 1868.[3]

The Lighthouse Board ordered the Baileys Harbor light discontinued and the lighting apparatus removed from the tower. On 1 December 1869, at the close of the navigation season, Darling extinguished the light for the last time. For whatever reason, he then left the employ of the Lighthouse Board and moved to Fish Creek. There he was appointed justice of the peace and later served several terms as county coroner. He moved to Sturgeon Bay in 1896 and died there in September 1915.[4]

During the summer and fall of 1869, a Lighthouse Board construction crew from Detroit, directed by Andrew Breitach, built the front and rear range lights. The keeper's house containing the rear range light was a 1½-story clapboard structure measuring thirty-five feet by twenty-four feet that rose from a full fieldstone basement with outside access. Stairs and a small porch provided entrance to the front door of the dwelling, and there was a room with a shed roof at the rear of the dwelling which was used as the kitchen. The rear range light tower projected from the roof at the front gable end of the house. Like the house, the rectangular tower was covered with clapboard painted white, and it had a red roof topped by a standard ventilating ball and lightning rod. The tower had small windows on both the east and west sides and a window measuring twenty-four inches by thirty-six inches with a semi-circular top on the south side. The lens and lamp were located behind this window.

Down the range some 950 feet to the south, the crew erected the front range light tower on a fieldstone base. The white tower was approximately ten feet square at the base; at a height of twelve feet, about halfway up, the corners of the tower were cut back to form an octagonal lantern room. The tower had two levels and was sheathed with vertically laid, matched flooring boards; it had a sheet-iron roof topped by a copper ventilator ball and a lightning rod. The lower level had an outside door and was used to store supplies for maintaining the light in the upper level. The lamp and lens were placed behind a single-pane window measuring twenty-two inches by thirty inches that faced the lake. Directly opposite this window was a small rectangular window facing the rear range light; this arrangement allowed the keeper to monitor the operation of the front range light without having actually to walk to the front tower. The lower level of the tower also had a window to provide light.

Breitach, the crew chief, left a signature board in the dwelling dated 21 October 1869,[5] but the range lights did not go into operation officially until the opening of navigation in 1870. The Lighthouse Board appointed Fabian Trudell the first keeper of the range lights on 1 December 1869. Trudell, who had been born in Canada, was 74 years old when appointed. He and his 69-year-old wife, also born in Canada, moved into the new lighthouse during the winter. Trudell received an annual salary of $540 for his lighthouse responsibilities, which included tending both the front range light (which used a steamer lens to exhibit a fixed red light that in 1870 was twenty-two feet above lake level) and the rear range light (which employed a 5th Order Fresnel lens made by Henry Lepaute Co. in Paris, France to exhibit a fixed white light thirty-nine feet above lake level).

Sailors entering Baileys Harbor were instructed to position themselves so the white light was directly over the red light and, keeping the lights so arrayed, to sail directly into the harbor.[6] The task of tending two lights that burned lard oil and thus were often hard to light in cold weather presented difficulties that probably made this station one of the more difficult ones. Whether it was the difficulties of the job, his advancing age, or some combination, Fabian Trudell resigned his position as keeper in September 1872 after serving only two years.

The Lighthouse Board appointed Marcus Shaler, a long-time Green Bay resident, to replace Trudell. Shortly after he and his wife arrived at the station, a devastating fire swept through much of the Baileys Harbor area, occurring just one year after the epic Peshtigo fire that also severely burned a large area of southern Door County. Fortunately, the range lights were not destroyed, though much of the surrounding area was burned. After the fire, life for the Shalers settled into a comfortable routine broken by occasional trips to Green Bay, to New London, and to Omro, Mrs. Shaler's home town. Some of these journeys occurred during the navigation season and lasted more than a day, so Shaler apparently found and trained someone to tend the lights while he and his wife were absent.

The navigation season ended early in December 1874 after a cool fall during which typhoid fever swept through the village of Baileys Harbor. The disease continued to ravage the village during the cold and snowy winter that followed. Whenever someone fell sick, Mrs. Shaler could be counted on to help; she was untiring in her assistance to victims of the disease, but finally she herself became ill; She died at the age of 43 in the evening of 26 January 1875. At the time, the *Door County Advocate* usually made only the briefest mention when someone died. Anything more than a simple death announcement was reserved for only the most prominent individuals — almost exclusively men. The respect Mrs. Shaler enjoyed is indicated by the fact that the newspaper printed several stories about her during the course of her illness. With the announcement of her death, the editor noted:

> She has been a great sufferer for a number of weeks past, but is now happily released from all further pain, trouble or care. She leaves a bereaved husband to mourn her departure, who has the sympathy of everyone. She was a very estimable lady and was loved and respected by all who knew her.[7]

She was buried in her former home town, Omro, Wisconsin.

Shaler had done a good job as keeper, but in April 1875 he resigned his position and moved back to Green Bay, an action no doubt related to his wife's death.

To replace Shaler, the Lighthouse Board appointed Joseph Harris, Jr. as acting keeper on 15 April 1875. Harris was born in England in 1841 and had come with his father to Sturgeon Bay in 1855 after living eight years in Rochester, New York. When the Civil War broke out, Joseph Jr. was one of Door County's first enlistees. Commissioned a corporal, he rose to the rank of captain before being discharged in 1864 due to severe wounds received in the assault on Petersburg. After returning to Sturgeon Bay, he married Rosalie M. Rice, daughter of Judge Daniel Rice, a prominent Sturgeon Bay resident, on 23 January 1865.

While his son was at war, Joseph Harris, Sr., the editor of the *Door County Advocate*, ran successfully for the Wisconsin State Senate in 1863. One of his motives was to promote a dream that he cherished — a ship canal that would connect Green Bay with Lake Michigan via Sturgeon Bay. Already involved in Republican Party activities, he became a friend and political operative for US Congressman Philetus Sawyer, a prominent Oshkosh lumberman. Sawyer was first elected to the House of Representatives in 1864 and was appointed to the US Senate in 1881. Once in Congress, Sawyer year after year adroitly championed internal improvement bills which provided federal money for Wisconsin projects. For as long as he was involved with the *Door County Advocate*, Harris faithfully supported Sawyer, as did succeeding editors.

In 1875, Harris, Sr. was Sawyer's private secretary. One of his jobs was to maintain Sawyer's support among the party faithful and to monitor Republican affairs in Wisconsin. When a lighthouse vacancy occurred, the area Port Collector and Superintendent of

Lights recommended to the Lighthouse Board who should fill the vacancy. Only rarely did the Board reject a recommendation, since presumably the local officials were the most knowledgeable about the possible candidates. Also, since the position was a political appointment, the Port Collector carefully consulted political leaders from the area and only rarely rejected their recommendations. In reality keepers' appointments were highly political, since no federal civil service covered the keepers at this time. No written record exists in this case, but Sawyer relied on Harris to nominate individuals for lighthouse keepers' appointments in Door County. It appears that Joseph Harris, Sr. took care of his son in obtaining for him a secure federal position; on 30 October 1875 the Lighthouse Board made permanent Joseph Harris, Jr.'s acting appointment as keeper of the Baileys Harbor Range Lights.[8]

Harris and his family, including his wife, who was pregnant with daughter Mable, and their two children, Edward, age 7, and Lottie, age 4, moved to the range light dwelling in April 1875. Harris proved to be both a skilled keeper and a popular figure. According to the *Advocate*'s local correspondent, "the range lights, under Mr. Harris' care, show for themselves that the right man is in charge. . . ." The Harrises lived only about a mile from the center of Baileys Harbor. They joined eagerly in the activities of the village, and their children attended the local school. Harris was active in veterans affairs, both in Baileys Harbor and in Sturgeon Bay, and helped organize the Henry S. Schuyler GAR Post in that city. He was also a founder of the Baileys Harbor Literary Club in 1876, a debating society, considering such topics as:

> — That the works of the Mechanic are of more benefit to the Farmer than those of the Farmer are to the Mechanic;
>
> — That foreign immigration should be encouraged; or

> — That solitary confinement is more effectual than Capital Punishment as a preventive of crime.[9]

Harris was the most active member of the group, debating almost weekly. During the winter, the Harrises made regular trips to Sturgeon Bay to visit family and friends, often staying for several days. During the navigation season, they entertained many friends and family members at the range lights. According to the *Advocate*'s editor:

> By the way, we happen to know that it is a nice place to visit; most always get lemonade! when you go there.[10]

In May 1881, Sam Drew, the original keeper at Green Island Light resigned his post after twenty years of service. The Lighthouse Board transferred Harris to the Green Island Light, and he and his family moved to the new assignment in June. Green Island is a small island located approximately seven miles southeast of Marinette, about halfway across Green Bay from Door County. Less than a month after Harris went to Green Island, the *Advocate* reported that he was

> not much pleased with his new location, owing no doubt to the complete isolation of self and family from the rest of the world. This, taken into consideration that Joe was raised in Door County, is quite enough to cause a species of homesickness.[11]

Considering his unhappiness and his father's position, it was not surprising that in February 1882 Harris was transferred to the Grosse Point Light in Evanston, Illinois. However, he was still attached to Door County, and in 1885 he became the keeper of the Dunlap Reef Light in Sturgeon Bay.

Hans L. Hanson replaced Harris at Baileys Harbor when the Lighthouse Board transferred him there in May 1881. Hanson was born 21 October 1835 and had worked seven years as a woodcarver before his 1876 appointment as first assistant keeper in Chicago. He married Hattie Thoreson of Chicago in 1881 before moving to Baileys Harbor. The winter of 1881–82 was mild and navigation remained open until January, preventing Hanson from taking a winter vacation, as many of the other keepers did. In mid-January when Hanson had to go to Chicago on business, his wife cared for the lights, assisted by two local helpers. The Hansons' stay in Baileys Harbor was relatively short; he was transferred to the Point au Sable Light near Manistee, Michigan in July 1882. He later served in Chicago and in Menominee, Michigan before retiring.[12]

The Lighthouse Board transferred George Larson from Michigan's Poverty Island Light to Baileys Harbor on the last day of August 1882 after Burr Caswell resigned his appointment rather than accepting a transfer to Baileys Harbor. Larson and his family sailed to Baileys Harbor in their own boat. They were very pleased with the change from the desolation of Poverty Island, especially since their two sons, Charles and Willie, could attend the local school. Like many of the keepers of the time, Larson, born in Denmark, was a Civil War veteran, having served in Wisconsin's famous Iron Brigade. After the war, he held several offices in the Wisconsin GAR.

For several years, shippers had been protesting that the harbor at Baileys Harbor often opened again after navigation had officially been closed and the range lights extinguished. In response to their pleas, the District Superintendent ordered the keeper at Baileys Harbor to re-light the range lights after the close of navigation if shippers requested that he do so. Keepers to the north as well as those on the west side of the peninsula could count on a three-month or four-month winter vacation from duty, the range light keeper at Baileys Harbor could not be sure he wouldn't have to relight his lamps unless the harbor was securely frozen over. Happily, the replacement of lard oil burners with kerosene burners in 1880 made the job of operating the lights easier.

In addition to his ordinary lighthouse duties, Larson took great pride in the grounds of the station. Only a few months after his arrival, the townspeople commented that he was putting the area around the lights in good shape. They predicted that in a few years the grounds would be one of the most beautiful places on the entire peninsula. In 1883 and after numerous requests, a Board crew made improvements and minor repairs to the station — a board fence was built around the 2½ acres surrounding the rear range light and a stable was built for the keeper's livestock. To help drain swampy areas, workers laid 300 feet of box drain. A well-driller put in a fifty-foot well lined with iron pipe and capped with a pump. That gave the Larsons had an abundant supply of water close to the house rather than having to carry water from the lake.[13]

To present a more professional appearance, in 1884 the Lighthouse Board adopted a uniform for the keepers; it consisted of a blue double-breasted coat, a single-breasted collarless vest, matching pants, and a blue cloth cap with a metal lighthouse badge in front and center. When the *Dahlia* delivered supplies for the range lights in June 1884, Larson received his new uniform free of charge, but the Lighthouse Board charged keepers for subsequent uniforms.[14]

George Larson's oldest son Charles became Sturgeon Bay's assistant postmaster in 1885, and the family began making regular trips to Sturgeon Bay to visit him. When the citizens of Baileys Harbor decided to organize a Sunday school, they asked George Larson to become superintendent; though at first reluctant to assume this new responsibility, he finally consented.[15] In late December 1887, local residents were surprised to learn that their efficient lighthouse keeper and esteemed townsman, George Larson, was contemplating leaving Baileys Harbor for a more southerly post. Apparently a case of rheumatism, developed during his army service, had flared up again causing him considerable pain.

> The village is extremely reluctant about losing him from its society and we doubt very much if another lightkeeper can be found who has been so untiring and public spirited in his efforts to improve and beautify the lighthouse grounds.

During his nearly five-year tenure at the range lights, several additional acres of grounds had been cleared, low spots were drained, much of the cleared area had been fenced, a well was drilled, and a stable built, and Larson had planted fruit and shade trees on the grounds. For all these activities, his successors will have much reason to be thankful in the many years to come.[16]

Larson remained at Baileys Harbor until March 1888, when the Lighthouse Board transferred him to the Racine lighthouse. Both he and his wife were pleased with the new assignment for he had lived in Racine previously and had many friends in the city. Moreover, Mrs. Larson was from Racine and had several brothers living there. As soon as his replacement arrived on 31 March 1888, Larson left for Racine; his family followed a month later, when navigation opened for the season. After several years at Racine, Larson resigned his position due to ill health; he later moved to the veteran's home near Waupaca, Wisconsin, and he died there in November 1899 at the age of 58 of tuberculosis.

> Capt. Larson was one of the noblest of men in all his dealings with his fellow-men and neighbors. Always kind and charitable he won a place in the hearts of all with whom he was brought in contact. . . .[17]

John Millidge, former assistant at Petite Pointe au Sable Light, located south of Ludington, Michigan, replaced Larson at Baileys Harbor. A native of Nova Scotia, Millidge lived alone in the rear range light for a month until navigation opened and his family could sail across Lake Michigan with their belongings. Apparently he did not become actively involved in Baileys Harbor activities as Larson had, but had the distinction of being an inventor. In December 1882, Millidge received a patent from the federal government for a new horse collar that he developed. Although he received numerous inquiries from outsiders in regard to his invention, his horse collar never became widely used. At various times during this tenure as keeper, Millidge suffered severely from attacks of asthma, some of which kept him confined to his home for long periods of time.[18]

As noted above, in 1880 the Lighthouse Board had replaced the lard oil lamps with ones that burned kerosene. Recognizing the increased flammability of kerosene, the Board recommended that fireproof oil houses be built at each station. However, despite the danger, the recommendation was implemented slowly because of a shortage of funds. Indeed, it was not until fifteen years later, in July 1895, that the *Amaranth* delivered the materials for the station's oil house. In August, Mr. Hunt, a lighthouse district employee, arrived at Baileys Harbor. He built a brick oil house measuring seven feet square some 105 feet north of the keeper's dwelling. It had a metal roof, a metal entrance door, and could house ninety five-gallon cans or butts on metal shelves.[19]

There were rumors in Baileys Harbor in November 1895 that a change of keepers at the range lights was imminent, but the stories of Millidge's departure seem to have aroused little local comment. The rumors were true; only the timing was incorrect. In May 1896 that the Board removed Millidge as keeper, though the reason for the action are not recorded. He and his wife moved to Chicago, but then moved back to Baileys Harbor to be near their daughter, Mrs. Joel Carrington. After returning, Millidge served as justice of the peace, dying on 2 June 1904.[20]

To fill the vacancy the Lighthouse Board transferred the first assistant at the Sturgeon Bay Canal Light Station, Henry H. Gattie, to Baileys Harbor on 1 May 1896 and promoted him to keeper. The son of Mr. and Mrs. Xavier Gattie, Henry was born in Belgium in 1865 and had come with his family to America in 1872. The family settled first in Kewaunee County, but soon moved to a farm near Sturgeon Bay. Gattie was a relatively slight man about five feet, eight inches tall, and spoke fluent French as well as English. In November 1888 he had become acting first assistant at the Sturgeon Bay Canal Light, receiving a permanent appointment as first assistant the following year. With the move to Baileys Harbor, his salary increased from $450 to $540 a year, the same salary Joseph Harris, Jr. had received twenty-one years earlier. The steam tug *Nelson* brought Gattie and his household goods to Baileys Harbor from Sturgeon Bay on 13 May 1896.

Gattie quickly settled in at the range lights, operating the station alone. Like many of the keepers, he was very handy, and among his first activities was painting the dwelling, inside and out. Richard Goll had been superintending repairs and improvements at Cana Island Light, and he arrived at Baileys Harbor on 4 September 1896 to spend two weeks making repairs to the dwelling, including re-shingling the roof and putting in new front steps. According to local observers:

> The range lights here are probably as pretty a place as can be found in this vicinity and the surroundings never looked better than since Henry Gattie took charge, everything in and about the premises looking as neat and bright as a new pin.[21]

The Baileys Harbor rear range light, with keeper Henry Gattie, his wife, and four visitors. The shade is drawn in the upper window to protect the lens; just to the right of Gattie is the station's oil house. Photo courtesy of Lee Traven.

Gattie began clearing by hand the 950-foot opening between the range lights to a width of 200 feet — 100 feet on each side of the walk connecting the two lights. While those familiar with today's much narrower swath between the lights might disagree, at the time it was felt this wider opening would contribute greatly to the beauty of the station and be of great benefit to navigators entering the harbor.[22]

Gattie was a hard worker, and he was also a very social individual. By all accounts, he quickly became a very popular figure in the village. To help relieve the late winter monotony, twenty-six of his male and female friends descended on his house for a surprise party one evening. The group played cards, games, and kindred amusements until a late hour. At midnight an oyster supper and refreshments were served before the guests departed. A score or more of Gattie's friends gathered a month later at his residence for an evening of talk and card playing. A fine spread, provided by the callers, was served about 8 PM. Those in attendance pronounced the affair one of the happiest held that winter.[23]

On 7 June 1897, the *Dahlia* and *Amaranth* both arrived at the same time to dock in Baileys Harbor. The crew of the *Dahlia* delivered supplies to the station, and the *Amaranth*'s crew brought ashore a new lighting apparatus to upgrade the front range light. Ten days later the district lampist visited the station. In order to improve the light's effectiveness, he removed the front range light's steamer lens and replaced it with a new 5th Order tubular burner and 5th Order locomotive headlight with a parabolic reflector.[24] The following July, when district lampist Wredge visited Gattie, he took the lamps and lenses from both the stations' lights with him for repair, leaving temporary replacements. Wredge returned to Baileys Harbor in March 1899 and installed the refurbished lenses and lamps. The lampist made regular visits to the stations during the navigation season and was available to the keepers if a serious breakdown of the lighting equipment occurred.

We learn from the keeper's log that, like many of the other men in Baileys Harbor, Gattie eagerly looked forward to the opening of deer hunting season every November. A few weeks before the 1897 season, Gattie went to Sturgeon Bay's Scholfield & Company, one of the city's major stores, and bought a new Daisy deer rifle. The third day of the hunt, he brought down a large buck that dressed out at 175 pounds. Then, as now, deer hunting was a yearly Wisconsin ritual, and Gattie went deer hunting nearly every fall for years.[25]

In the 1890s, several ships a week were usually in port loading lumber, ties, and cordwood, but, as farmers cleared the land and forests dwindled before the lumbermen's onslaught, agricultural products — potatoes, peas, and grains — became more important as cargoes. During stormy weather, numerous ships, both sail and steam, sought shelter in the bay. The schooner *Nancy Dell* was one of the last of the schooners making weekly trips to Chicago carrying lumber throughout the season; each winter she laid up in Baileys Harbor. Federal purchase of the Sturgeon Bay Canal in 1893 turned the canal into a free waterway. This meant that Goodrich Line steamers, the major carriers of passengers and freight, now rarely stopped at Baileys harbor; they preferred to sail into Green Bay through Sturgeon Bay rather than around Deaths Door. By 1900, as other forms of transportation developed and the forests receded even more, boat traffic declined as both farmers and townspeople turned to overland transportation. Baileys Harbor had begun its long slide into obscurity as a commercial port.

Gattie's name continued to appear often in the newspaper as correspondents mentioned his travels to visit friends in and out of Door County, his attendance at parties and gatherings in the area, and his work at the range lights. In early December 1899,

Gattie and Misses Edith Ehrke and Eva and Clara Hendrick, all of Baileys Harbor, drove over to Liberty Grove to spend the day with friends.

> It must be conceded that Henry is having more than his share of good things, but it is supposed to be merely accidental in this instance. However, everybody will hope to see him here again, and that soon and often. He is also privileged to bring as many of the nice girls from Bailey's Harbor as he sees fit.[26]

After dating a number of women, Henry's friends began noting that he was paying special attention to Eva Hendrick as the new century began. Born in Baileys Harbor in 1879 of German immigrant parents, Eva and her twin sister Nellie had grown up in Baileys Harbor. Both Eva and Henry were well-liked and popular, and their friends were pleased when they announced their engagement.

On 18 February 1901, Gattie made the following entry in his log, "My Wedding at 4 PM H. Gattie." That was all he wrote, nothing more, but the wedding was one of the social highlights of the year in Baileys Harbor. The ceremony was conducted by Ephriam's Rev. John Greenfield and was held in the sitting room of the bride's mother's home with only family members in attendance. Even though it was mid-February, the bride, attired in white silk, wore a wreath of fresh orange blossoms and carried a bouquet of live roses. Her sister, the maid of honor, carried yellow roses. After the ceremony, the wedding party had dinner, and then joined a large number of invited guests for a ball at the Baileys Harbor House. The Duclon Orchestra, made up of members of the Eagle Bluff Lighthouse keeper's family, furnished the music.

> Both young and old made merry well into the following morning when the dancers departed with

> regrets that Mr. and Mrs. Gattie could not be married at least once a month.[27]

Many newly married Door County couples took wedding trips, and mid-February would have been an ideal time to leave the range lights, since navigation was closed, but the couple apparently immediately went home, since Gattie's entries in his log continued on February 19 without any interruption.

Continued operation without interruption would generally also characterize activities at the range lights. Each year Gattie painted the range light buildings — the oil house, the barn, the privy, and the woodshed — and the wooden board fence which now enclosed about 2½ acres. Except for the barn, which had red walls, all the buildings were white with red roofs. In 1909 a new four-inch well, seventy feet deep was drilled. Each spring Gattie cleaned out the cistern in the basement of the dwelling. Together the Gatties maintained their garden (sixty feet square) which provided fruits and vegetables for the couple's table. The walks to the immediate outbuildings were made of concrete, but the keeper had to maintain the wooden plank walk between the range lights. In addition to the 2½ acres within the fence, another 5½ acres around the dwelling were more or less cleared. According to a 1909 description of the station, the general surroundings of the station were swampy for most of the year, although the healthfulness of the station had always been good. Catarrh and colds, generally in fall and winter, were the most prevalent diseases at the station and in the vicinity. The inspector attributed the diseases to the low swampland surrounding the station, and he suggested the premises could be greatly improved by trenching from the swamps to Lake Michigan. He felt that this action would also prevent the fog that sometimes arose from these swamps to obscure the rear range light when the front light, closer to the shore, was still visible.[28] Fortunately for visitors to The Ridges today, the inspector's recommendation was not followed.

Life was good for the Gatties as they kept the range lights burning. However, the scene continued to change. Improved cars and trucks, improved highways, and the nearness of the railroad terminus in Sturgeon Bay meant that fewer and fewer ships entered the harbor. Nevertheless, because it was a harbor of refuge, there was justification for maintaining the range lights. In the 1920s the Lighthouse Bureau began looking for ways to save money, including reducing the number of keepers and experimenting with means of illumination to replace kerosene. The engineers developed a system using acetylene gas which required new lamps, but could utilize the existing lenses. The system had a pilot light and a so-called sun valve that turned on the gas. When light was needed, the valve opened the gas line and the pilot light ignited the gas in the lamp. The system was virtually automatic and required only periodic (usually monthly) inspection and cleaning. At a cost of $2,331, the Baileys Harbor Range Lights were converted to an unmanned acetylene system in September 1923.

Since they no longer needed a keeper at the range lights, the district inspector began looking for a place to transfer Gattie. Fortuitously, in August, the assistant keeper at Cana Island quit the service, and Gattie transferred a few miles east to the vacancy at Cana Island. On 4 September 1923 the Gatties moved out of the rear range light dwelling to Cana Island. Thus, in September 1923, the Baileys Harbor Range Lights no longer had a resident keeper to attend them, but they still continued to guide mariners into the harbor. Operation of the Baileys Harbor Range Lights became a duty of the Cana Island keepers; barring unexpected difficulties — i.e the lights not operating — they came there only once a month to check the pressure in the acetylene tanks and to replace them if necessary. The buildings were closed, shuttered, and locked.

The Gatties remained at Cana Island only until 26 November 1923, when Henry was transferred to the Two Rivers Pier Head Light in Two Rivers, Wisconsin. Eva had already become lonely living at Cana Island, and she was particularly pleased with the move. Gattie remained at the Two Rivers station until 1931 when he retired after 45 years in lighthouse service. After retirement, he and Eva returned to Baileys Harbor to live. Henry Gattie, the last resident keeper at the Baileys Harbor Range Lights, died 27 April 1948, but he was survived by his widow, who lived until 1963.[29]

The monthly task of driving from Cana Island to the Baileys Harbor range lights to clean the lenses and check the acetylene tanks, usually took two to three hours. If the range lights went out, personnel at the Baileys Harbor Coast Guard Station, which was located east along the shore from the range lights near the original Baileys Harbor light, would telephone the keepers at Cana Island to come to relight them. On 5 November 1926, the Eagle Bluff Light also was converted from kerosene to an unattended acetylene light, and it too became the responsibility of the Cana Island keepers.

In 1930, the federal government leased the dwellings at both Baileys Harbor and Eagle Bluff stations to private individuals. In November 1930 a lighthouse crew strung electrical wire between the rear and front range lights. A lighthouse electrician from Milwaukee then installed electric lights in the range lights, and on 24 November 1930, the Baileys Harbor station switched from acetylene gas to electricity. The Cana Island keepers disassembled the old acetylene equipment and trucked it to Sturgeon Bay for disposal. Though a timeclock at the station automatically switched the lights on and off, the Cana Island keepers continued to clean and polish the lenses and to clean and paint the rear lantern and front tower.

The Secretary of Commerce granted the Immanuel Lutheran Church of Baileys Harbor a revocable license to use the rear range light dwelling as a parsonage, and the church rented the dwelling from 1930 to 1956, taking responsibility for upkeep and maintenance of the premises. Specifically, the minister or member of his family or a custodian was responsible for replacing burned-out bulbs in the two range light lenses, changing burned-out fuses, and adjusting the automatic clock switch; they called the Cana Island keeper when his services were required to maintain the Baileys Harbor Range Lights.[30]

In January 1934, on the recommendation of the deputy commissioner of Lighthouses, the Secretary of Commerce granted the Door County Park Commission permission to occupy and use the approximately thirty acres which comprised the Baileys Harbor Light Station Reservation as a park. Except for two small plots actually surrounding the front and rear range light buildings, the property had been declared surplus to the needs of the Bureau of Lighthouses.

The reservation and surrounding land had long been recognized as a very unusual and interesting geological and botanical area that contained many rare plants. When the park commission began to clear part of the land for a trailer park, there was an outburst of opposition to the destruction of this unique area which halted work on the park. The opponents joined together in 1937 to form The Ridges Sanctuary for Plant and Animal Life Incorporated in order to preserve the area. The Ridges Sanctuary also began acquiring additional land around the reservation, and in 1972 the county leased the light station reservation to The Ridges.[31]

After the church relinquished use of the dwelling as a parsonage, the building stood unused and empty for nine years. In 1965 The Ridges Board asked the Coast Guard to lease them the dwelling to use as a residence for their naturalist. The Coast Guard agreed, and in the spring of 1966 Roy Lukes moved into the empty rear range light dwelling.

During the summer of 1969, the Coast Guard built a concrete pad between the shore and the road south of the front range light. One evening in early November, Lukes returned home and smelled cigarette smoke in the house. The only other persons having access were coast guardsmen. He went upstairs to the tower to see what they had been doing in his absence. He was shocked to discover that they had removed the light and the Fresnel lens. When he went to the front range light tower, its light and lens were also gone. Shortly thereafter, the Coast Guard erected the present metal tower with its directional light on the pad south of the front range light.[32]

Thanks to the work of Alanson Sweet, an accomplished mason and building contractor, the Baileys Harbor Lighthouse tower and dwelling still stand, nearly a century and a half after they were originally constructed. The lighthouse is now a monument to the early history of Baileys Harbor, rather than a beacon for the boats that still sail in and out of Captain Bailey's harbor, and the range lights that once guided mariners into the security and safety of the harbor also have been extinguished. The front and rear range light buildings remain, however, reminding all who see them of the days when faithful keepers tended their lights.

The Cana Island lighthouse about 1940. Notice that the summer kitchen has been removed. Photo courtesy of US Coast Guard.

Chapter 6
Cana Island Light

Summer visitors to Cana Island today can sometimes walk across the 300-foot natural causeway from the mainland with dry feet, but at other times they may have take off their shoes and wade through water covering the causeway — it all depends on the level of Lake Michigan. In the past, keepers have sometimes had to use boats to make the crossing from the island to the mainland, though at other times they used horse-drawn vehicles or cars. Throughout the history of Cana Island Light, the choice has depended on Lake Michigan, not on those making the crossing.

Cana Island light has been a popular spot for visitors from the time of its construction. It is perhaps Door County's most sketched, painted, photographed, and videotaped lighthouse. Cana Island Light is beautiful, and it looks the way most people think a lighthouse should. It has a gleaming white tower surmounted by a large black lantern that soars above the attached keepers dwelling and reminds visitors of well-known lighthouses on the east and west coasts.

We have already mentioned in the previous chapter that the original Baileys Harbor Light was not ideally located for either of its jobs — i.e. to serve as both a coast light and a harbor light. As that became apparent, the Lighthouse Board began searching for a new location for a lighthouse along Door County's Lake Michigan shore. Northeast of Baileys Harbor are two well-protected bays which, like Baileys Harbor, open to the southeast. These two natural harbors — Moonlight Bay and North Bay — both had good holding ground for anchoring ships; they are separated by a peninsula of land which terminates on the southeast with the sometimes flooded causeway to Cana Island.

Cana Island is a rough triangle about 8.7 acres in size; it measures approximately 840 feet east-west by 700 feet at its widest point north-south. The lighthouse stands on the east side of the island about 60 feet from the water's edge; it is on a part of the island that juts out into the lake, thus exposing the station to waves from three sides. The gently dipping limestone bedrock creates broad shallows around the island, making it extremely difficult to approach the station directly by water. There was once a small pier in front of the light, but the station's boathouse and main landing pier were located on the southwest corner of the island, just south of the present causeway, where slightly deeper water made it possible for shallow-draft vessels to land in good weather. As noted above, Cana Island sometimes is an island, sometimes simply an extension of the peninsula, depending on whether the Lake Michigan water level is high or low.

The island itself looks quite different today than it did when the station was built in 1869. At that time it had a very thin covering of soil and rocks over the bedrock that barely raised its surface above Lake Michigan's waters. This helps to account for some of the perhaps exaggerated stories told by the early keepers of terrifying storms that actually swept over the island and into the lighthouse dwelling. Also, when the light was manned, the keepers kept much more of the island brushed out and clear than is the case today.

In March 1867, Congress appropriated funds to repair and renovate the 15-year-old Baileys Harbor Lighthouse. However, as we have noted, the Lighthouse Board eventually decided to abandon that station entirely and to build a new light four miles to the northeast on Cana Island. The Board also decided to designate the new light a coast light with a more powerful 3rd Order lens, rather than a harbor light with a less powerful 5th Order lens, though it also marked the approach to Baileys Harbor and Moonlight Bay to the south and North Bay to the north.

For a number of years the Board also sought funding from Congress to build a harbor light at the entrance to North Bay. The requested funds were never approved, however, and the entrance was only marked with a buoy. The Federal government had never transferred ownership of Cana Island to the State of Wisconsin, and the Board requested President Andrew Johnson to reserve the island for a lighthouse; on 7 April 1868 the President complied with the request. The Board next went to Congress for funding, and, in July 1868, Congress approved abandonment of the Baileys Harbor Light and at the same time increased the previous appropriation to cover the cost of the new lighthouse station on Cana Island.

Lighthouse Board crews were busy in the area during 1869. One crew was hard at work building the range lights at Baileys Harbor. Another crew, under the direction of Charles Crossman, foreman of the Lighthouse Engineers, began preparation of the site at Cana Island; they cleared trees and brush from about three acres on the eastern portion of the island, blasted out a hole for the basement of the keeper's dwelling, and cut a path from the landing on the southwest side of the island. After building a full basement from the shattered rocks, the crew began erecting a 1½-story keeper's dwelling measuring forty-two feet by twenty-seven feet, and a covered way connecting the dwelling to the light tower that measured eight feet by ten feet.

The tower itself was built on an eight-foot foundation, four feet of which were below ground level. The tower was eighteen feet in diameter at the base with double walls for ventilation. The outer wall narrowed from a thickness of two feet at the base to fifteen inches at the base of the watch room, about sixty-five feet above the foundation. At that point, the tower tapered to a diameter of sixteen feet. The inner core of the tower (with walls a foot thick) remained eight feet in diameter from top to bottom; the crew installed six windows, each sixteen inches in diameter, in the tower to provide light during the day.

The entire complex — dwelling, connection, and tower — was built of cream-colored Milwaukee brick; in 1869, the sixty-five-foot brick tower was the tallest brick structure in Door County. The dwelling had five rooms for the keeper on the first floor and three rooms on the second floor for the assistant keeper. The keeper's kitchen was located on the west end of the dwelling; it had an outside door and was nearly at ground level, about two feet lower than the rest of the first floor.

Cana Island's lantern had two levels, the watch room or service room at the top of the tower and the still higher lantern room. Metal brackets attached near the top of the tower supported the lantern's floor. The watch room ceiling was six feet nine inches high and the room was five feet in diameter; it had a balcony enclosed by a steel railing that extended out another three feet from the wall. A stairway led to the lantern room which was six feet high and nine feet in diameter, with a balcony two feet wide and surrounded by a steel railing. A copper dome three feet high stood atop the lantern room; a ventilating ball that allowed gases from lamp to escape, and a lightning rod added another nine feet to the height of the structure.

The Lighthouse Board contracted for a cast-iron and glass lantern, which was shipped in pieces to Cana Island, hoisted to the top of the tower and assembled in the fall of 1869. The lantern itself was ten-sided with vertical iron bars holding glass panes, each of which was 5/16 of an inch thick, 69¾ inches high and 31⅜ inches wide. On a cast-iron pedestal, the district lampist positioned a 3rd Order Fresnel lens which had been built by Henry Le Paute of Paris, France. The light was fixed, so no revolving mechanism was needed. The lens had five panels of 72 degrees each, one of which was on the west side and was silvered so the light did not illuminate the land side of the island. The focal plane of the lens was some seventy-five feet above the base of the tower which was several feet above ground level; in 1911 the focal plane was calculated to be eighty-two feet above mean lake level. The lampist installed a Joseph French 3rd Order hydraulic float lamp that burned lard oil in the lens. The crew finished work at the station late in the fall, and the light was lit officially for the first time on 28 January 1870 when navigation opened.[1]

The Lighthouse Board appointed William Jackson keeper on 3 November 1869, as the station was being completed. The same day the Board appointed his wife Caroline as assistant keeper. Their annual salaries were $600 and $400 respectively, rates that did not change for over thirty years. Jackson had been born in Wisconsin in 1835. His wife was the same age and was born in Prussia; she had come to the United States as a girl. Since Caroline was the assistant keeper, the Jacksons occupied both floors of the dwelling with their four sons and one daughter.

One of the keeper's duties was to log the number and type of ships that passed the station. Jackson reported that 4,862 ships passed the Cana Island station during daylight hours of his first year at Cana Island. This was before the opening of the Sturgeon Bay ship canal and also before the area south of Sturgeon Bay was served by railroads. Using his telescope, Jackson could observe much of the ship traffic sailing in and out of Green Bay from ports to the south, especially Milwaukee and Chicago. He logged more than 3,000 schooners and 100 barks, and already in 1870 he noted more than 300 steamers that passed the light. The next year 4,264 ships passed Cana Island.[2]

On 29 August 1872, Jackson and one of his sons had to swim to shore when the station's boat capsized in a northwest gale and was lost about 1½ miles from the old Baileys Harbor light. Jackson and his family left Cana Island shortly after this incident.

Julius Warren took charge of the station 15 November 1872; he was a farmer from Clay Banks, Wisconsin, south of Sturgeon

Bay on Lake Michigan. As was often true in the years after the Civil War and before the advent of the Civil Service System, being a veteran and a Republican often played a key role in obtaining a light keeper's appointment. According to the newspaper, Warren's appointment was:

> another instance in which the Republican administration at Washington, takes care of the wounded soldiers who volunteered to save the nation from rebels and traitors.[3]

In mid-June 1873, the Lighthouse Board appointed Warren's wife Sarah as assistant keeper, a position she had already been filling unofficially. While Warren served as keeper, his father and brother from Clay Banks visited Cana Island several times a year.

The fall of 1874 was a particularly stormy one and Lake Michigan's level was high; Warren's log contains the first of a long series of accounts of tremendous storms that raked the exposed island. On September 14 there were heavy southerly gales and, on the morning of the 15th "the sea ran mountain high;" six weeks later a gale that began about two in the morning "blowed down about one third of the timber on the Island;" a few weeks later a terrific southeast gale hit that lasted from 1 AM to 6 AM before swinging around to the southwest. Warren complained that the resulting sea was so heavy that it swept completely over the island. Shortly after the storm, Warren closed the station for the winter; he and his wife spent the winter at their Clay Banks farm.

Traffic was heavy during 1874; Warren logged 4,115 vessels of various types powered by sails or steam that passed Cana Island. Charles Crossman, who had directed the construction of the station, visited in June to make minor repairs, which included fixing the woodshed floor. In September, the *Dahlia* brought district lampist Crump to check the station's optics. The Warrens also received a visit from Joseph Harris, Jr., his wife, and their son and daughter. Harris was appointed keeper of the Baileys Harbor Range Lights less than a year later, and the two families became good friends.

During a gale on 16 September 1874, the steam-barge *Ira H. Owen* hit the reef off the mouth of Baileys Harbor and broke her rudder off. The crew of the disabled *Owen* cut adrift the *Jessie Linn*, a large barge they had been towing. The barge drifted at the mercy of the winds and waves until shortly after 10 PM when she struck the reef south of the Cana Island lighthouse; the light was plainly visible, and the crew made their way safely to the station with Warren's assistance. The next morning the *Owen*'s captain came to the light and picked up the crew. Since it was so late in the year, they decided not to attempt to refloat the *Linn* until spring. Warren noted in his log on 26 May 1875 that, after several weeks of work, two steamers and a tug had released the barge from the reef.

The district lighthouse engineer visited the station in April 1875 and delivered materials for the construction of a boathouse and boat ways. Prior to this time, there had been only a pier built on the west side of the island some 750 feet from the lighthouse. In mid-September, foreman of engineers George Dobson and a construction crew built the boathouse and made minor repairs to the rest of the station.

Warren made entries in his official log rather sporadically, and he apparently did not keep a daily weather log. There were long lapses between entries, yet the entries are written next to each other with no indication of any missing material. The first entry in the log after the mid-September note about building the boathouse was dated 7 November 1875, when William Sanderson wrote:

> Wm. A. Sanderson takes charge of the Cana Island Light Station, Viz. Julius Warren.

The official records say only that Julius and Sarah Warren were "removed," with no indication as to why. Warren and his family returned to their farm in Clay Banks where Julius remained until his death in 1914. Sarah died in 1924. Except for the three years they had served at Cana Island, both spent their entire adult lives on their Clay Banks farm.[4]

William Sanderson arrived at Cana Island on 7 November 1875, though the Lighthouse Board had officially given him a probationary appointment on 14 October 1875; a year later on 10 November 1876 the Board made the appointment permanent. At the same time the Board appointed Sanderson's wife Sarah as assistant keeper with the same two-stage process. Sanderson was born 2 December 1843, in New York, the son of a Scottish Episcopal minister. During the Civil War, he enlisted in the 44th New York Infantry and moved to Sturgeon Bay to teach school after mustering out in 1866. On 4 April 1867, he married Sarah Rice, then 25 years old, a Sturgeon Bay native and daughter of Judge Daniel Rice, one of Door County's earliest residents. Sarah Rice's sister was married to Joseph Harris, Jr. whose father was a political ally of Congressman Philetus Sawyer and later Senator Sawyer's secretary. When the vacancy at Cana Island occurred, Sanderson apparently had an inside track on the job due to being a war veteran, a Republican, and related to Harris by marriage.

When appointed to Cana Island, the Sandersons had three children — Clifford William, age 7; Herbert J., age 2; and Jennie, age 5. Since Mrs. Sanderson was her husband's assistant, the Sanderson family occupied the entire house and must have found the lighthouse dwelling spacious.[5]

Whether due to instructions from his superiors or on his own initiative, Sanderson's log was much more professionally kept than Warren's, with daily weather observations and many more comments; though his log has fewer comments than those of later keepers. During his sixteen-year tenure at Cana Island, Sanderson's log shows his interest in the weather, but it records very little of the day-to-day routine of the keeper or of his personal activities.

Sanderson took charge of Cana Island on 17 November 1875 and a month later extinguished the light for the winter, the navigation season having ended. Later in his tenure Sanderson and his family usually spent the winter in Sturgeon Bay, but they stayed this first winter at the lighthouse, though they made a number of visits to Sturgeon Bay during the course of the winter.

The Sandersons witnessed more serious storms with more dramatic effects than did any of the other Cana Island keepers. At times during their stay, Lake Michigan's water levels were high, and Cana Island was truly an island, terribly exposed to winds and waves ranging from northeast to almost southwest. Gales from those directions swept across long stretches of open lake, pushing the water before them and thus raising the water level even higher and building huge waves. The shallow water around the island caused the waves to break offshore, but this only partially lessened the effects of storm waves. Also, the level of the land immediately around the lighthouse buildings was lower at that time, and these factors combined to produce some particularly eventful times for the Sandersons; they had five major storms in one season.

Sanderson's first entry in his log for 1876 was on March 16. According to him, the wind had begun blowing from the northeast on the evening of the 15th. By 9 AM on March 16, the wind had increased to almost hurricane strength and continued to increase until 6 PM. It was impossible to stand up or face the wind outside, so everyone stayed in. According to Sanderson's log, it was "the heaviest gale of wind experienced in this section of the country in years." Sanderson did not exhibit the light that season until March 28, and he mentions no flooding despite the strength of the gale, so Lake Michigan apparently was still covered with ice.

On May 15 a three-day gale struck from the northeast. The sea rolled over the bank where the ground met the stones of the beach and carried away the wooden sidewalks around the dwelling. At times the water stood as much as four feet deep on the station's grounds. On June 19 another gale set the sidewalks adrift with the water as much as eighteen inches deep around the dwelling. Five weeks later, on July 26, waves from a heavy southerly gale swept away the piers protecting the boathouse on the southwest side of the island; the water rose to a depth of twenty-two inches around the house and tower and once again set the wooden sidewalks adrift.

August was calm. The *Dahlia* delivered supplies and two visitors: Commander William P. McCann, the district inspector, and lampist Crump, who inspected the station. September also began on a calm note, and Mrs. Joseph Harris, Jr. visited her sister early in the month, but all that soon changed. On September 9, the wind began to blow from the northeast, shifted to the east and rose to gale strength the next day, and then went back to the northeast before calming. The water was so high during those three days, that it came into the kitchen and also flooded the basement. But, it was the last major storm before Sanderson extinguished the light and shut down the station for the winter on 15 December 1876.

Extinguishing the lamp did not mean that navigation ceased, however. A mild winter allowed commerce to continue on Lake Michigan, and fishermen still went out in their boats. In mid-January, at the time the Sandersons went to Sturgeon Bay for a visit, the ice bridge to Washington Island was not safe enough to travel across. Sanderson and his family remained all winter at Cana Island, but they made another trip to Sturgeon Bay in January for a special reason, to meet his father, the Reverend James Sanderson from New York City.

Baileys Harbor several times. The visitor apparently made a very favorable impression in the village; at the beginning of April, the *Door County Advocate's* Baileys Harbor correspondent wrote:

> Mr. Sanderson is a remarkably intelligent gentleman, and during his short stay amongst us has made a host of warm friends, and as the time draws near for his departure we feel sorry to think that he cannot remain with us.[6]

One wonders what this Door County visitor told his friends in New York City about his son's situation on Cana Island and about his visit to Wisconsin.

Sanderson exhibited the light for the first time that spring on April 6, which marked the official opening of navigation. Apparently, 1877 was a calm year in terms of the weather, and the log indicates only that the Sandersons went about their routine lighthouse-keeping duties. The *Dahlia* delivered supplies, and Captain J.N. Miller, the new inspector, paid a visit to the station in late July. Lighthouse foreman T.W. Taylor came to see what repairs were needed, and returned with a crew of laborers on September 8 to stay for two weeks of repairs at the station. During that time the Sandersons had to provide room and board for the workers. On Christmas day, the family celebrated both the holiday and the close of navigation; for the next three months, the light in the tower was dark.

For several years Sanderson's activities followed a settled routine. Navigation usually opened about mid-March and the light was exhibited at that time for the season. The *Dahlia* brought supplies and the lighthouse inspector made his annual inspection in late June or early July. October or November brought foreman Taylor's visit with his crew to paint the buildings and make minor repairs before moving on to another station.

There were some serious storms during those years, but, until 16 October 1880, none caused the level of flooding and damage that had occurred in the 1876 storms; on that day, the wind began to blow from the northwest before shifting to the southeast and increasing in velocity. This storm is one of the most severe in Lake Michigan history and became known as the "Alpena Gale" in memory of the Goodrich Transportation Company side-wheeler *Alpena* which was lost in it along with eighty-six passengers and crew. The shift of the wind to the southeast exposed Cana Island to the full fury of the storm; on 16 October 1880, Sanderson wrote in his log:

> The most Severe Storm Ever Known on the Lake — Eleven wrecks in the Vicinity of this Station.

And he later added,

> The 16th day of this Month Prevailed the Heaviest Gale of Wind and the most destruction ever known on the lake. The Sea at this Station made a clean break into the House and back into [illegible].

Two days later the *Dahlia* stopped at Cana Island, and Captain Watson and his crew visited the station. When Watson returned to Sturgeon Bay, he gave a reporter a rather more dramatic account,

> At Cana Island the water dashed into the lower part of the lighthouse, ten feet above its level and fifty feet back from the shore. The keeper had to flee with his family into the boathouse farther back. The water tore up the walks around his home, drowned his chickens, and smashed things up generally.[7]

And further graphic details were added as time went on. The Sandersons apparently had a friend with them at the lighthouse when the storm struck. Three months later, the friend wrote to the *Advocate* editor:

> We had a terrible time of it here Cana Island the night of the storm, the sea at times almost making a clean break over the house. The lantern at a height of one hundred feet was continually enveloped in spray throughout the night, but not withstanding a good light was maintained.[8]

From this more dramatic account, rather than from Sanderson's official log or his superior's report, have come the repeated stories of the waves sweeping over the dwelling and almost putting out the light. Keeping the light lit, no matter what the conditions, was an almost sacred responsibility among the keepers, some of whom perished rather than abandon their posts. While Sanderson's position was not threatened to that degree, he kept the faith and maintained the light throughout the storm. When calm returned, Sanderson counted eleven shipwrecks in the vicinity of Cana Island. The shift in the wind during the storm had pinned a number of ships against the north shores of North Bay and Baileys Harbor after they had sought shelter there. More than thirty vessels were reported ashore on Plum Island to the north.

Tending the light became much easier for the Sandersons in 1882 with the shift to mineral oil for the lamps. On 12 March 1882, lampist Crump arrived at Cana Island to fit the new lamps. The alterations to the lighting equipment were quite extensive and required five days of work before he left to convert the apparatus at Eagle Bluff Light. Among the supplies the *Dahlia* delivered at the time of the annual inspection on 30 June 1882 was the mineral oil for use in the new lamps, and Sanderson began burning the new fuel that night. The *Dahlia*'s crew removed the old lard oil tanks from the station in November, but they did not take away the actual lard oil lamps and attachments until the following May.

Burning mineral oil may made it easier to light the burner, but the job of the Cana Island keeper became more difficult in October 1882. Sarah Sanderson lost her position as assistant keeper on October 1; the assistant keeper positions at Cana Island and at seventeen other stations, including Pottowatomie, were abolished at that time because Congress had failed to appropriate sufficient funds to pay their salaries. In fifteen years, this was the only time that Sanderson allowed his emotions about personal affairs to creep into his log book; he wrote that this

> cannot be considered less than a disgrace to any Civilized Government on the face of the earth.

For the Sandersons, loss of the assistant keeper's salary was an immediate and serious financial jolt. Their annual income went from $1,000 to $600, while their children continued to grow. In the fall of 1882, their oldest son Clifford left home to board with family friends in Sturgeon Bay while he attended high school; up to that time he had attended school in North Bay with his siblings.

The winter of 1882-83 was the last one that the Sandersons spent at Cana Island, for several reasons. One was a concern for their children's education. Another was that Mrs. Sanderson, who was pregnant, fell ill in July 1883 and was taken to Sturgeon Bay to recover. Her husband made no mention of it in his log, which was for official business, but the newspaper reported that she had been in poor health for some time and speculated that her illness

> was doubtless brought on by continuous confinement to her household duties and in traveling up and down stairs while assisting her husband in keeping the light.[9]

Sanderson was very busy that fall. On September 30, Charles Dobson (Mr. Taylor's replacement as lighthouse foreman) with his assistant Christian Thiele and a work crew arrived to work on several major projects after they completed their work on the new Sherwood Point Light. The crew spent three weeks at Cana Island. During that time they renewed the lining of the watch room in the tower and laid 750 feet of sidewalk from the dwelling to the boathouse; they built a crib twelve feet wide and seventy-five feet long at the boathouse that extended from shore into five feet of water to serve as a boat landing, and they built a wooden breakwater on the shore in front of the light.[10]

In 1883, Door County was still in many ways not far removed from earlier frontier times. On October 21, Sanderson received a telegram informing him that his pregnant wife was seriously ill and that he should come at once. The message had been sent the previous day and had taken nearly two days to travel from Sturgeon Bay to Baileys Harbor because the telegraph wire was down. When Sanderson finally reached his wife's bedside, he was relieved to find her much better than expected, and he also found that he was the father of a healthy new son, T.A. Sanderson, born after the telegram was sent.[11]

Sanderson extinguished the light for the season on 19 December 1883 and rejoined his family in Sturgeon Bay. In the years that followed, like most other Door County keepers, Sanderson chose to winter away from his assignment.

In January 1884, Sanderson and his 16-year-old son Clifford traveled to the small town of Plover, Wisconsin, just south of Stevens Point, to visit D.H. Rice, a brother-in-law, who had a successful mercantile business. Sanderson apparently found a job for his son there, because he returned a week later, while Clifford remained with Rice in Plover. What Clifford's future in the business world might have been will never be known; that spring the Lighthouse Board, two years after abolishing the position, decided to reinstate the assistant keeper position at Cana Island, and helping to tend the light apparently was more attractive to Clifford than being behind a counter. Exactly how he secured the appointment is unclear, but William Sanderson's relation with Joseph Harris, Jr. undoubtedly played a large part in obtaining the coveted position. The Lighthouse Board granted Clifford a probationary appointment on 22 March 1884 and made the appointment permanent four months later. Thus did Clifford W. Sanderson begin a career as a lighthouse keeper that did not end until his retirement in 1933, nearly 50 years later. He remained as assistant keeper at Cana Island for five years before being transferred to the Cedar River Light Station.[12]

In 1884 the Lighthouse Board had become concerned about the repeated flooding of the Cana Island Station and finally decided to attempt to improve the situation. District foreman Miller came to the island on October 4 to take measurements of the grounds and to estimate the cost of filling in low spots around the station. The fact that Miller did not leave for Pilot Island until October 12 suggests that the proposed project was quite extensive, but approval of the funds to undertake it was slow in coming. The need for the changes was again shown on 8 September 1885, when a terrific northeast gale produced huge waves that washed away the bank in front of the lighthouse, allowing water to encircle the house and flood the kitchen during the night. Again on October 19 and on November 6, heavy northerly gales and high seas caused flooding of the grounds around the house.

In an effort to cut costs, the Lighthouse Board decided to make a major change in its maintenance policy in 1885. Prior to that time, virtually all station maintenance and repair was done by district crews that visited the stations periodically. The Board now ordered the keepers to do the required maintenance, especially painting, and to make minor repairs at their posts in addition to performing their normal duties. Most of the keepers were quite handy and many already had been doing many of their own minor repairs rather than waiting months for the Lighthouse Board crews to come. Now, however, they were officially responsible for such work, and painting the buildings became one of their most time-consuming tasks. The engineer's office in the Detroit headquarters gave permission for Sanderson to build a small barn to the west of the dwelling, allowing him $15 for materials but nothing for labor.

There was no relief from the flooding of the station in 1886. On April 23, a heavy northeast gale sent seas rolling in around the dwelling. Four days later waves surged again around the dwelling, brought this time by a southeast gale. On November 17, an even more severe gale struck from the northeast, and waves broke over the bank to flood the grounds and dwelling with water yet one more time.

In July 1888, the Lighthouse Board offered Clifford Sanderson the keeper's position at a new lighthouse being built at Gladstone, Michigan, but he decided to stay at Cana Island. However, the Board transferred Clifford to the Cedar River Michigan Station in November 1889, and Patrick W. Chambers became assistant keeper at Cana Island.[13]

On 18 April 1890, Captain Miller, a district official, and one G.L. Clark from the government harbor and pier works and a brother of district lighthouse inspector Commander C. E. Clark, arrived to superintend a general renovation of the Cana Island station. A crew of twenty-five men and five teams went to work filling in nearly a half acre of the low, swampy land around the lighthouse with about 3,500 cubic yards of stone, gravel, and dirt. The men also built a 400-foot wooden breakwater, running parallel to the shore, to help to prevent waves from washing around the dwelling during storms. The dwelling roof was reshingled, the floors inside were torn out and replaced, and other repairs were made. Apparently there were problems with the tower because a number of bricks were replaced and the mortar repaired. Workmen installed iron pipe for a hand railing on the tower stairs.

In 1883, when they began using kerosene for fuel, the Lighthouse Board had ordered that fireproof oil houses be built to store the more volatile fuel as money became available. Now, seven years later, workers built a hexagonal brick oil house nine feet in diameter and located ninety feet west of the kitchen. The fireproof oil house had a capacity of 240 five-gallon cans of kerosene.

The last project of the 1890 season was carried out by eight men and two teams who built a footbridge on the causeway connecting Cana Island to the mainland. Mr. Clark and his crew left Cana Island after ten weeks work on July 2, having completed their work. The cost of all these projects was approximately $3,500.

Even before they left, the *Advocate* commented:

> . . . the Cana Island station will hardly bear a resemblance to what it formerly was. Certain it is that the person who visits this island only periodically will have to look twice before he can recognize a familiar object in the surroundings.[14]

The 1890 changes gave the station much the appearance it has today, though one major improvement still remained — the brick tower would be encased with steel plates in 1902.

In September, Chambers resigned as assistant keeper and was replaced on an acting basis by Joseph Kilgore of Baileys Harbor. The appointment marked the beginning of Kilgore's long lighthouse career.

Despite all the improvements to the station, William A. Sanderson resigned as keeper of the Cana Island Light and left the lighthouse service on 14 January 1891, two weeks after he had extinguished the light for the season. When asked why he resigned, Sanderson responded with more than a hint of bitterness that

> Cana Island is one of the most inhospitable and undesirable places that can well be imagined. Being quite isolated life becomes almost unendurable, as the keeper's family cannot stand to live in such a place for any length of time. The greatest difficulty in this respect is the dampness of the interior of the rooms, the water dripping from the walls the year round.

Despite these comments, Sanderson served as keeper at Cana Island for fifteen years and he and his family lived there year round for many of these years. When their children got older, Mrs. Sanderson lived in Sturgeon Bay during the school year so the children could attend school, but she and the children returned to Cana Island in the summer. Later, Sanderson joined his family in Sturgeon Bay from mid-December to mid-March. Being away from his wife and family was certainly part of the problem, but there was clearly a more serious difficulty, as Sanderson further remarked:

> Then the salary of the keeper and his assistant has been reduced to such a figure now that the most rigid economy has to be practiced in order to make both ends meet.[15]

Actually, Sanderson's salary had not been reduced — it remained at $600 per year for his entire career — but the family lost Mrs. Sanderson's assistant's salary of $400 per year in 1882 when the position was abolished. Clifford served as assistant keeper at the same $400 salary from 1884 to 1889, and perhaps he contributed to the family's income during that period, but, when he went to Cedar River in 1889 at age 21, he had his own expenses. It may well be that William Sanderson decided that, without his son's help, they could no longer manage on his salary alone, for only a little more than a year after Clifford was transferred, Sanderson resigned his position.

In April and May 1891 a severe diphtheria epidemic struck Sturgeon Bay, and like many others, the Sanderson residence was placed under quarantine. According to Sanderson, this circumstance cost him a position that he had secured in the Chicago, Minneapolis, and St. Paul Railroad office in Milwaukee; since he could not leave his home, the railroad gave the job to someone else. William Sanderson remained in Sturgeon Bay working at various jobs until his death on 14 June 1922.[16]

A new era for the newly renovated Cana Island station began in 1891. Charles Young, second assistant keeper at Pilot Island and a Door County native, had expressed an interest in the job, but he had only recently joined the service, and there were too many keepers and first assistant keepers ahead of him. In late January the Lighthouse Board appointed Jesse Thomas Brown, assistant keeper of the Point Au Sable Light at Ludington, Michigan on the eastern shore of Lake Michigan, keeper of the Cana Island Light. However, Brown's wife Hannah and their sons did not join him until late June when a schooner from Ludington brought them and their furniture to the island.

Jesse Brown was born in Sheboygan on 16 November 1842, the third child of six born to Joshua and Betty Brown. In September 1862, he enlisted in Peoria, Illinois, as a private in the 14th Illinois Cavalry, giving his residence as Chicago and his occupation as sailor. He remained a private until he mustered out at Pulaski, Tennessee in July 1865. In August 1868, Jesse Brown married Hannah Foster at the Baptist Church in Leamington, Ontario, and, while the couple lived there, four sons were born — Roland, Volney Clair, Lawrence E., and Albert Foster — the latter three of whom would all serve in the Coast Guard. The Browns had two more children, Marion Loyd and Maxwell Ray, who were born in Ludington, Michigan after Brown entered the lighthouse service.

James McIntosh of Kewaunee, Wisconsin, who had been assistant keeper at Twin River Point (Rawley Point) Light, replaced assistant Joseph Kilgore at Cana Island. Kilgore was transferred to the Green Island Light in Green Bay. McIntosh resigned two years later in March 1893, never having moved his family from Kewaunee to Cana Island.[17]

Probably because he had served longer in the service than Sanderson before becoming keeper, Brown's log was very different from his Sanderson's. Brown recorded much more of the ordinary activities that took place at the station, and he seemed especially to note when he or his assistant left the station and returned. Absences from the light were always supposed to be recorded, but some keepers were more faithful about this than others. Like most keepers, however, Brown went through periods when he recorded things in very great detail alternating with shorter periods when his entries were skimpy.

Sanderson had complained about being isolated, but for many years Brown and his assistants made trips at least once a week to Baileys Harbor for mail and supplies, and they often went more frequently. Keepers had to mail monthly reports to headquarters, but many trips were made to visit friends or purely for pleasure. The Browns had many friends who paid them regular visits in return, including Mr. and Mrs. John Millidge from the Baileys Harbor Range Lights and Mr. and Mrs. John Kneskin and

Dr. and Mrs. Hendricks of Baileys Harbor. During their first year at Cana Island, Miss Johnson, their sons' school teacher at North Bay, also came to call. Groups from Baileys Harbor and Sister Bay often came to the island to picnic.

Work fell into a daily and seasonal routine; the usual chores involving daily preparation of the light were supposed to be completed by 10 AM. During April, May, and June, Brown and his assistant usually cleaned and painted the buildings. Once a month Brown changed the wicks and burner in the light. In the early years, much of October was devoted to gathering wood and sawing and piling it for winter use. Putting on storm windows was another fall task.

Rather than move into Sturgeon Bay or Baileys Harbor for their first winter, the Browns chose to stay at the light. McIntosh spent the winter with his family in Kewaunee, returning in March 1892.

In that same month, Brown applied for a veteran's pension under the newly liberalized Pension Act passed by Congress. He claimed he was suffering from rheumatism, heart disease, and a lame back as a result of his service, though they did not prevent him from successfully performing his duties as keeper. Brown was granted an $8 monthly pension which had increased to $40 a month by the time he died in 1924, and Hannah then received a widow's pension of $30 a month until her death in 1938. The Pension Act was a notorious attempt by the Republican Congress to reward Union veterans, and Brown simply did what thousands of other Union veterans did.

After a busy spring, Brown became ill in May and went to see his friend Dr. Hendricks in Baileys Harbor. On 20 May 1892 his log simply reported "Keeper Brown sick. Volney Brown standing watch for him." Volney was the keeper's 19-year-old son. Brown had a severe attack of erysipelas and was dangerously ill, and it was not until June 14, over three weeks later, that he stood his own watch again.

Not surprisingly, considering their common interests and circumstances, close ties often developed among lighthouse keepers. In late June, Mrs. William Sanderson, wife of Brown's predecessor, came to Cana Island for a three-day visit along with Joseph Harris, Jr., his wife, and their son and daughter. By this time, Harris had left the lighthouse service and was Sturgeon Bay's postmaster. The log indicates that a steady stream of people came to visit the Browns during that fall. In 1892, they again remained at Cana Island for the winter. Jesse extinguished the light on December 20, eighteen days after assistant keeper McIntosh left for the winter; rather than returning the next spring, McIntosh resigned his position in March 1893. The Light House Board appointed the Brown's son Lawrence, age 18, as the new assistant keeper, a position he held for six years before being transferred to Pottowatomie Light.

The year 1893 was routine at Cana Island until the fall. On September 30, the 104-foot schooner *Windsor*, bound for Chicago with her hold and decks piled high with cedar poles, posts, and ties, attempted to sail into North Bay to escape a heavy storm; she went aground at 2 AM on the reef off the southeast side of Cana Island. Heavy seas swept over the schooner and threatened to break her up, and a call went to the Life Saving Station crew at Sturgeon Bay for help. Lake Michigan was too rough for them to sail to Cana Island, and they were forced to haul their equipment overland some thirty miles over poor roads; they reached the scene after midnight and, with great difficulty brought the ship's crew safely ashore and took them to the lighthouse for shelter. A series of storms continued to batter the *Windsor*, and her owners stripped and abandoned her. Captain David Clow, Jr., the youngest son of Captain David Clow, Sr., one of Door County's earliest settlers, was hired to bring in a crew of men to pick up the cargo of cedar that had washed ashore — Clow was available because he had lost his schooner in the same gale that wrecked the *Windsor.* In November, Clow was captain of the *A.P. Nichols* that went ashore on Pilot Island; as discussed earlier, keeper Martin Knudsen heroically saved Clow, his father, and the rest of their crew in a dramatic rescue.

The *Windsor*'s cargo also attracted the attention of the owners of the schooner *E.F. Royce.* On 26 November 1893, the *Royce* had spent several days alongside the abandoned *Windsor* being loaded to the rails with cedar when she also was caught by a storm and driven on the beach at Little Harbor, just south of Cana Island. Her crew got safely ashore without help and made their way to Baileys Harbor. The *Royce* was abandoned, and the cargo of cedar was washed out into Lake Michigan and lost.[18]

There were no sinkings near Cana Island during 1894, but an incident in Baileys Harbor almost brought tragedy to the Browns. In mid-June, Lawrence Brown took his small canoe-like boat to Baileys Harbor to pick up his friend Leroy Hendricks, the oldest son of Dr. and Mrs. Hendricks, friends of the Browns and frequent visitors to Cana Island. As the men got about halfway across the harbor on their way back to the station, a squall suddenly swept across the area. Their boat filled with water and began to sink. Neither of the young men were strong swimmers, but fortunately, several fishermen had been watching from shore, launched their boats and reached the young men just as their boat sank.[19]

The crew of the *Dahlia* unloaded 1½ tons of coal at the boathouse landing in April 1895, and the keepers moved the 50-pound bags of coal from the landing across the island to the dwelling using wheelbarrows. Previously, wood had been used to heat the dwelling and for cooking; Mrs. Brown may have continued to use wood in her cook stove, but from this point on coal was used for heating.

During 1896 there was a great deal of activity at the station. Richard Goll was in charge of making repairs at Baileys Harbor and Cana Island, he arrived on the island on August 8 with a five-man crew; the steam barge *Liberty* brought supplies from Sturgeon Bay, including lumber, shingles, brick, cement, pumps, etc.[20] The men used the materials to rebuild the barn and then used it for living quarters, though Mrs. Brown cooked for them. The crew also built a summer kitchen measuring twelve feet by twenty feet several feet west of the dwelling kitchen. This wooden structure has since been removed, though the cement sidewalks built around it still remain. The boatways leading from the boathouse to a water depth of five feet were rebuilt and new rollers were provided.

The residents of Cana Island had always used Lake Michigan water for household use, and in an effort to remedy this situation, Edward Schreiber, a local well driller, began drilling in early September. After a week, he struck water, but of poor quality; he returned in late September and spent another week drilling to a depth of fifty-five feet, where it seemed that good water was available for a time. However, two years later in 1898, Schreiber returned to redrill the well, and he returned still again the following year, to drill a completely new seventy-two foot well. To prevent contamination, this last well was cased with four-inch galvanized pipe and cemented at the surface. Even so, in 1911 an official description of Cana Island station noted that the water in the well was not generally used because of its poor quality and that the keepers relied on water from Lake Michigan.[21]

Despite the treacherous reefs and shallows around Cana Island, very few ships actually went aground near the island. Its 3rd Order lens provided a light that was visible in good weather for eighteen miles and most captains stayed safely out in the lake, away from the shallows. However, heavy fog could confuse even an experienced skipper, and on 11 May 1899 at 4:30 PM the steamship *Thomas Davidson* of more than 2,000 tons ran onto the rocks at the southwest end of the island while heading in an east-northeasterly direction. The *Advocate* marine reporter observed that "it seems very queer the manner in which the *Davidson* fetched up."[22] The captain said he thought his vessel was heading through Deaths Door at the time, on a northwest bearing, though actually she was miles to south and heading between the mainland and Cana Island. As the waters shoaled, the captain changed his course to the northeast, away from the mainland until his vessel went aground. Wrecking tugs were summoned and, after having used hydraulic jacks to raise the ship, the *Davidson* was released nine days later and sailed to Manitowoc for repairs.[23]

The Lighthouse Board promoted assistant keeper Lawrence E. Brown to keeper in July 1899 and transferred him to Pottowatomie Light on Rock Island. Brown replaced Louis Hutzler, who was transferred to Green Bay's Green Island Light as replacement for keeper Captain Gaylord, who had died. Henry Bevry, a watchman at the Sturgeon Bay ship canal, became the new assistant keeper at Cana Island. Bevry was born in Sturgeon Bay in 1874 and had just married his wife, Jessie. The newlyweds moved into their second floor quarters in September 1899.

During that month, lampist Wredge arrived to work on the lantern and engineer Edward Guest came with a crew to paint the outside of the tower and to make other repairs. Wredge came back in November and on the 13th, Brown began using the new 3rd Order burner that Wredge had installed. The new light was more complicated than the old wicked burner, and it took the keepers some time to adjust to its peculiarities. In December 1899, Brown took a three-week leave of absence and traveled to Saugatuck, Michigan, where his brothers lived. However, the primary purpose of the trip was medical, not to visit relatives. Brown had developed

Cana Island lighthouse, 1914. Note the summer kitchen attached to the dwelling's kitchen and the passageway connecting the dwelling to base of the tower. Photo courtesy of the Milwaukee Public Library/Wisconsin Marine Historical Society.

a cancer on the bridge of his nose, which the doctors in Saugatuck removed. He and his wife spent the holidays there, returning after the beginning of the new century, which got off to an uneventful start at Cana Island.[24]

On 9 August 1901 Jesse Brown's brothers and their families from Saugatuck, Michigan arrived for a visit. After a week's stay, Jesse accompanied the visitors back to Michigan, where he remained for two weeks. Keepers rarely left their stations for extended periods of time during the navigation season unless there was a serious reason, so Brown probably had received permission to be absent to again visit his doctors in Saugatuck. Brown left the station again on September 25, this time so that he and his wife could attend their son Albert's wedding.

Earlier that year, lighthouse engineer Edward Guest arrived with a crew of men to repair the boathouse and to move it from the land to a crib located in the water. However, of greater significance was his visit in late July, when he carefully measured the outside of the brick lighthouse tower.

The deteriorating condition of the brickwork had become a concern of the engineering department. Rather than attempt to restore the brick or to tear the tower down and build a new one, the engineers decided to enclose the brick tower in a casing of steel plates. Based on Guest's measurements of the tower, detailed plans and specifications were drawn and a contract was let for the fabrication of the steel casing. On 17 May 1902, the first load of materials arrived at Cana Island, and an engineering party and more materials arrived a month later.

The plates of the metal casing were placed around the tower and riveted together at the joint flanges. The casing did not fit tightly to the bricks; instead a space was left to be filled with concrete. The men built a scaffold around the tower as they went higher. On August 13, the crew finished riveting the steel casing and filling it with concrete; nine days later, they finished painting the tower and the project was complete. Before leaving, however, the crew also extended the boatways, installed a boat carriage, and made various other repairs around the station.

With its tower encased in steel plates and painted white, the Cana Island Light looked much as it does today. Few visitors to Cana Island today realize that the tower and the dwelling originally were constructed of identical cream-colored brick; from the outside, no evidence remains of the tower's brick construction.

A month after the working party left, Henry Bevry was transferred to the Wind Point Light in Racine, Wisconsin. His replacement, Emil Mueller, arrived at Cana Island on 1 October 1902. Mueller remained at Cana Island until 27 January 1905 when the Lighthouse Board transferred him to the Chicago Harbor Light.

Reinhart Pfiel was Mueller's replacement as assistant keeper at Cana Island; he was born 23 December 1879, the son of Mr. and Mrs. John Pfiel, early settlers in Ellison Bay. A former sailor and part owner of the schooner *Sardina* (wrecked at Hedgehog Harbor in 1900), Pfiel had entered the lighthouse service in 1902 at the Grosse Point Light in Evanston, Illinois. He reported for duty at Cana Island on 4 April 1905. Thirteen months later he married Anna Johnson, a native of Sister Bay.

In addition to the weather, keepers were expected to log any unusual natural phenomena; this often amounted to nothing more than keeping records of the first snow or frost, of when the ice began to form or clear, or of particularly severe thunder and lightning. However, sometimes the events recorded were much more striking and unusual. On 30 August 1905, Brown logged that he had seen a rare eclipse of the sun at 5 AM; he also reported seeing Halley's Comet in the eastern sky at 3:30 AM on 1 May 1910.

Late in August 1906, an engineering department steamer delivered timbers and cement to Cana Island, and, on 21 September 1906, engineering superintendent Louis Comfort and a crew of men arrived to remove the old, wooden walks and replace them with 459 running feet of concrete walks, most of which are still in place. When the walks were finished on October 2, part of the working crew went to make repairs at Pilot Island. The rest of the crew spent a week repairing the footbridge on the causeway from the island to the mainland, originally built in 1890. The crew also built the present brick outhouse, and they put a steel rod through the keeper's dwelling between the first floor joists to prevent the south wall from bulging out. The last of the crew left for Pilot Island on October 15, after twenty-four days of work.

Three years later one of the last major maintenance efforts took place on Cana Island. Superintendent Comfort again came to Cana Island on 22 April 1909 with a working party that painted the tower and made repairs to the dwelling. They put in eight doors, plastered the rooms, cemented the outside of the cellar, and shingled the dwelling. They laid about 80 additional feet of cement walk, shingled and strengthened the storehouse, and rebuilt and repaired the dock at the boathouse. After completing these tasks, Comfort and the working party left on May 23 to make repairs at the Eagle Bluff Light.

The Lighthouse Board transferred Reinhart Pfiel from Cana Island to the Kewaunee Light Station on 30 July 1909. Pfiel retired from the lighthouse service in 1917 and returned to Ellison Bay where he built up a restaurant business before dying in August 1941.[25] To replace Pfiel, the Board appointed Wisconsin native Joseph J. Stodola, age 26, whose wife Ida was 17, but their stay at Cana Island was relatively short; the Lighthouse Board transferred Stodola to the Kewaunee Light on 22 May 1911.

The last major change (before electrification) in the lighting apparatus at Cana Island occurred in 1910. On June 6 of that year, crew members from the supply steamer *Hyacinth* brought ashore a new incandescent oil vapor (IOV) burner. A week later the supply steamer delivered 120 five-gallon cans of oil or kerosene for the new burner, and lampist Wredge arrived on June 15 to install the new IOV burner, which operated like a Coleman gas lantern. On June 30, Brown lit the new burner; it produced a more brilliant light, but also was more complicated to operate and maintain. Several times that summer, the keepers had troubles when the vaporizer nozzles in the burner became plugged, forcing them to use the old-style wick burner to finish a watch.

When assistant keeper Stodola and his wife left for his new assignment at the Kewaunee Light, the Lighthouse Board replaced him at Cana Island with Morris Weiss — the official records show his name as Morris Weiss, but according to his daughter, Ruby Weiss Cornell, her father's name was Moritz. He arrived from the Plum Island Range Light Station in Deaths Door on 22 May 1911. The move involved a promotion from second assistant to first assistant and also brought him closer to his wife and family in Baileys Harbor. During school terms his family lived on the family farm, and Weiss visited them at least once a week. During the navigation season, when school was not in session, the family lived at Cana Island.[26]

Brown and Weiss tended the Cana Island Light without major incident until 25 April 1913, when, after twenty-two years at Cana Island, Jesse T. Brown was transferred to Michigan's South Haven Light. Brown served there until he retired; he and Hannah then moved to Florida. Jesse Brown died 26 on March 1924, while visiting his son Albert at the South Chicago Light, and was buried in Leamington, Ontario. After her husband's death, Hannah Brown moved to Jacksonville, Florida to live with her son Roland;

she died there 4 June 1938 and was buried next to her husband in Leamington, Ontario.[27]

Cana Island's new keeper was Captain Conrad A. Stram, who was at the beginning of a long and distinguished lighthouse career. Not long after his birth, on February 20, 1880, Stram's parents moved from Green Bay to a farm 2½ miles east of Sturgeon Bay. He entered the lighthouse service in 1903, enlisting as a common seaman on the *Lansing Shoal Lightship*, and subsequently served at the South Fox Light, Kewaunee Light, and Racine Light. Stram rose rapidly in the service and in 1908 became captain of the *Peshtigo Reef Lightship*. Prior to taking command, he received a letter from his supervisor, the inspector of the 9th District, Chicago, Illinois dated 8 April 1908:

> Remember that you are in command and treat the men under you, as you would want to be treated, and do more than your share of the work. . . . Do not get the "big head" for there is always some one left who can fill you place; no man is indispensable. . . . Glad you like your new place, and I consider you a very lucky boy.[28]

Stram took this advice to heart, helping the crew raise the kerosene-burning light up the mast at night and taking his turn cranking the lightship's manual fog horn during bad weather. He married Elnor Dier of Sevastopol on 6 September 1911 while he was the Captain of the *Peshtigo Reef Lightship*. Stram arrived at Cana Island on 2 May 1913, but his family did move in until mid-June.

During these six weeks Stram and Weiss spent much of their time cleaning, repairing, and painting from the top of the lantern's dome down to the cellar drain. The walls, floors, doors, and woodwork in the dwelling were scrubbed and painted or varnished. The barn, workshop, and boathouse were cleaned.

Broken window panes were replaced and sashes painted. The black outside parts of the tower received a coat of paint, and they white-washed the inside of the tower. They even took down the flag pole down to be painted. The men also cut the grass in the yard with a scythe, began making flower beds, and pulled the pump from the well to clean it. Just before his family came, Stram went into Sturgeon Bay to get their furniture.

After his family took residence, Stram and Weiss shifted their activities to other parts of the station. The Browns apparently had not used the cistern for some time, and when Stram pumped it out, he found it thick with dirt and filthy from decayed rats, mice, and birds. He cleaned it, patched the holes in its cover, and put screens over the down-spouts to prevent birds from being washed into the cistern. The keepers cleared the underbrush on the south side of the island, repaired the boathouse and dock, painted the station's gas launch, tore down and rebuilt the launch's engine, removed logs and stones that had been deposited by waves on the road to the mainland, and blasted out stumps so they could plow up a vegetable garden. Stram made almost weekly trips to Baileys Harbor for groceries, but he built a coop so the family could raise chickens and a seasonal ice house to store ice for the family's icebox. The family had a cow, and Stram harvested and also purchased marsh hay for feed. What they did with the cow after December 15, when Stram closed the station and the family moved to Sturgeon Bay, was not recorded.

In 1914 Stram lit the light on April 2, marking the opening of navigation. He spent much of April cleaning up, burning brush, preparing the the flower and vegetable gardens, and fencing around them. Painting the tower, the dwelling, and various outbuildings, inside and out, occupied much of May and June.

In May, the lighthouse foreman came to check the old well, still an unsatisfactory source of potable water. Stram took him to well drillers in Baileys Harbor, Jacksonport, and Egg Harbor to solicit bids for a new well. The foreman accepted the bid of William Fischer of Baileys Harbor. Fischer began drilling on June 11; a month later and 113 feet down, he struck water. However, a pump quickly pumped the well dry, and, to get more water, Fischer drilled an additional nine feet. The well was completed on July 24. In his log, Stram declared the water "ok".

In 1914, Stram began submitting weekly weather reports and monthly supply reports to district headquarters. Navigation remained open on the lake all winter, so Stram and Weiss remained on duty at the island. Stram's family spent part of the winter in Sturgeon Bay, and Weiss's family moved to Baileys Harbor in the fall so that the children could attend school. During the winter, the Strams made several short trips; while he was away from the light, Joseph Weiss, Morris's younger brother, served as a substitute.

After two years, work at Cana Island had settled into a routine for Stram. April usually was spent putting the grounds in order and building the wood pile for the stoves. May and June were devoted to cleaning and painting the buildings, concurrent with taking care of the lawn and gardens and at least weekly trips to Baileys Harbor. The district inspector periodically visited the station and, throughout the summer, lighthouse supply steamers called with supplies of oil, coal, and other materials needed to maintain the station. Fall was a time to harvest the remaining vegetables and to prepare for winter.

After 1914 the keepers stayed at Cana Island year round and kept the light throughout the winter for the larger, more powerful steel-hulled ships — especially railroad car ferries — that continued to sail across Lake Michigan in all but the most severe weather. Stram and Weiss had become so skilled with their IOV burner that district lighthouse inspector L.M. Stoddard sent Stram a letter of commendation for burning the same mantle for eighty days.

On 29 October 1917, Stram wrote to Stoddard informing him of the birth of a son. Belying the fearsome reputations held by inspectors, Stoddard clearly had a good sense of humor. He responded to Stram on 2 November 1917:

> Receipt is hereby acknowledged of your letter of October 29, 1917 reporting a visitor at your station, which is contrary to the instruction contained in District Circular Letter No. 101. You are advised that under the circumstances the regulations will be waived in your case and you are authorized to give the visitor a permanent residence.[29]

In March 1918, a few weeks less than five years after he arrived at Cana Island, Conrad Stram received a new assignment — master of the *Lansing Shoal Lightship* — the station at which he began his career in 1903. The Lighthouse Bureau transferred Oscar H. Knudson, age 56, to Cana Island from the Milwaukee Pierhead Light. Knudson was a small, wiry man; born in Drammon, Norway 25 October 1862, he had spent much of his early life at sea, sailing around the world five times. He then opted for fresh water and sailed the Great Lakes before becoming a keeper. He married Maud Minor, daughter of E.S. Minor, a well-known Sturgeon Bay businessman and politician who had served in both the Wisconsin State Assembly and the US House of Representatives. Maud had been born in Fish Creek in 1878 and was 39 when she moved to Cana Island; she was very pleased to be back nearer her home. The Knudson's had one son, Ansel, who was 11 in 1918.

Another person who was thrilled with the move was Mrs. Marion Augustine. As a young girl, Marion spent summers with her grandmother, Mrs. E.S. Minor, and a highlight of the summer now became the portion of the vacation she would spend with her aunt and uncle at Cana Island. She remembers these as very special times and ones which helped to kindle her continuing interest in the lighthouse — Marion and her husband Bud own and operate the Spikehorn Campground on Cana Island Road several hundred yards from the entrance to the causeway to Cana Island.

Like Stram, Knudson spent much of the spring and early summer each year cleaning up the grounds and painting the station's buildings. They planted a large vegetable garden, but the Knudsons went to Baileys Harbor at least weekly for groceries. They usually went on Saturdays in the station's gas-powered launch, but Oscar and Maud also enjoyed an occasional walk to Baileys Harbor. When they went by boat they tied up at Mr. Brann's dock and shopped at his store. Mrs. Augustine remembers these trips because Mr. Brann always gave her a piece of candy as she left the store with her aunt and uncle.[30]

Whether he enjoyed it or not, Ansel Knudson had to walk to school at North Bay, about four miles away. Partway there was Eastman's corner where the lighthouse mailbox was located, and it was Ansel's job to put the outgoing mail in the mailbox on his way to school. One morning, his mother forgot to give him some letters to put in the mailbox, and she decided to take them herself. Imagine her surprise when she opened the mailbox and found Ansel's shoes inside. When he got home that afternoon, his mother asked him why she had found his shoes in the mailbox; Ansel admitted that he left his shoes there because all the other boys at school were barefoot, and he didn't want to be different.[31] In September 1918, Ansel went to live with his grandmother in order that he could attend the Sturgeon Bay public schools. After that the Knudsons often walked to Baileys Harbor and then took the bus to Sturgeon Bay to visit their son and other relatives.

In February 1919 Lake Michigan demonstrated once again its mighty strength. The footbridge on the causeway between Cana

Oscar H. Knudson (1862–1960) was keeper of the Cana Island light 1918–1924. Photo courtesy of Marion Augustine.

Island and the mainland was still in place, but Knudson decided to build a more substantial structure. He and Weiss began to build a series of cribs on the causeway with logs that they gathered from the beach. They filled the cribs with stone to strengthen and anchor them, spending two weeks on the project. However, before they had laid decking on the cribs, a northeast gale struck, and Knudson cryptically recorded in his log "cribs washed away in storm." The footbridge offered less resistance to the waves and was damaged, but not destroyed. From then on Knudson confined his building projects to dry land.

Maud convinced Oscar that they needed a cow so that the family could have fresh milk and butter. Manure for the gardens was surely a welcome by-product as well. It is not reported who milked the cow night and morning, but Oscar was in charge of making hay. The cow pasture apparently was on the island, and Weiss at times brought a team from his farm to help put up hay in the station's barn. Like Stram before him, Knudson also bought hay from area farmers. During the summer of 1919, Knudson also began building the stone walls that still stand around three sides of the station.

When kerosene was delivered that summer, Knudson and Weiss had to haul it from the boathouse to the oil house, and they also used wheel barrows to move twelve tons of hard coal from the boathouse to a bunker in the workshop. On 7 August 1919, Morris Weiss resigned his position as assistant keeper, but the resignation was not related to the workload. His wife Agnes had become convinced that he was about to be transferred from Cana Island to one of Minnesota's Lake Superior lighthouses, which she characterized as isolated rocks far from anything. This was an apt description of many of the lighthouses on Lake Superior. Her main objection was that there would be no nearby schools for their children to attend. After he resigned, Weiss opened a blacksmith shop (his father had been a blacksmith) and later a garage; he also continued to operate the family farm. He died shortly before his 65th birthday in 1950.[32]

The Bureau replaced Weiss with Mr. Louis Picor who arrived by boat on 24 September 1919. In the early evening of 2 October 1919, Knudson noticed first smoke and then flames shooting up from an unknown freighter about 2½ miles offshore. The ship was the wooden steamer *Frank O'Connor*, 301 feet long with a 42-foot beam, built in 1892. At that time the *O'Connor* was one of the largest freighters on the Great Lakes; on September 29 she had loaded 3,000 tons of anthracite coal at Buffalo, New York and set sail for Milwaukee. After passing through the Straits of Mackinac, Captain W. J. Hayes sailed down the west shore of Lake Michigan into a light head wind. While off Cana Island a watchman discovered smoke seeping from one of the after hatches and sounded the alarm.

When the crew removed the hatch cover, smoke and flames erupted from the hold before their fire hoses could be effective. To reduce the draft fanning the fire, Captain Hays came about and with the wind at his stern headed for North Bay, though it soon became apparent that the fire was out of control. In an effort to save as much of the ship and cargo as possible for salvage, Hayes ordered the sea cocks opened in order to sink the vessel as rapidly as possible. The crew got into the lifeboat and abandoned ship.

Meanwhile Knudson and Picor had gotten the station's launch underway and were hurrying to provide assistance. The Baileys Harbor Coast Guard Station had also received word of the *O'Connor*'s plight and launched one of their own boats. Knudson passed a line to the *O'Connor*'s lifeboat and began towing it to Cana Island, getting to about a quarter of a mile from the station before the Coast Guard arrived. Because they were better equipped to take care of the twenty-one survivors and were closer to transportation facilities, the Coast Guardsmen took the crew back to Baileys Harbor rather than to Cana Island.[33] The *O'Connor's* anchor, later illegally removed from the sunken ship, has been placed on the grounds at Cana Island as a reminder of the dramatic events of 2 October 1919 and of the role the lighthouse keepers played in the rescue.

At this time, Lake Michigan water levels were at a high point in their cycle. For the first time since Brown's days as keeper, Knudson reported in November 1919 that after an east-south-east gale, the cellar was flooded with water. Assistant Picor submitted his resignation in December and left Cana Island on 1 January 1920. Assistant Sullivan replaced Picor on 22 January 1920, but he resigned after only two months on duty and left Cana Island with his wife on 31 March 1920. The Board then appointed John P. Hahn assistant keeper at Cana Island; he arrived at the station on 19 April 1920, and his wife followed eleven days later.

During these personnel shifts, there were other important changes at the Cana Island station. Lake Michigan was high enough to cause continued flooding of the basement after severe storms, but it was still low enough that, during April, Knudson cleared the larger stones off the causeway across to the mainland. On April 9, he and Maud walked to Baileys Harbor to take the bus to Sturgeon Bay, and the next day the Knudsons rode back across the causeway to the lighthouse in their new car.

Having a car vastly changed the Knudson's lives. They continued to use the launch to go to Baileys Harbor, but the Knudsons now had the means to travel throughout the county, and, except during the winter when Oscar put the car up on blocks and removed the tires, travel they did. They took even more frequent trips to Sturgeon Bay to see their son, relatives, and friends, and in late summer they went to the Door County Fair. They took trips to Northport, Sister Bay, Fish Creek, and other county communities. Also, rather than arriving by boat as in the early days, other keepers increasingly brought the lighthouse inspectors to Cana Island by car, and Knudson would then drive them on to their next visit, unless, of course, the inspector was going to an island station. In a move that must have shocked some people, Maud learned to drive and began driving by herself or with Mrs. Hahn to Sturgeon Bay and other places.

When not involved with other duties, Knudson continued to build stone walls along the shore, while his assistant cut underbrush on the island. Together they tore out the rotten timbers remaining from the old wooden breakwater, and, during September, spent much of their time helping a Coast Guard crew install poles and string telephone wire to Cana Island. The telephone was meant to be only for official business, but, like their car, it helped to reduce the sense of loneliness and isolation. With its hand-cranked magneto, a telephone was much simpler to install than electricity, which did not come to Cana Island for another fourteen years. The Knudsons were avid readers and they continued to read by the light of kerosene lamps the newspapers and magazines that Mrs. Augustine's parents saved for them.

Knudson finished the stone wall on the south side of the lawn during 1921; not content with a simple gate in the wall, he made stone pillars on each side and connected them with a stone arch. The arch has long since been removed in the interests of safety, but the base of the pillars still remain and visitors use the old opening to go from the lawn to the rocky beach to the south.

On the last day of 1921, the Hahns left Cana Island to go to his new assignment at North Manitou Light Station in Michigan. Charles Lensmeier came from North Manitou to become the new assistant keeper. On 15 August 1922, Knudson recorded in his log that the assistant left the station at 5:30 AM for Sturgeon Bay; the next day, Lensmeier telephoned that he had quit the lighthouse service. He returned the next day, packed his furniture, and left

Cana Island, though he apparently later rejoined the lighthouse service and had a long career at other Lake Michigan lights.

Lensmeier's abrupt departure was fortuitous for another Door County keeper, Henry Gattie of the Baileys Harbor Range Lights. The range lights had just been converted to an unwatched acetylene gas system, and responsibility for their maintenance had been shifted to the Cana Island keeper. The district inspector had been seeking a new assignment for Gattie, and, when Lensmeier left, Gattie was shifted temporarily to Cana Island, until longer term arrangements could be made. Gattie served at Cana Island from the beginning of September until the end of November, when he and his wife moved to Two Rivers, Wisconsin, where he had charge of the Two Rivers Pierhead Light.

Knudson handled Cana Island Light alone until 19 January 1923 when his new assistant, Sam Hanson, arrived. Hanson had tragically lost his wife and two sons while serving as assistant keeper at Chambers Island. He had left the lighthouse service for several years before returning and coming to Cana Island, but working at the light apparently brought back too many memories for him. He once again severed his connection with the lighthouse service on 30 June 1923 and moved to Sister Bay.

Theodore Grosskopf, who arrived at Cana Island on 12 July 1923, would remain there somewhat longer. Grosskopf was a native of Milwaukee, where his mother and sister lived, and a bachelor. He joined Knudson on the monthly trips to check the pressure in the acetylene tanks at the Baileys Harbor Range Lights; except for an occasional cleaning, checking the gas pressure was the main maintenance responsibility. Shortly after he arrived at Cana Island, Grosskopf also bought himself a car so that he too could have more freedom of movement.

One of the burdensome aspects of life for keepers at Cana Island was that the lighthouse supply steamers off-loaded kerosene for the lamp in barrels at the boathouse dock on the west end of the island. The keepers then had to tap these barrels and transfer the fuel into five-gallon cans before they transported it to the oil house. At most other stations, kerosene arrived in the smaller cans and went directly into the oil houses, but at Cana Island the landing was so far from the oil house that the kerosene was shipped in barrels. In an effort to save time and effort for the keepers and to take advantage of bulk deliveries of fuel from private suppliers, the Lighthouse Bureau directed Knudson and Grosskopf to prepare concrete cradles for two bulk oil tanks near the boathouse, which were delivered in October. During the fall, the keepers also spent several days hauling and spreading gravel on the road across to the mainland.

The 1923–24 school year was Ansel Knudson's senior year at Sturgeon Bay High School, and his father apparently told the district inspector that Ansel was interested in attending Northwestern University in Evanston, Illinois and that he and Maud would like to be transferred if a vacancy occurred at one of the lighthouses in the Chicago area. On 4 March 1924, Knudson recorded in his log "Telephone call from the office." The phone was reserved for official business, and two days later, when Mr. Grosskopf returned from leave, the Knudsons began packing their furniture, so the phone message Knudson received probably informed him that he was being transferred to the Grosse Point Lighthouse in Evanston, Illinois, only a few blocks from the Northwestern campus. Ansel was able to live with his parents at Grosse Point Light until he graduated in 1928.

Before Knudson left Cana Island on 29 April 1924, he and Grosskopf spent their time washing and cleaning in preparation for turning the station over to the new keeper. Oscar Knudson retired as a lighthouse keeper in 1930, freeing the couple to travel and live for a time on the West Coast before they returned to live in Sturgeon Bay. Mrs. Knudson died in October 1959, and Oscar Knudson died six months later on April 20, 1960.[34]

Clifford William Sanderson, son of William and Sarah Sanderson, took charge of the Cana Island light from Oscar Knudson on 29 April 1924. Sanderson was not a stranger to Cana Island since he had lived there and even served as assistant keeper there from 1884 to 1889. After leaving the island in 1889, he spent one year at Cedar River Light and then returned to Door County to serve as keeper of the Dunlap Reef Range Lights in Sturgeon Bay for thirty-four years from 1890 to 1924 when the station was closed. Sanderson was 56 when he and his wife, Hedwig, returned to Cana Island.

Even with a new keeper, much remained the same. Spring was still a time for cleaning, painting, varnishing, and taking care of the grounds. Like their predecessors, the Sandersons and Grosskopf traveled to Baileys Harbor for supplies and to Sturgeon Bay and other communities to visit friends and relatives. Grosskopf's mother and sister usually spent July and August with him on the island. Among the routine jobs was checking the gas pressure at the Baileys Harbor Range Lights, and checking the telephone line after every storm to remove any fallen trees or branches, but there were new things as well. Sanderson was very handy, and he soon began the project of installing new hardwood floors throughout the dwelling. He and Grosskopf spread some 133 cubic yards of gravel on the road from the Eastman's house to the station.

In mid-November, Sanderson received official word that an acetylene winter light would be installed and that the station, which had remained open all year for several years, would now be closed during the winter months. A lighthouse engineer with the appropriate name of Marine arrived on November 18 to install the acetylene apparatus. The gas tanks were installed inside the tower with a pipe that connected them to the burner in the lens. The light worked like those at the range lights, with a sun valve and a pilot light that automatically lit the burner when it became dark. It took two days for Marine to complete the installation, but Sanderson did not actually switch to the acetylene system until 20 December 1924. Two days later the Sandersons closed the station and left for Sturgeon Bay, while Grosskopf went to his home in Milwaukee. Sanderson visited Cana Island and Baileys Harbor once a month during the winter to see that everything was operating properly at both stations.

The Sandersons and Grosskopf returned to the Cana Island station on 2 April 1925 and on April 13 changed from acetylene gas to the IOV lamp, beginning a largely routine year for the keepers. In the fall they took the smaller of the oil tanks (750 gallons) off its foundation near the boathouse and dug up the foundation blocks. In December Mr. Eastman brought a team of horses and hauled the foundation blocks and oil tank to a new location near the oil house, but the ground was frozen too deep to bury the foundation blocks and reset the tank. The footbridge to the mainland had now become so deteriorated that the men received permission from headquarters to dismantle it; Grosskopf finished taking the planks from the old bridge in December, which they would burn in the spring. On December 15, Sanderson changed to the acetylene gas winter light and two days later left the station for Sturgeon Bay.

In early January 1926, Sanderson made his first winter visit to the station, but on January 27 he fell and severely injured his knee. Unable to travel, he called Grosskopf in Milwaukee and asked him to come to check the Cana Island and Baileys Harbor Lights. On February 9, Grosskopf found everything in good order at both stations, but on March 9, the chief of the Baileys Harbor Coast Guard Station called Sanderson to inform him that the Cana Island Light was out. Because of the need for quick action, rather than calling Grosskopf, Sanderson asked Claud Chapman, his friend and fellow keeper from Chambers Island who was in Sturgeon Bay for the winter, to go to Cana Island. After a difficult trip from Baileys Harbor through deep snow, Chapman found that the pilot light was out. He relit it and returned to Sturgeon Bay. A month later when Sanderson and Grosskopf came to open the station, they drove to Baileys Harbor but had to leave their cars in the village and hire a team to take them and their supplies to the light because the deep snow on the road had not been plowed.

In May, the keepers mounted the oil tank they had not been able to set during the winter. The keepers laid a pipeline from the tank through a hole in the oil house base to its interior where they could fill the five-gallon cans they carried up to the lantern. When the thousand-gallon tank near the boathouse was empty, the crew of the *Hyacinth* removed it. Rather than depending on oil from the *Hyacinth,* the Lighthouse Bureau signed a contract with the local Standard Oil Company dealer who delivered oil to the station with his tank truck.

On 5 October 1926, Sanderson acquired a new responsibility; the Eagle Bluff Light Station was converted to an unwatched acetylene light and placed in charge of the Cana Island keeper. Now the keeper and/or the assistant had to drive not only to Baileys Harbor, but also across the peninsula to Fish Creek and then to Eagle Bluff to check and maintain that light as well. In December the keepers extinguished the Eagle Bluff Light for the season, prepared the Baileys Harbor Range Lights for the winter, and shifted the Cana Island Light from oil vapor to acetylene gas before leaving for the winter.

Life for the Sandersons and Grosskopf at Cana Island settled into a comfortable routine during 1927 and into the fall of 1928 until, at 1 PM on October 4, with a heavy afternoon fog concealing the lighthouse and all other landmarks, Sanderson realized that a ship had gone aground on the south side of the island. Not until two hours later did the fog lift enough for the astonished keepers to discern that the 352-foot steamer *Michael J. Bartelme* was at their very doorstep. Built in 1895, the *Bartelme* was a typical Great Lakes ore-boat and had been owned by several companies before being purchased by the Valley Camp Coal Company earlier in 1928. She had just delivered a load of coal from Ashtabula, Ohio, to Milwaukee, and was running light on her way through Deaths Door to the ore docks at Escanaba to pick up a load of iron ore.[35]

Sanderson immediately telephoned the Baileys Harbor Coast Guard Station. Despite heavy seas from the south that delayed them and drove the *Bartelme* closer to shore, the Coast Guardsmen arrived at 4 PM to lend assistance. Wrecking tugs arrived the next day to attempt to pull the *Bartelme* off the rocks, and a large number of spectators came to watch the effort. On October 5, the Coast Guard took the crew off the ship because of the danger from the heavy seas. The next day, part of the crew went back aboard only to be removed the following day. Representatives of the company arrived on the scene as the crew shuttled back and forth. Finally on October 26, the captain received word that he and the crew were to strip the vessel and abandon her. On November 5, a south gale and heavy sea finally broke the back of the once proud *Bartelme*.

Three weeks after they began to strip her, the crew had taken all the salvageable material ashore and left for Sturgeon Bay. In June 1930, a wrecking crew salvaged the engines and broilers from the wreck, but the *Bartelme* story was not over yet. Salvagers had removed much of the ship, but on 16 July 1932 Henry C. Berg of West Allis was caught in an undertow and drowned while swimming out to the wreck. Sanderson called the Coast Guard, and they came and dragged for the body but did not find it until the following morning.

When the keepers returned to Cana Island in April 1929, they found Lake Michigan so high that the causeway was under water. They nevertheless went about their usual tasks, preparing the lights for the coming season. In May the high water and a heavy sea combined to wreck the top of the boathouse dock, but by September the water level was low enough that the Standard Oil Company tank truck had no difficulty in driving across the causeway to deliver five hundred gallons of fuel for the lantern.

In 1930, the Lighthouse Bureau decided to make better use of the vacant Baileys Harbor and Eagle Bluff dwellings. On June 30, the department leased the Eagle Bluff dwelling to the Fruit Growers Cooperative for use as an office, and with the leasing of the dwelling, the Cana Island keepers became responsible only for the maintenance and operation of the acetylene light. A month later the Lighthouse Bureau leased the dwelling at Baileys Harbor to the Immanuel Lutheran Church of Baileys Harbor for use as a parsonage and the minister and church became responsible for upkeep of the dwelling for the next twenty-six years, although the keepers continued to make sure the lights were operating.

This responsibility became much easier on August 25 when Mr. Ealison, a Lighthouse Bureau electrician, completed conversion of the acetylene gas lights at the range lights to electricity. A clock switch now controlled the operation of the range lights. Periodically the lenses had to be cleaned, and bulbs had to be replaced when they burned out, but this was a far cry from what Gattie and other range light keepers originally had to do to guide ships into the harbor. After a few years, the ministers were even made responsible for changing the bulbs.

The lighthouse engineers had decided that the danger of an explosion at Cana Island was too great should one of the acetylene tanks leak inside the tower during the winter. So, while he was at the station, Ealison moved the gas line from inside to outside the tower and moved the tanks outside as well so that any leaking gas would be dissipated harmlessly.

With improved roads and cars, Cana Island, then as now, was a popular place to visit. Sanderson noted that from 1 June to 1 November 1932, he had taken 1,970 people up in the lighthouse tower. Countless other visitors enjoyed picnicking, swimming, or simply admiring the scene. Sanderson and Grosskopf had cleared virtually all of the underbrush from the island and maintained the area inside the stone walls as lawn. They also had several vegetable and flower gardens.

After nine years service at Cana Island, Theodore Grosskopf received a new assignment at the Sturgeon Bay Canal Light on 30 April 1932. The Lighthouse Bureau transferred Ross F. Wright - who was to be the last civilian keeper at Cana Island - from the Manitowoc Light to replace him. Wright was born 7 November 1877 in Sturgeon Bay, had worked on various boats in Sturgeon Bay as a young man, and later ran a local bicycle business for a Green Bay firm. In November 1905 and again in 1906 he worked as a laborer during the winter at the Sturgeon Bay Canal Light, receiving an appointment as first assistant at the Milwaukee Pierhead Light in May 1907. After three years in Milwaukee, he was transferred on 11 April 1910 to North Manitou Island Light, Michigan. On 22 June 1910 he married Grace Kellogg, age 30, a native of Reedsburg, Wisconsin, who had taught school in Reedsburg, Two Rivers, and Manitowoc. The couple stayed at North Manitou only until 1 June 1911, when the Lighthouse Bureau transferred Wright to the Manitowoc Light. A man of many skills, Wright built a cabin cruiser that he named *Old Dog* and used in numerous rescues off Manitowoc, earning official citations from the Lighthouse Bureau for six of these efforts.

Keepers were allowed to have outside jobs as long as they did not interfere with the performance of their lighthouse duties, and Wright had one of the more unusual situations. While at Manitowoc, he built and operated a dance pavilion on the lake shore called the "Grasshopper"—an extremely popular destination on warm summer nights for people in the area. When he moved to Cana Island, Wright sold the "Grasshopper" but kept *Old Dog.*[36]

One of Wright's first duties was to go to Eagle Bluff with Sanderson to learn the intricacies of the unmanned acetylene system. Sanderson and Wright spent about a week cleaning, chipping, priming, and applying two coats of paint to the inside and outside of the lantern. This was the most extensive maintenance work that had been carried out at Eagle Bluff since the light became unmanned in 1926. During the 1932 season, the popularity of the station brought almost 1,900 people to climb the tower for a bird's-eye view of the surrounding territory. On December 11, the Sandersons and Wrights left Cana Island for the winter.

Sanderson arrived at the station for his final season as keeper at the beginning of April 1933. Though the spring was largely uneventful, lightning struck the telephone line on April 30 and followed the line into the dwelling. Fortunately, no one was injured, and the damage was repaired the next day. On June 13, the US Navy Airship *Macon,* which was visiting the Chicago World's Fair, passed over the station going north at 12:30 PM and returned 2½ hours later. The passage of the huge airship was a memorable experience for people in Door County.

On 1 July 1933, Clifford W. Sanderson recorded his own retirement in his log and turned the station over to assistant keeper Ross F. Wright, thus ending a long and distinguished career that began in 1884 at Cana Island when he became his father's assistant. The Sandersons moved to their home on South Cedar in Sturgeon Bay where his wife died 23 October 1940. On New Year's Day 1942, Sanderson entertained his brother Bert, who worked as a local newspaper man, and his family at dinner. His other brother, T.A. Sanderson, a local attorney, was unable to join them since he was in a Milwaukee hospital. After the company departed, Mrs. Dora Stewart, his housekeeper, left Sanderson sitting in his favorite chair reading. The next morning when she came to the house, she found the retired lighthouse keeper dead on his living room floor dressed in his

> jacket and scarf as though having looked out to see how bad the New Year's storm had become — just as if he was back on duty at the lighthouse checking visibility.[37]

With Sanderson's retirement, the Lighthouse Bureau promoted Ross Wright to keeper and transferred Michael Drezdon in from the Green Island Light as assistant keeper. When they left the station for the winter 1933, the snow was so deep that Drezdon got his car stuck on the causeway and had to leave it there until spring. In 1934 Lighthouse Bureau crews strung electrical wires across the causeway from the mainland to the dwelling. Electric lights soon took the place of the old kerosene lamps in the living quarters, and the burner in the lantern was replaced with a special electric fixture, completing the transition at Cana Island Light from lard oil to kerosene to electricity.

Life for the keepers was considerably less demanding in the 1930s than in former times, but in 1935 Mrs. Wright's health began to decline. After a full day of activities, she suffered a stroke at the supper table and died several hours later on 18 August 1939. She was survived only by her husband and two aunts. According to the newspaper, however, she left

> a host of friends, for her sunny disposition instantly made and kept all as friends with whom she came in contact.[38]

In 1939, as part of a government reorganization plan, the Coast Guard absorbed the Lighthouse Bureau, and Coast Guardsman Donald Langohr was assigned to work with Wright. In June 1941, keeper Ross Wright retired as the last civilian keeper at Cana Island Light; Langohr over took as keeper, and Michael Drezdon remained as assistant keeper. After thirty-four years as keeper and assistant keeper, Wright moved back to his home at 431 South 4th Avenue in Sturgeon Bay, and he and *Old Dog* soon became familiar sights in the community. On 17 February 1944, Ross Wright married Mrs. Mae Donovan Purdy, and 1½ years later on 12 September 1945 he died unexpectedly at his home at the age of 67.[39]

When World War II broke out, the Coast Guard took over the Cana Island Station completely and has maintained the light there ever since. At that time the dwelling was sealed off from the tower and the south side entrance was added. During the war, the Coast Guard conducted training activities at the station. The light was later automated completely with a mechanism that automatically rotates a new bulb into position when a bulb burns out, and the station now is rarely visited more than once a year by Coast Guardsmen.

In 1945 the Coast Guard put Cana Island up for lease, and Ralph McCarthy, owner of Flur Wire and Metal in Milwaukee, rented the island and dwelling for $19 a year. For the next twenty-five years the McCarthys and their three children spent their summers on Cana Island. During that time, the Coast Guard removed the barn, boathouse and pier, summer kitchen, and oil tank. In 1970, their children grown, the McCarthys gave up their lease. The Door County Maritime Museum, wanting to preserve a part of the maritime heritage of Door County, leased the Cana Island Light from the Federal Government and opened the island (though not the dwelling or tower) to visitors.[40]

Since 1976, Louis and Rose Janda and their children have served as caretakers on the island during the summer months. They have restored the dwelling where they live and take care of the grounds, as well as answering the questions of the thousands of visitors who come to enjoy the beauty of the Cana Island Light Station. The light is turned on automatically at dusk and still shines out across the water to guide mariners and warn them of the nearby shoals, just as it has done since William Jackson first exhibited a light at Cana Island light in 1870.

Chapter 7
Eagle Bluff Light

Eagle Bluff easily has the greatest number of visitors of all the Door County lights. Restored by the Door County Historical Society, each year it is toured by thousands of visitors who the wander over the station's grounds. Although the clearing around the dwelling is much reduced in size and the barn and summer kitchen are gone, inside the dwelling people can glimpse a view of what life was like for the keepers and their families in the days when Eagle Bluff was manned and its light guided sailing vessels and steamers through the Strawberry Channel to the west.

The usual channel for mariners sailing to the city of Green Bay from Lake Michigan passes west of Chambers Island, but a second, more narrow and difficult channel, lies between the Strawberry Islands east of Chambers Island and the mainland north of Fish Creek. With the growth of settlements along the bay north of Sturgeon Bay, an increasing amount of shipping passed through this eastern channel.

Shipping activity in and around Door County slowed somewhat during the Civil War, but it did not stop. Maritime interests continued to request more navigational aids to make shipping safer in the area, and the Lighthouse Board sent a special committee to the western Great Lakes in 1865 to ascertain the needs and wants of the commercial interests and to study the navigational situation in the waters of Green Bay. Upon their return to Washington, they made a number of recommendations to the full Board, including one calling for a coastal lighthouse on Eagle Bluff, a prominent bluff north of Fish Creek, that would help shipping using the east channel to pass through it more safely. To build the lighthouse, the Board asked Congress for a special appropriation, and on 28 July 1866 Congress designated $12,000 for the proposed lighthouse.[1]

By executive order on 19 October 1866, President Andrew Johnson reserved twelve acres from the public domain for the site of the Eagle Bluff Light. The reservation was to extend some distance along the shore north of the lighthouse and as far as lighthouse or Tennison Bay on the south. However, the site of the new station provided a challenge for the builders. The engineers wanted to build the lighthouse on the extreme westerly point of Eagle Bluff adjacent to the channel, but the front of the site was an almost sheer, forty-foot cliff overlooking a narrow, stony beach that was open and exposed to the waves and that would often make landings impossible. Fortunately, the land to the south sloped gently down from the proposed building site to the shore of Lighthouse Bay.

The Board intended to build the lighthouse during the 1867 navigation season, but that spring the Board decided that construction of a light at another location in the district was more urgent, so the Eagle Bluff working crew was transferred there. However, contracts for building supplies for the construction at Eagle Bluff were let, and most of the necessary materials were delivered in the fall of 1867 to the north shore of Lighthouse Bay, so as to avoid hauling them up the cliff.

As soon as navigation opened in the spring of 1868, a working crew from Detroit arrived in Lighthouse Bay with additional building supplies. A path was cut from the water to the lighthouse site and almost an acre of land cleared of the birch, poplar, and fir trees growing there. After blasting out a hole five feet deep for a basement, the crew used some of the shattered rock to build a full basement. They also excavated a hole for a cistern ten feet south of the kitchen. Masons then put up a two-story dwelling measuring twenty-six feet by thirty feet with an attached kitchen wing measuring twelve feet by twenty feet several feet lower than the first floor; the entire structure was built of cream-colored Milwaukee brick. The first floor had four rooms —

Eagle Bluff light, 1914. Notice the oil house to the left and the summer kitchen at left center. Photo courtesy of Milwaukee Public Library/Wisconsin Marine Historical Society.

now restored as a dining/living room, a formal parlor, a music room, and a master bedroom from the time of the Duclons — as well as a hallway and formal front entrance on the bay side. On the second floor there was a single closet, a small front room, and a large bedroom across the rear of the dwelling. The masons built the walls thicker than usual, and the window casings were set deep, giving extra depth to the sills. Later, screens, storm windows, and shutters were added.

The tower for the light was built diagonally into the northwest corner of the house. Made of the same Milwaukee brick as the dwelling, the tower is nine feet four inches square from top to bottom with a four-inch projecting brick cornice at the top; the walls of the tower are thirteen inches thick, and inside them is a circular lining four inches thick to provide ventilation to the tower. A spiral cast-iron stairway with fifty-five steps rises from the basement to the lantern deck and fills the inside of the tower. There are landings at the first and second floors and doors at the entrance to each floor and the basement which allowed the keeper and his family to use the tower stairs to move between floors. The masons installed three windows in the tower to provide light during the day.

In the middle of the rear wall of the dwelling, between the living quarters and the kitchen wing, is a massive square brick chimney oriented, like the tower, diagonally to the wall. The diagonal arrangement and four flues made it possible for there to be stove openings in the parlor, in the living/dining room, and in the kitchen on the lower level, and in the large bedroom on the second floor. Northeast of the dwelling, the masons built a substantial six foot square privy of the same cream-colored bricks as the lighthouse.

The Detroit Locomotive Works built the cast-iron lantern in Detroit, Michigan in 1868 and shipped it in pieces to Eagle Bluff;

the company had ceased building locomotives ten years earlier, but the owners had retained the firm's original name when it became a custom iron foundry and machine shop. When the tower was finished, the crew hoisted the pieces of the lantern up and reassembled it in place. The square, cast-iron lantern deck rested directly on the brick tower and had an entrance through a trapdoor in the deck. As in all the other Door County lighthouses of this style, there was no watchroom. The ten-sided cast-iron lantern was seven feet in diameter. A cast-iron roof and a ventilator ball with a lightning rod completed the lantern. It was forty four feet from the base of the tower to the center of the ventilator ball, and the focal plane of the light was seventy-six feet above mean lake level. A metal railing circled the edge of the lantern deck forming a gallery where the keeper could stand to clean the lantern glass, paint the lantern, or observe activities in the surrounding area. Each of the ten panes of glass in the lantern was 26¾ inches by 40 inches in size and 3/16 of an inch thick. Two panes on the landward side of the lantern were opaque so that no light shown into the forest behind the station. The lantern originally contained a 3½ Order Fresnel lens built by the Henry Lepaute Company of Paris, France, and a 3½ Order Funcks two-wick burner illuminated the lens. The light itself was a fixed white light of 860 candle-power, visible for sixteen miles in clear weather.[2] On the night of 15 October 1868, newly appointed keeper Henry Stanley officially exhibited the light from the new Eagle Bluff Light Station for the first time. The light was operational approximately six months after the work crew arrived to begin construction, a remarkable feat under the circumstances.

Henry Stanley was the first of only three keepers at Eagle Bluff from the time it became operational in 1868 until an unmanned acetylene light was installed fifty-eight years later in 1926. He was born 19 October 1823 in Norway, and like many young Norwegian boys, he followed the sea until he immigrated to America in 1844. Five years later, after hearing about the discovery of gold in California, he boarded a ship bound for San Francisco. When the vessel arrived, the crew deserted and joined the passengers looking for gold. Stanley remained at the diggings for some time, but finally returned without a fortune. He met Katherine Hesh, whom he married in 1854, back in New York City. Katherine had been born in Heidelberg, Germany on 2 December 1837 and had come as an 8-year-old with her parents and five siblings to settle in New York State. After their marriage, the Stanleys moved west, and Henry sailed the Great Lakes. He also became part owner of several ships, but once he received the keeper's appointment at Eagle Bluff, he abandoned sailing and began selling his interest in his ships. In the fall of 1868, Henry, Katherine, 10-year-old John, and 8-year old Elizabeth moved into their new home at Eagle Bluff.[3]

Very little is know of what occurred at Eagle Bluff during the Stanleys' first four years there, as the earliest surviving log begins in August 1872. Stanley must have performed the usual routine duties of a keeper successfully, since he kept his job. Young John Stanley apparently died sometime between 1870, when he was listed in the US Census, and August 1872 when the log picks up; Stanley later carefully logged family illnesses and his daughter's later death, so his son's death presumably would have been mentioned if it had occurred after 1872. Also, mention was made of the death of their two children in obituaries of both Henry and Katherine.

Before 1872, there was only one item in the *Door County Advocate* concerning the lighthouse; a serious squall hit Fish Creek and blew the roofs off several buildings, destroyed trees and fences, and damaged a portion of the lighthouse roof.[4] The damage was not serious enough, however, to be mentioned in the yearly Lighthouse Board report.

Beginning in 1872, the story of the Eagle Bluff Lighthouse and those who lived there slowly comes alive. In that year there were four entries in Stanley's log, three in August and one in September. Three commented on heavy, but apparently not damaging, winds; the fourth recounted the district inspector's visit, delivery of annual supplies, and overhaul of the lamps by the district lampist. During 1873, 1874, and 1875, Stanley again made only three-to-four entries a year, but after the annual inspection in August 1876, Stanley began recording a great deal more about the activities at the lighthouse in his station log. A picture emerges of a very friendly, social family with a large circle of friends who enjoyed visiting the lighthouse, sometimes staying for extended periods of time — hardly the lonely, bleak, and isolated life that we sometimes picture keepers and their families enduring. Today, the location of Eagle Bluff Light within the confines of Peninsula State Park gives visitors the impression that the lighthouse was extremely isolated because anyone arriving there either from Ephriam to the north or from Fish Creek to the south will have driven for miles through the park. However, even as late as the 1950s several families had homes and cottages within the park, and Nicolet Bay was once known as Shanty Bay because of all the buildings that lined the bay's shore, many inhabited by fishermen and their families. Even one of the station's original outbuildings, located south of the present cleared area, was remodeled into a cottage. Blossomberg Cemetery lies within the park's boundaries south of the light and represents the remains of another settled area.

There never was a boathouse at Eagle Bluff, and the pier at the foot of the stairs in front of the station was usable only by small boats in good weather. The keepers kept their boats in Lighthouse Bay, using a pier at the end of the path from the lighthouse. Visitors coming by boat also used this pier. Prior to 1883, when the Lighthouse Board's official survey map was drawn, there was a road running from the station to Fish Creek, and the amount of company the Stanleys had seems to indicate that this road was in place much earlier than 1883.

Until near the end of their tenure at Eagle Bluff, the Stanleys lived there year round rather than moving to Sturgeon Bay or some other community in the winter, perhaps because they did not feel isolated or cutoff from friends and activities, even in winter. If the road was not clear of snow, the frozen waters of Green Bay provided an easy route for travel either to the north and to the south.

In October 1876, lighthouse foreman J.W. Taylor came to Eagle Bluff and stayed for three weeks. During this time, he built a wooden fence that enclosed the clearing in the forest around the lighthouse and performed miscellaneous minor repairs. The Stanleys had many visitors from Ephriam, Fish Creek, Sister Bay, Green Bay, Sturgeon Bay, Milwaukee, Marinette, and Menominee, Michigan. One group of twenty-one men and women arrived on August 12, and Stanley noted they "all had a social time until the next day." Though Stanley extinguished the light for the season on 12 December 1876, friends from surrounding communities continued to visit the lighthouse after that time. Among them were Captain Davidson, the Pilot Island keeper, and his wife who stopped on their way to Sturgeon Bay. Mrs. Stanley also visited Sturgeon Bay for several days at a time, staying with friends and acquaintances.

Seventeen-year-old Elizabeth had several friends who seemed to be regular visitors. Elizabeth became a school teacher, and many of the young women who visited also were teachers. Ula Noble was her most frequent visitor and often stayed for several days during vacation times; Ula was a native of Fish Creek who later taught school in various communities, including Baileys Harbor, Washington Island, Jacksonport, and Sevastopol. Lizzie Remington and Lucy Graham of Sturgeon Bay were also teacher friends. Other visitors included Jennie Blakefield, a merchant's daughter from Fish Creek (and whose parents also were frequent visitors), various Kilgore daughters from Baileys Harbor, and G.L. Schulz of Appleton. Until 1881, when Katherine Stanley was ill and Elizabeth got married, it was a tradition for the Stanley friends to have a surprise party at the lighthouse in February or March; fifteen to thirty guests, married and unmarried, would come in the evening from Fish Creek, Ephriam, Egg Harbor, Sister Bay, and the surrounding area to have "a social time until the next morning."

Lighthouse foreman Taylor arrived on 7 June 1877 for a six-week working visit. According to Stanley, "he made great improvements" during that time, though he unfortunately made no mention of what the improvements were. Taylor did build a wood shed for the station and all or part of the stone fence that still stands immediately to the west of the lighthouse at the top of the cliff overlooking the water. While at Eagle Bluff, Taylor lived and ate with the family.

A "grand celebration" at the lighthouse on 8 September 1877 marked the arrival of a piano for the Stanleys. Fortunately the weather that day was favorable. Despite Francis Badtke's account:

> Great difficulty was encountered as they lifted the huge piano up the cliff and sixteen men were required to carry their heavy burden up the steep steps at the front of the lighthouse,[5]

Stanley's log is clear about what really happened. The piano was brought ashore at the pier in Lighthouse Bay where the original building materials were brought ashore and where Stanley kept the station's boat. Sixteen men then carried the instrument up the path through the woods to the lighthouse. The Stanleys provided their helpers with dinner, and the group then "had quite a social time with music."

That fall and winter were unusually mild, and the Stanleys had visitors at least once a week and sometimes three times a week. And visitors rarely came alone, but usually in groups of three or four. It was so warm that on December 28 Stanley took a boat ride since there was no ice on the bay. Not until 1 January 1878 did Stanley extinguish the light for the season, an unusually late closing for Eagle Bluff. The mild winter continued throughout January, and on January 22 the keeper was able to sail to Ephriam since there still was no ice on the bay. On 11 March 1878 he once again resumed his normal duties when he exhibited the light in the lantern for the season.

Stanley tended the light faithfully, the lighthouse inspectors made their annual inspections and delivered supplies, and numerous visitors continued to come to Eagle Bluff. Then in 1880, Mrs. Stanley suffered the first of a series of illnesses that seemed to plague her at various times for the next thirty-five years. After a number of fruitless visits to doctors in Sturgeon Bay, Mrs. Stanley went to Fort Howard (now part of Green Bay, but then across the Fox River from Green Bay) for medical attention in May 1880. Stanley did not mention her absence in his log until he noted on November 2 that "Mrs. Stanley returned home after an absence of five months and a half." The only hint as to the nature of her illness was a note in the newspaper in June that she was so ill that it was feared she might die from cancer.[6] At that time a diagnosis of cancer was given to a wide variety of illnesses that today we would label as something else. A month later the newspaper reported that she was out of danger and that her recovery was almost certain. However, after that was in type, but before it was published, the editors learned she was once again seriously ill.[7]

The name of Mrs. Stanley's doctor in Fort Howard was not recorded, but in light of events that followed, her physician probably was Dr. Frank L. Lewis. Lewis was born 22 September 1840 in Hardwick, Vermont. He studied medicine with a local doctor after graduating from high school in Montpelier, Vermont, and then went on to serve as a hospital steward during the Civil War. He moved west after the war and, in May 1867, married Jennie Brandt of Eureka, a small town west of Oshkosh, Wisconsin. In March 1869 he graduated from Rush Medical College in Chicago, and for a short time practiced medicine in Eureka. Dr. Lewis relocated in August 1870 to Arcadia, thirty-five miles north of La Crosse, in western Wisconsin, where he quickly built up the largest practice of any doctor in the area. Known for his skillful diagnoses and treatment, he also was a respected surgeon. In 1876 he was a Republican, a Master Mason, and the father of two young children.[8] His wife died shortly thereafter; he moved to Fort Howard and quickly became known as one of the area's leading practitioners.

Although a lighthouse paint crew came in September to paint the station's buildings, the big news for the Stanleys was the return of Mrs. Stanley on November 2. One month later, after handling the duties at the station by himself for most of the season, Stanley extinguished the light.

Elizabeth seems to have met Dr. Lewis and his children during the time her mother was in Fort Howard, though she did not stay all summer in Fort Howard, because the log indicates that her friends continued to visit the lighthouse. Elizabeth and Dr. Lewis apparently continued communicating after her mother's return, and Dr. Lewis began a four-day visit to the lighthouse on 4 June 1881. He returned a week lateron July 24 and Stanley wrote in his log:

> July 31 — Dr. F.L. Lewis and my Daughter Lizzie Stanley left on there [sic] wedding trip for Green Bay.

Mr. and Mrs. Stanley accompanied the couple to Lewis' home in Fort Howard where that evening Rev. Father Walsh married the couple in front of members of the families. Mrs. Stanley was Catholic, although she became more active in her church after the couple moved to Sherwood Point in 1883, and Elizabeth was brought up in the Catholic faith. Since a priest married them, Lewis must have been so in love that he converted to Catholicism and left the Masonic order.

In September, Mrs. Lewis came back to the lighthouse for a two-week visit with her parents. This would be the last time Henry Stanley saw his daughter alive. On the night of Thursday November 10, a friend brought a telegram to the lighthouse with shocking news; the message from Dr. Lewis informed the Stanleys that their daughter was extremely ill and requested that Mrs. Stanley come immediately. She did her best, but Mrs. Stanley did not get to her daughter's bedside until Saturday afternoon, just three hours before Elizabeth died. The suddenness of her death was a terrible shock — only a few days before, apparently strong and robust, she had seemed to be in perfect health. She had lived in Fort Howard only a short time, but she had made a large number of friends who were deeply saddened. Henry Stanley sorrowfully wrote in his log,

> November 14 — I received a Telegraph Dispatch from Fort Howard that Mrs. F.L. Lewis was Dead. She died the 13th day of November 1881.

Though he wrote that his daughter died on the 13th, her tombstone gives the 12th as the date of death, and this seems more to be correct likely since her mother's journey should have taken a 1½ rather than 2½ days. The *Advocate* reported that her remains would be brought back to Fish Creek for burial, but Mrs. F.L. Lewis was buried in the Allowez Catholic Cemetery.[9]

The shock of her daughter's unexpected death was so great that Mrs. Stanley became suddenly and violently ill. Despite the best efforts of her son-in-law, in whose house she was confined, her recovery was considered hopeless.

Stanley extinguished the light at Eagle Bluff on 1 January 1882 for the season, and three days later he was granted a leave of absence from the station during the winter due to his wife's illness. He left immediately for Fort Howard to be at his wife's bedside. Under Dr. Lewis' care, Mrs. Stanley slowly began to improve. On 8 March 1882, Stanley opened the door of the lighthouse, returning home for the first time since January to resume his keeper's duties, but not until May 31, 6½ months since she had been called to her daughter's deathbed, was Mrs. Stanley well enough to rejoin her husband at Eagle Bluff.[10]

In March, a week after Mr. Stanley returned to the lighthouse, district lampist Crump arrived to make a significant change in the light at Eagle Bluff. He removed the original lard-oil lamp from within the Fresnel lens, made the necessary modifications, and installed a new mineral oil or kerosene-burning lamp. The Lighthouse Board recognized the danger of storing the new fuel in the lighthouses and earlier had ordered construction of fireproof oil houses when the money was available. However, money was scarce, and for nearly twenty years the mineral oil at Eagle Bluff had to be stored inside the lighthouse in the small basement at the foot of the spiral stairs in the tower. Fortunately no accident occurred, for if a fire had broken out, the Eagle Bluff Light would undoubtedly have been destroyed.

Even before completion of the Sturgeon Bay ship canal, shipping interests had begun demanding that additional aids to navigation be installed in Sturgeon Bay. The Lighthouse Board responded to the demands by building the Dunlap Reef and Sherwood Point light stations. As early as May 1882, before the Sherwood Point Light was even begun, there were rumors that Stanley would be transferred to the new station.

Dr. Lewis and the Stanleys remained very close. Perhaps because of the length of her stay in their house, the Lewis children and Mrs. Stanley had become very fond of each other, and the children came to spend the fall of 1882 at Eagle Bluff. Their visit ended late in October, when the little girl became sick, and the Stanleys asked Dr. Lewis to come and take his daughter back to Fort Howard.

Sherwood Point Light was still awaiting construction, but the editor of the *Advocate* noted in February 1883 that Captain Davidson, keeper at Pilot Island, would be transferred to Eagle Bluff and that Stanley would be moved to the Sherwood Point Light when it was completed. The editor was premature and only partially correct. In early July, Stanley made a trip to Sturgeon Bay, and he did go to Sherwood Point while he was there to see how construction was progressing before returning to Eagle Bluff. Stanley was not officially appointed to be keeper at Sherwood Point until 20 September 1883. His fifteen-year tenure as the first keeper at Eagle Bluff ended on 30 September 1883, when he signed the station's log for the last time. Except for the deaths of their son and daughter, the years at Eagle Bluff had been good ones for the Stanleys, and there had been no serious problems with the lighthouse, even though it was new when they arrived. As they packed to move, the Stanleys could look back on the many times the house had been filled with the joy, laughter, music, and fun they shared with their many friends.

Exactly how the appointment took place was a mystery, but the Lighthouse Board appointed William Henry Duclon to replace Henry Stanley at Eagle Bluff; appointment of lighthouse keepers, postmasters, and other federal government officials was a highly political matter, and Duclon apparently had no local political connections whatever. He was born 27 March 1845 in Alexandria Bay, New York, a small community on the St. Lawrence River. His father Claudius was a fisherman, and William was the eldest of six children. As a youth, he was five feet eight inches tall, with a light complexion, and brown hair. He enlisted in the army at the outbreak of the Civil War and served with several units, including Company K of the 14th New York Regiment Heavy Artillery. After his discharge, Duclon made his way to Mackinac Island, Michigan, where he married Julia Davenport on 2 May 1867. She had been born on the island on 25 April 1845; her father, Ambrose Davenport, was reputedly a full-blooded Ottawa Indian and may have worked at one of the lighthouses in the area. The couple named their first child Ambrose, in honor of the bride's father; the boy was born in February 1868. On 22 September 1873, the Lighthouse Board appointed William Duclon 2nd assistant keeper at the Waugoshance Light west of the Straits of Mackinac, which began a lighthouse career that did not end until forty-five years later in 1918. Two years later, after two more sons were born, Duclon was transferred to Beaver Island Light, on the south shore of Beaver Island, west of Waugoshance Light in northern Lake Michigan. While at Beaver Island, the Duclons had four more boys. On 20 September 1883 Duclon officially took charge of Eagle Bluff Light and signed the log for the first time as keeper; he signed the log for the last time thirty-five years later.[11]

During Duclon's long tenure at Eagle Bluff many changes took place in the county, state and nation. Fishermen continued to mind their nets, farmers replaced lumbermen, and many more people settled in Door County; passage through the ship canal at Sturgeon Bay became free; steam replaced sail as vessels became larger; and ever fewer ships passed the lighthouse on their way to and from the city of Green Bay. The Progressives captured control of state government, the nation weathered a severe depression, and the US fought a war with Spain and was engaged in World War I. Changes also occurred at Eagle Bluff, though a visitor in 1918 would have found things little different there from 1883.

Captain Duclon, as he was often called, did a commendable job of maintaining and operating the light at Eagle Bluff, and he received several citations from the inspectors for his work. He was, however, very haphazard in the keeping of his log. The official instructions to keepers required that two facing pages were to be used per month; if carefully written, one line per day was considered sufficient unless there were unusual occurrences. Keepers generally recorded weather observations on the left page, and wrote comments on the right-hand page about what they did that day and listed visitors, noteworthy events, absences from the station, visits of inspectors, and other such information. However, Duclon often disregarded the instructions; he would write down events for a number of years and then follow them with pages of weather data that was generally from the same period of time. The log was supposed to be strictly chronological, but he sometimes wrote things completely out of order. However, none of the inspectors seem to have regarded his casual record-keeping to be sufficiently important to dismiss him, though he was reprimanded for not recording when, why, and for how long he left the station. Of the three keepers, his was the most casual station log.

Life at the lighthouse must have been hectic when the Duclons moved to Eagle Bluff, for all nine family members lived together at the lighthouse, with the seven boys sharing the large upstairs bedroom. The boys probably were not allowed to help their father in the lantern, but there was plenty for them to do around the station. There was no well, and water was hauled in yoked buckets up the long stairway from the shore of Green Bay, and there was a large garden to tend and animals to be fed and watered. The older boys probably helped their father take care of the grounds and paint the buildings, and they must have helped to cut and split wood for the wood stoves inside. They hunted deer with their father in the fall, and from very early on the boys fished throughout the year.

The younger boys also helped their mother around the house. Julia was well-known in the area for cooking, sewing, and needlework. She made many of her sons' clothes, but was best known for the beautiful quilts she pieced during the long winter nights. As her sons married (only Frank remained a bachelor), Julia gave each bride a quilt, and as grandchildren arrived she made quilts for them as well. The aroma of freshly baked bread, cakes, pies, and other foods often wafted through the rooms from the kitchen at the east end of the dwelling, and she made great numbers of cookies that she stored in large crocks for later consumption.[12]

During the summer, Julia and her family cooked and ate in the white-walled, red-roofed summer kitchen measuring sixteen feet by twenty feet that was located to the southeast of the dwelling. At first, Captain Duclon and Julia seem to have stayed pretty close to home. The *Advocate* reported his arrival at Eagle Bluff in October 1883, but made no further mention of the new keeper until February 1885, when Duclon came to Sturgeon Bay for several days. After 1885 there were regular accounts of visits to Sturgeon Bay. Duclon was a loyal member of Sturgeon Bay's GAR Post, and he attended its functions as often as possible.

Duclon early recognized opportunities to earn extra money by fishing during the winters. In the spring of 1887, he and his sons caught some more than 2,000 pounds of lake trout through the ice off Eagle Bluff. The boys had grew up close to water and boats, rather than on farms, and it is perhaps not surprising that several of them became successful fishermen as they grew older.

While 1887 began well for Duclon, it did not end that way. On November 11, he wrote:

> A very nice day wind from the W light and clear. I have been laid up four weeks i am going down to fish creek to day with a horse.

Apparently the trip to Fish Creek brought little relief; a month later the *Advocate* reported that he had been ill nigh unto death for several weeks past, and it was feared after one particularly bad episode in December that he would die. "He says another such siege would finish him," reported the *Advocate*.[13] The cause of his illness was never mentioned, but he finally recovered fully and attended the veterans ball in Sturgeon Bay in February 1883.

In March 1887, 21-year-old Ambrose brought his new bride Ada Belle Richter home to the lighthouse to live. According to family tradition, as the boys married, each daughter-in-law came to Eagle Bluff to live for a time.[14] Whether true for all the sons who married or not is unclear, but it was true in several cases.

Thanksgiving day, 28 November 1889, began as a joyous family occasion at Eagle Bluff but ended dramatically with a threat of tragedy. The night before, a northeasterly storm had forced the Goodrich steamer *City of Ludington* to seek shelter in the lee of Horseshoe Island, 1¼ miles to the northeast of the light. Horseshoe Island is literally horseshoe-shaped, and its open side is to the south opposite Nicolet Bay. Both the bay of Horseshoe Island and Nicolet Bay offered excellent anchorages. In the late 1870s the Flint and Pere Marquette Railroads leased Goodrich ships to take passengers and freight from Milwaukee to Ludington, Michigan, and the *City of Ludington* was built in 1880 to sail this route. She was 180 feet long with a 34-foot beam and had forty-four passenger staterooms. She was used year round and was heavily reinforced to prevent damage from ice in the winter. Several times during the 1880s she was frozen in the ice for weeks and drifted without harm.

As the storm worsened, Captain Gilman abandoned the lee of Horseshoe Island and headed into the island's bay. As is the practice with modern sailboats, he nosed his ship's bow up onto the beach and secured the vessel with lines to trees on shore. Normally this would have been a sound maneuver, but the wind continued to build until gale force winds snapped her lines and blew the ship off the beach at 4 AM. Before her engines could give Gilman a chance to maneuver, the big steamer's bow was driven aground on a large submerged rock off the west shore of Nicolet Bay, though her stern lay safely in deep water.

When Duclon received word of the grounding, he and his older sons made their way through the woods to Nicolet Bay. Shortly before noon, Gilman decided to get the only woman passenger and her son ashore if possible, since his vessel was pounding badly on the rocks. The crew passed a line ashore, and the Duclons tied the line to a sleigh attached by a second line to shore. The sleigh was pulled back to the ship, the two passengers got on, and the Duclons pulled them safely ashore and took them to the lighthouse. When the storm was over, the Goodrich steamer *Depere* removed the cargo from the *City of Ludington* and picked up the woman and her son.

The company hoped that the removal of her cargo would permit three tugs to free the ship, but this failed and they decided to leave her there until spring. They hired Ambrose Duclon as shipkeeper of the steamer, and he was responsible for making sure that no further damage or vandalism occurred. Using hydraulic jacks, wrecking tugs were able to refloat the vessel in May 1890. *City of Ludington* was repaired and placed back in service, and she did not retire from service until 1927.[15]

As they grew up, Ambrose and his brothers turned to fishing as a livelihood. By 1892 Duclon Brothers was among Fish Creek's leading commercial fishing groups. In the winter, when the ice closed navigation, Captain Duclon joined his sons. The Duclons were excellent fishermen and were regularly mentioned in the *Advocate* for their outstanding catches of lake trout, herring, bass whitefish. Today the herring fishery has all but disappeared, but in December 1894,

> The Duclons caught so many herring off Eagle Bluff they couldn't find time to take them to the fish sheds, so they shovelled them aside and let them freeze on the bank. They say you couldn't see sun some days from the gulls and hawks flying around.[16]

Obviously, a good fish story could make the newspapers even then. The sons generally fished out of Fish Creek and Nicolet Bay, but Ambrose and Frank lived for a time at Jackson Harbor and fished in the waters around Washington Island. They operated several fishing tugs, and they ran both sail and steam yachts for charter. For several years in the early 1890s Ambrose also was a member of the Sturgeon Bay Life Saving Station's crew.

Several of the Duclons were quite musical. Family tradition has it that William ordered a baby grand piano for his family for $50, but when it arrived it was too big and had to be returned for the smaller one now on display at the lighthouse.[17] Large dances and masquerade balls were the rage in Door County during the 1890s, and the Duclon brothers organized their own band and traveled through-out the area to provide music for such events. In January 1893, they played at the Sturgeon Bay masquerade ball and were highly praised by those in attendance. For that performance the band consisted of a first and second violin, a base viol, and a guitar.[18] Again according to family lore, they sometimes took the legs off the family piano, loaded it on a sleigh or wagon, and reassembled it at the hall where they were playing, and then reversed the process to return home. Charles' wife Edith sometimes

The seven sons of William and Julia Duclon in the early 1880s; from left they are Ambrose, Walter, Frank, Joseph, William Jr., James, and Charles. Photo courtesy of Peg Foster.

was the pianist. At first the Duclons simply provided the music, but later they actually organized the dances in Fish Creek's People's Hall. By all accounts, the grand masquerade ball held 25 January 1896 was the social event of the Fish Creek season.

Another popular venue for the Duclon family band was Baileys Harbor, where it seems that a regular part of their appearances was a fight with the sons of Jesse Brown, keeper of the Cana Island Light. The accounts of who won usually depended on whether the observer was from Baileys Harbor or Fish Creek. The Duclon boys didn't confine their fighting to the Browns, however, and after a dance at the Fish Creek Town Hall held on 14 March 1896, Dr. Eames of Egg Harbor swore out a warrant against Frank, Charles, and Joseph Duclon, charging them with mayhem; the Duclon boys were aged 25, 20, and 18, so this was a serious incident and not just a boyish prank. Eames charged that the three brothers had assaulted him during the dance, broken his nose, and caused other injuries. They each posted a $100 and returned to Fish Creek. Captain Duclon argued that Eames was acting out of spite and that his sons were innocent. The outcome was not published.[19]

The 1890s brought change to the family at Eagle Bluff. Ambrose and his wife moved first to Sturgeon Bay, then to Fish Creek, and then on to Washington Island. William married his wife Ruth in 1894, and Joseph and Charles apparently found reasons to visit Baileys Harbor other than fighting keeper Brown's sons. On 10 January 1896, Joseph married Augusta Spring, a very popular Baileys Harbor native, at St. Mary's Catholic Church. Charles was a groomsman and two years later married Edith Ehrke, who was one of the bridesmaids.[20] By 1900, only Frank, Walter, and James and his wife Lillian were living at the lighthouse with Captain Duclon and Julia, though Joseph and his wife had built a home at Shanty Bay. At that time, those three brothers were engaged in fishing, as were Ambrose, Joseph, and Charles; William had become a licensed engineer on a steam tug.[21]

There were also changes at the light station itself. Eagle Bluff was well-built and required only minor maintenance through the years. It was struck by lightning several times — not too surprising since its lantern rose high above the surrounding area — but each time there was only incidental damage. At one point Duclon reported that a heavy squall had blown some stones off the top of the stone fence, but he mentioned no damage to the lighthouse itself.

In 1893 a work crew came to the station and built a 1½-story barn measuring sixteen feet by twenty-four feet south of the dwelling. The crew painted the barn buff and white and put a red roof it. They also added a wooden plank walk to the new building. Two years later Board engineers hired a local well-driller to put in a well thirty-six feet south of the dwelling. Using a horse-powered drilling rig, the driller bored a four-inch well down seventy feet. The water quality was reported to be excellent, so the family members no longer had to carry water up the long stairway from the bay, though Julia continued to use rainwater collected in the cistern when she wanted soft water.

Most lighthouses had flag poles and keepers used them to salute passing vessels, but it was not until 1895 that the Lighthouse Board had a flagstaff erected at Eagle Bluff. It was put in while a working crew made minor repairs at the station. In July 1899, seventeen years after the light began burning mineral oil, a lighthouse tender delivered brick for construction of an oil house at Eagle Bluff. However, the metal work for the structure was delayed; it arrived too late for construction in 1899 and was stored at the Sturgeon Bay Canal Light for the winter. The following summer, a Lighthouse Board crew built a cream-colored brick oil house measuring seven feet by nine feet about eighty-nine feet south of the lighthouse. They capped the building with a metal roof and fitted the inside with metal shelves to hold ninety five-gallon cans. Building the oil house in 1900 was the last major project the Lighthouse Board or its successors undertook at Eagle Bluff, except for laying the existing cement walks at the station in 1916. From 1900 on the government made only minor repairs to the lighthouse on the east channel.[22]

Life for William and Julia Duclon continued its usual pattern of tending the light and maintaining the station, punctuated by visits from the district inspector and from friends and family. In 1900, Frank, Walter, and James and his wife Lillian lived at the lighthouse. The sons fished and helped their father in their spare time. Ten years later James and Lillian had moved out and been replaced by Charles and his wife Edith. Shortly after that, William and Julia, who had both turned 65 in 1910, had a home built for themselves in Fish Creek and, like many other keepers, began to spend their winters away from the lighthouse. For a time their sons and families also lived in Fish Creek. Walter and William Jr. became engineers on tugs working in the Green Bay harbor. James worked at various jobs in the Black Creek area west of Green Bay. Ambrose moved to Green Bay and worked in a paper mill there. Charles was a licensed Great Lakes pilot and later served as a caretaker for the Maltman family on Fish Creek's Cottage Row. After working as a fisherman, barber, and rural mail carrier, Joseph became the long-time caretaker of the Friedmann Estate in Fish Creek. Frank was a sailor who lived with his parents during the winter, and, after they died, he helped Joseph at Friedmann's.[23]

On 21 April 1917, William Duclon drove out from Fish Creek and opened the lighthouse. The bay was still full of ice, so he did not light the lamp for the first time in 1917 until three days later. A week after that, district lampist Butler arrived and installed a new incandescent oil vapor lamp (IOV). The new light apparently was putting out more light than was needed for navigation — it burned with a brighter and more intense light than did the old Funcks burner it replaced — for Butler returned on 30 April 1918 and replaced the original 3½ Order Fresnel lens with a new 5th Order

Keeper William Duclon (1845–1926) and his wife Julia Davenport Duclon (1845–1922). Photo courtesy of Bill Guenzel.

Fresnel lens and 5th Order IOV lamp. This change reduced the effective range of the light to near what it had originally been.

William Duclon made his last official entry in the Eagle Bluff log on 15 December 1918 when he wrote, "I closed the Light in the Tower this morning for 1918." This entry also closed his career as a lighthouse keeper, a career that had begun forty-five years earlier in 1873. In retirement, William and Julia enjoyed the company of their children and grandchildren, and Julia became very active in the Fish Creek Baptist Church, especially in the Ladies Aid Society. She died on 20 September 1922 after a long illness, and her funeral at the Baptist Church "was probably the most impressive and well attended of any ever held at Fish Creek." Her body was buried in the Blossomberg Cemetery several miles south of the lighthouse which had so long been a part of her life. Four years later, in mid-July, William was hospitalized in Sturgeon Bay. He was moved from there to his son's home in Green Bay where he died 2 September 1926. James was unable to return in time, but William's six other sons acted as pallbearers. After services in Sister Bay, the veteran light keeper may well have been borne past the Eagle Bluff Light for a final time on the way to the Blossomberg Cemetery for burial next to his wife.[24]

With Duclon's departure in 1918, the Lighthouse Bureau transferred Peter Coughlin from the Green Island Light to Eagle Bluff to become its third and last keeper. Coughlin was born in Canada in 1856 of a Canadian father and an Irish mother. He came to the United States in 1878 and became an American citizen in 1892. While serving as a keeper in Alpena, Michigan, Coughlin met Mrs. Margaret Sullivan McLaughlin of Alpena, a widow with three adult children. Margaret Sullivan was born in 1858 near Port Huron, Michigan, to Irish-American parents and had married Mr. McLaughlin of Alpena. Their two boys and a girl were still very young when their father died, leaving Margaret to raise the children alone. Peter Coughlin served at several lighthouses in

Michigan before the Lighthouse Bureau transferred him to Green Island Light in 1915 as assistant keeper. He arrived at Eagle Bluff on 5 February 1919 at the age of 62 and officially took charge of the station on March 1.[25] His wife arrived four days later, but their furniture did not arrive from Green Island until April 27; the boat crew landed the furniture at the pier in Lighthouse Bay, and Coughlin spent two days moving it through the woods to the lighthouse.

Coughlin's logs give a much clearer and more detailed picture of activities at Eagle Bluff than do Duclon's entries. Every day he was at Eagle Bluff, Coughlin recorded the weather and logged whether his old station, the Green Island Light (15 miles to the SW) and the Cedar River Light (17 miles to the NNW near Cedar River, Michigan) were visible. The Chambers Island Light was on the island's west side and so was never visible despite being closer. Until near the end of his tenure, Coughlin rarely had a day when he failed to enter what he was doing or what was happening at the station.

Like most new keepers and despite his age, Coughlin spent the first few months of his assignment cleaning and painting the station from the cellars to the domed roof of the lantern. He painted every room in the dwelling, the outside of the tower, the oil house, the privy, and the storms and screens, and he whitewashed the fence and summer kitchen. He also painted the ice house, which Duclon seems to have built on his own, since there is no record of any official approval or appropriation for the structure.

It is not recorded exactly when wires were strung to the lighthouse and a telephone for official business was installed, though it probably happened shortly after the turn of the century — and therefore during Duclon's tenure — when telephone lines were extended from Sturgeon Bay to the towns and villages to the north.

The Coughlins had a garden, and during the summer Coughlin spent time cleaning the yard, cutting the grass, and sawing wood. In addition to the garden, the Coughlins also kept chickens and pigs which were butchered in November. After their arrival, the crew of the *Dahlia* delivered a new cooking stove and a heating stove which Coughlin installed.

The lighthouse continued to be a popular destination for visitors, especially on Sundays when Coughlin confined his activities to what he referred to as "general duties" — this meant extinguishing the light in the morning and preparing it to be lit in the evening. Among the frequent visitors were members of the Duclon family. The Coughlins made several trips a week into Fish Creek for mail, groceries and supplies, so their life was not as isolated as it had been at the Green Island Light.

The waters of Green Bay were often tranquil, though sometimes tragedy replaced tranquility. After performing his general duties on Sunday 11 May 1919, Coughlin took one of the station's boats and made his way around the islands bordering the channel on an unsuccessful search for the body of a crew member from the *Hyacinth* who had fallen overboard and drowned. Later in the year, on October 25, a severe storm with northwesterly winds had capsized a fishing boat manned by Hiram Cornell and Jerome Murphy, and both men were drowned. Nine days later (another Sunday), Coughlin searched along the shore for the men's bodies. He eventually found Murphy's body floating near a buoy in front of the lighthouse, but not until the following July.

As their first year at Eagle Bluff drew to a close, the Coughlins prepared for cold weather. Coughlin cut and stacked wood, put on storm windows, and shoveled the walks to the outbuildings. After several weeks of very cold, snowy weather, the bay froze over, and on 15 December 1919 he stored the lighting apparatus and closed the station for the winter.

Coughlin exhibited the lamp in the tower for the first time that season on 11 April 1920, and life at Eagle Bluff settled into its regular routine. Coughlin worked in his garden and cut grass all summer, but he finished cleaning, painting, varnishing, and white-washing the buildings in July and turned to cutting wood. In the fall, he painted roofs, harvested the garden, and generally got the station ready for winter. He closed down the light after a cold, clear Christmas day, and the Coughlins left Eagle Bluff to spend the rest of the winter in Detroit, Michigan.

The 1921 navigation season opened on March 30. The year got off to a normal start with Coughlin doing his usual cleaning and painting, though someone other than Mrs. Coughlin was at the lighthouse with him and whether Mrs. Coughlin was ill and remained in Detroit was not clear. In late April, the handwriting, spelling, and style of comments change noticeably in the log — Coughlin apparently dictated his entries to another person who actually wrote them in the log. In late May, Coughlin made the entries himself for several days, but someone else wrote in his log during June and July, though he continued to perform his duties at the station. On July 27 Coughlin noted, "My wife came home from Detroit." and he made the following entry in his log on August 15: "The keeper left the station sick." It would appear that Coughlin had been having health problems for several months; perhaps he was finally willing to admit he needed help after his wife returned. After a five-day stay in the hospital in Sturgeon Bay, Coughlin returned to his post, and, two weeks later, seemingly fully recovered, he once again began performing his usual activities around the station. Just before Christmas, Coughlin closed Eagle Bluff for the 1921 season.

The Coughlins moved back to the lighthouse on 8 March 1922, before the ice had gone out and navigation opened. One month later tragedy struck. Clifford Hanson, the 18-year-old son of Sam O. Hanson who was assistant keeper at the Chambers Island Light, fell through the unsafe ice between Chambers Island and Fish Creek and drowned. Coughlin witnessed the accident from the tower at Eagle Bluff. Snowfall had blocked the road to town, and he was unable to call for help and arrange the boy's rescue because a tree limb had fallen across the telephone line somewhere between the station and Fish Creek. The anguish Coughlin experienced is clearly apparent in his log:

> The Hanson boy drowned in the Channel near Fish Creek. I tryed my best to save Him. Had to walk to Fish Creek for Help, the telephone out of order.

Two days later Coughlin wrote:

> Keeper lit the light in the tower to night for a Small boat going to Chambers Island to get Sam Hanson the assistant there to attend His boys funerl.

The spelling and grammar are not perfect, but the emotion clearly shows. Keepers took great pride in making every effort to prevent accidents and deaths in the waters around their lights, and lighthouse keepers and their families were a closely knit group; Clifford Hanson's death was especially hard because it affected one of their own. Not until 16 April 1922 did Coughlin officially light up Eagle Bluff for the season.

After this tragic beginning, life at Eagle Bluff in 1922 settled into the established routine. However, after the superintendent's inspection visit in July 1922, Coughlin's log took another turn. Probably at the superintendent's direction, Coughlin began to use only one page in the log instead of two; he recorded the visibility of the Green Island Light and some weather data, but no longer did he log his daily activities or make comments. Inspection visits, the opening and closing of the light, and the names of some visitors were reported, but it can be assumed that Coughlin continued to carry on day-to-day activities much as in the past when he faithfully recorded them.

On 19 December 1925, Peter and Margaret Coughlin closed Eagle Bluff for the last time together. Mrs. Coughlin spent the winter with her daughter and family in Detroit. Despite the urging of friends and relatives to stay longer in Detroit, she seemed anxious to get back to the lighthouse, and she was planning to start back for Eagle Bluff on 5 April 1926. However, on the afternoon of April 1, Mrs. Coughlin was visiting with some friends at her niece's home when she suddenly fell forward and died. She was 67. Her funeral was held on April 5, and her body was taken to Port Huron, Michigan, for burial with other family members. Commenting on her death, the *Advocate* noted that Mrs. Coughlin had many warm friends in Door County:

> None ever came to the light that Mrs. Coughlin did not have time to be courteous and kind to them and every one went away wishing they might come again at no distant day.[26]

Peter Coughlin returned to Eagle Bluff and lit the light in the tower on 29 April 1926, but his wife's death was a devastating blow. Instead of his usual firm strokes, Coughlin's handwriting in the log was so shaky that it was hard to recognize. He reported only visibility of the Green Island Light and the weather, with no comments. In June 1926 Coughlin turned 70 and began receiving retirement benefits. In the interest of economy, the Lighthouse Bureau decided to convert Eagle Bluff from an IOV light to an unmanned acetylene gas light, though Coughlin was given the privilege of living at the lighthouse for as long as he wanted. He could have left in June, but he remained until September 15 when he made the last entry in the Eagle Bluff log: "Green Is light not vis. rain and fog N wind."

He ended 38 years of service without a note or comment. Neither did he make any comment about the fact that Eagle Bluff was being converted to an unmanned station. As soon as the conversion was made, Coughlin made his last log entry, closed the dwelling, and left to spend the winter in Mankato, Minnesota, where a nephew lived.[27]

Coughlin stayed in Minnesota for four years and then returned to Green Bay and bought a home. On 31 August 1934, he stepped into the street while walking near his home and was hit by a passing motorist. He died from his injuries six days later on 5 October 1934, the last keeper at the Eagle Bluff Light. He had no family in the area; his body was shipped to Mankato, Minnesota for burial.[28]

The Eagle Bluff Light officially became an unmanned acetylene gas light on 20 September 1926. Since there was no longer a keeper at the station, someone had to do routine monthly maintenance and make sure the apparatus functioned properly, though the acetylene system worked remarkably smoothly through the years. These duties became the responsibility of the Cana Island keepers who also took care of the unmanned Baileys Harbor Range Lights. The lighthouse remained vacant until 1930, when the Fruit Growers Union Cooperative leased the dwelling for use as an office for a short period of time.

The Wisconsin State Conservation Commission was the agency in charge of Peninsula State Park which surrounded the twelve acres reserved for the Eagle Bluff Light. In the early 1930s, they began inquiries into acquiring the property since operation of the light was automatic and the station vacant. The Commission was successful, and Congress authorized the Commerce Department's Commissioner of Lighthouses to convey by quit claim deed the 10.98 acres of the Eagle Bluff Reservation to the State of Wisconsin for inclusion as part of Peninsula State Park. The Lighthouse Bureau felt it was in its best interest to have someone occupy and maintain the dwelling in connection with the operation of the park in order to prevent it from deteriorating. With Congressional approval, the Lighthouse Bureau leased the remaining 1.02 acres of the reservation and all the buildings on the property except the light tower and lantern to the State of Wisconsin. The federal government maintained ownership of the lighthouse yard and buildings, but the state was allowed to use the property except the lighthouse tower itself for park purposes. On 9 May 1936, the transfers were completed.[29] Under the terms of the lease, the Lighthouse Service had access to the tower and lantern at any time and the right to establish and maintain other aids to navigation on the premises. The State of Wisconsin was to provide a custodian, preferably resident on the property, to guard and protect the property from damage and to maintain the buildings in good repair. For a while, park employees lived in the dwelling during the summer season, although there was no electricity, running water, or telephone, and a large screened porch was added to the south side of the house. However, once the property had been transferred to the state, federal interest and concern about Eagle Bluff almost faded away; despite the terms of the lease, the dwelling stood vacant in the 1950s, subject to the ravages of weather and vandalism.

By the 1950s, the once active Door County Historical Society had also fallen on hard times. However, in 1956 Bert Sanderson (a partner in the *Door County Advocate*, a son of William Sanderson and a brother to Clifford Sanderson, both longtime Cana Island keepers) and Conrad Stram (the retired keeper of Cana Island, Sturgeon Bay Canal Station, and Sherwood Point) helped breathe new life into the society. Once they had put the organization back on its feet, the members felt they should undertake restoration of an historic building. Not too surprisingly, Sanderson and Stram thought a lighthouse would be an ideal project, and Lowell Hansen, Peninsula State Park superintendent, suggested the vacant Eagle Bluff Lighthouse. The historical society accepted the suggestion and began negotiations with the federal government through the Coast Guard and the State of Wisconsin.

In 1960, the parties signed an agreement allowing the Door County Historical Society to restore and operate the lighthouse site as a museum, with the Coast Guard maintaining the aid to navigation. The Coast Guard replaced the acetylene gas system with a battery-powered electric light and then installed a solar-powered beacon on the lantern's railing. The Fresnel lens remains in the lantern, but is no longer illuminated. State park personnel were to maintain the grounds.

Under Mrs. Ida Bay's direction, efforts began in January 1961 to restore the dwelling to its appearance in 1868, though it now in fact looks more like it did when the Duclons lived there than when the Stanleys did because several of Duclon sons and grandchildren donated furniture and other articles to the project. Walter Duclon, who lived in Green Bay, was especially interested and provided a great deal of useful information. The structure was faithfully restored except that the old wooden shingles were replaced with asphalt shingles and the walls were covered with wallpaper appropriate to the period rather than being repainted. Finally, after more than 2½ years of difficult and at times discouraging labor, the Society opened the Eagle Bluff Light to the public in September 1963.[30] During the years since 1963, Eagle Bluff Light has become once again, as it was when the Stanleys, Duclons, and Coughlins lived there, an extremely popular destination for visitors. Thousands of people, young and old, have visited the site to learn and experience what it was like to be the keeper and his family at Eagle Bluff Light in the 19th century.

Chapter 8
Chambers Island Light

Visiting the Chambers Island Light was easier when you would have been welcomed by one of the keepers as you tied your boat up to the station's pier. After securing your boat, you could then take a short walk across the well-kept lawn and go into the dwelling. Most visitors now arrive on the *Quo Vadis*, which lands at the Holy Name Retreat House pier on the east side of the island, and then follow the track across the island to the lighthouse on its northwest coast. The station is now a quiet town park, that gradually is being reclaimed by nature. Once witness to heavy commercial shipping, the light today guides only a few freighters on their way to the city of Green Bay or to Sturgeon Bay, for most of the traffic is recreational.

As the size of the ships and the volume of traffic through the Rock Island and Deaths Door Passages increased, mariners on their way to the city of Green Bay sailed farther west before turning south to pass on the west side of Chambers Island. This west channel replaced the east channel along the shore of the Door County peninsula as the main route for ships traveling to and from the city of Green Bay or to Oconto, Peshtigo, and Marinette-Menominee. Smaller ships and those with reasons to touch on Door County's western shore used the narrower, reef-strewn Strawberry Passage east of Chambers Island. The wider western channel was much easier for tacking sailing vessels to negotiate.

Chambers Island is the largest island in Green Bay. It received its name in 1816 when Colonel John Miller sailed into the bay with 500 men in four sailing vessels; his objective was to build Fort Howard on the west bank of the Fox River at the head of Green Bay. The British ceded this area to the newly independent United States in 1783 but retained control until 1815. The new Fort Howard would firmly establish the United States in control of the area. As Colonel Miller and his men sailed through the area, they gave names to many of the places they passed; Chambers Island was named after Miller's second in command, Colonel Talbot Chambers, who remained in charge of Fort Howard when Colonel Miller returned to Mackinac.

Chambers Island is about eleven miles in circumference and roughly trapezoidal in shape; it is 2 miles wide, 1½ miles long on the west side, and 3¾ miles long on the east side. Hanover Shoal tails away on the southeast corner. There is a large bay on the north side of the island, and the lighthouse stands on the northwesterly side of a peninsula on the west side of the bay. It is an outlier of the Niagara Escarpment to the east which forms the Door County peninsula, although the bedrock is covered with sand and gravel glacial drift. The island is somewhat unusual in that it contains Lake Mackaysee, a small lake on the east side of the island with two small islands of its own. The lighthouse site is 9 miles northwest of Fish Creek, 13 miles northeast of Menominee, Michigan, and 6 miles from the mainland directly across the west or main channel. The light is only 6½ miles from the Eagle Bluff Light on the Door Peninsula, but it is not visible from that location.

In 1837 a Board of Navy Commissioners sent Lieutenant G.J. Pendergast to make a survey of the need for lighthouses on the western Great Lakes. He reported that there was already a lighthouse on Rock Island and that a light was needed in the Deaths Door passage, but he judged that there was an even greater need for a light nearer the head of Green Bay. Pendergast concluded that a light on Chambers Island would be desirable, but that a light on Grassy Island near the mouth of the Fox River was even more critically needed.[1]

Vessels on their way to and from what is now the city of Green Bay continued to sail past the west side of Chambers Island, but it was not until the late 1840s that settlement on the island began when Stephen A. Hoag, a Quaker, built a small cabin there. In 1851 Nathaniel Brooks and David Clow, both ship's carpenters and new partners in a boat-building venture, moved with their families to Chambers Island. It is very likely that Brooks had seen the potential of the site when he visited Hoag in 1849. They were soon joined by a number of other families, including that of Lewis S. Williams. Most of the people settled around the large, sandy bay on the north side of the island and combined farming with fishing, lumbering, and boat building. David Clow became the best-known of the boat builders; we have discussed above how Martin Knudsen later rescued Clow and his son when their vessel went aground on Pilot Island.

The settlers successfully petitioned the county board in 1858 to set aside Chambers Island as a separate town, and at the first township election the voters elected Lewis S. Williams supervisor, treasurer, and assessor. Things went smoothly until the later 1860s, when internal bickering rose to such a level that the county board in November 1869 dissolved the Town of Chambers Island and attached it to the Town of Gibraltar, which included the area around Fish Creek.[2]

The Civil War was still in progress when the Lighthouse Board sent a special committee in 1865 to determine the wants and needs of the commercial interests in the western Great Lakes. The committee members were particularly directed to examine the situation in Green Bay. On their return to Washington, DC the members made a number of recommendations including that a lighthouse be built on Chambers Island, that range lights be erected at the entrance to the Fox River, and that a beacon be placed on Peshtigo Shoal. The Board asked an appropriation of $25,000 from Congress to accomplish this, which was approved on 28 July 1866. However, further discussion by the Board indicated that the appropriation was insufficient for the proposed projects, since the Chambers Island light with a 4th Order Fresnel lens and suitable keeper's dwelling would alone cost an estimated $15,000. Plans for the light were thus placed on hold pending further review.

However, lighthouse engineer Colonel W.F. Raynolds came from Detroit to select a possible site, and he chose a location on the peninsula that forms the west side of the harbor on the north side of Chambers Island. In November 1866, Lewis S. Williams offered to sell the ten acres of land at that location to the government for $100. The chairman of the Board approved the site Colonel Raynolds had selected but was disappointed by the quantity of land involved. He directed Colonel Raynolds to attempt to purchase more land, not to exceed fifty acres, at the same price per acre. Why the chairman wanted a reservation so much larger than many other stations is unclear, but Colonel Raynolds approached Williams again. On 8 May 1867 Williams and his wife Anna deeded 40.04 acres of land to the federal government in return for $250, according to the survey of the US Land Office in Menasha, Wisconsin. This was $150 less than Colonel Raynolds had been authorized to offer, though actually a later survey in 1883 by lighthouse engineer A.R. Flint revealed that the land included in the deed's description totalled only about 30 acres instead of 40.[3]

With the site now in hand, the Board decided to move ahead with the Chambers Island Light, delaying action on the other proposed navigation aids until later. The Board had received an appropriation in 1866 to build the nearby Eagle Bluff Light. Plans had been drawn and contracts let for materials for this project in preparation for construction in 1867, though the project was delayed until the following year. Board engineers apparently used the already completed plans for Eagle Bluff to build the Chambers Island lighthouse, modifying the tower only slightly; except for the towers and a few other minor details, the lighthouses are virtually identical.

In early June 1868, the steamer *Rocket* delivered a crew of men along with a large quantity of cut stone, bricks, lime, and other building materials at the site of the Chambers Island Light. The crew from Detroit immediately set to work clearing several acres of land, digging a basement from the coarse gravel, and building a pier so that additional materials could be brought ashore. The men dug a basement 245 feet from the shore, and masons laid up stone walls. They then erected a 1½-story dwelling measuring twenty-six feet by thirty feet and an attached kitchen wing several feet lower than the first floor and measuring twelve feet by twenty feet from cream-colored Milwaukee brick. The main floor had five rooms, a pantry, a closet, a hall, and a front entrance facing the bay, while the second floor contained a small closet, a small front room, and a large room across the rear of the dwelling.

The masons built the tower for the light diagonally into the western corner of the dwelling. The first and second stories of the tower were ten feet square on the outside with buttressed corners, while the balance of the tower to the lantern deck was a ten-foot octagon. The octagonal top of the tower served to distinguish the Chambers Island Light from the Eagle Bluff Light (which has a square tower) for mariners. The tower is double-walled with outside walls thirteen inches thick and a circular inner wall four inches thick. As at Eagle Bluff, the only stairway in the dwelling is a fifty-five-step cast-iron structure that leads from the basement to the lantern deck, with landings and doors on the first and second floors. The men also constructed a large, square, brick chimney near the rear of the dwelling oriented diagonally to the rear wall.

At the top of the tower, the workmen constructed an octagonal cast-iron deck and a ten-sided cast-iron and glass lantern, which they hoisted up and bolted together in place. Above the lantern, they bolted on a cast-iron dome roof to which they attached a ventilator and lightning rod. The deck had a trap door that allowed entrance from the stairs and one of the lantern panels was fitted with a cast-iron door that gave access to the deck outside the lantern. There are ten panes of 5/16 inch glass, each twenty-seven inches by forty inches, but the one that faces inland was covered so that the light shone out over an arc of 324 degrees. The tower was 245 feet from the shore and was forty-four feet nine inches tall from the base to the center of the ventilating ball. The focal plane of the light was sixty-eight feet above lake level and was designed to be visible for sixteen miles. The lantern has been destroyed, but it likely was built by the Detroit Locomotive Works in Detroit, the same firm that built the lantern at Eagle Bluff. With the lantern in place, the district lampist installed a 4th Order Fresnel lens imported from Paris, France, and connected the clockwork which rotated the mechanism to give the fixed white light a flash every sixty seconds. The crew built a wood-frame privy east of the dwelling and a wood-frame boat house; they also lengthened and strengthened the original landing dock. The dock had little protection from the waves building up on the bay — a continual problem at the station — and the boathouse was located on shore; boatways were installed to enable the station's boats to be drawn ashore and into the boathouse.[4]

On 1 October 1868, less than four months after construction began, the new Chambers Island Light officially went into service when the keeper lighted the burner in the lens for the first time. Three weeks earlier, the Lighthouse Board had appointed Lewis S. Williams, who sold the land for the lighthouse to the government, as the first keeper. One wonders whether some sort of deal regarding that appointment figured in the land purchase; However, it was the port collector at Milwaukee who recommended that Williams be appointed keeper, not Colonel Raynolds, who had handled the purchase of the site.

Williams was 48 and his wife Anna was 40 when he became keeper. They both had been born in New York state, where their

Chambers Island light in about 1940. Notice the oil house to the left of the flagpole along the sidewalk and the boathouse with boatways extending out to the water. Photo courtesy of the US Coast Guard.

parents were natives. Like so many men at that time, Williams was an army veteran. The couple had at least four children including one, Sherman, who was born after his father's appointment. As at other stations, life for Williams quickly settled into a regular routine, although his duties were more complicated than Stanley's at nearby Eagle Bluff because, in addition to tending the burner in the lens, the clockwork at Chambers Island had to be wound several times each night. For most of Williams' career, the family lived at the station year round, although the light was extinguished when the bay froze over and navigation ceased. Since Marinette-Menominee was only slightly farther away but was much larger and had many more stores, the Williams family went there more often than to Fish Creek or Sturgeon Bay. Consequently, he was not as well known in Door County as were keepers who regularly visited Sturgeon Bay or wintered there.

The islands east of Chambers Island are known collectively as the Strawberry Islands, apparently because many strawberry plants grew there, and there also were several areas with strawberries on Chambers Island. Williams developed a very extensive strawberry patch in his spare time. It was so large in fact that he became well known for it in the area. During the summer, groups often came to the island to picnic; the station pier provided one of the few good landings for visitors, and by all accounts Williams was a gracious host. A group of twelve Menominee residents visited the island in 1875, but realized they had forgotten several things when they got there. Williams helped them out and also gave them a strawberry pie and strawberries and cream. After lunch, the keeper took the party for a stroll around the island and showed them his strawberry patch. According to one visitor,

> We had heard fabulous stories about this patch before, but were not prepared for the sight that met our gaze. The ground was literally red and it was impossible to step out without treading on them.

Williams invited his visitors to pick and eat as many berries as they wanted. The picnickers described the keeper as

> one of those blunt, happy, hospitable persons who make all feel at home under any circumstance, and it was the universal opinion of our party that he was the right man in the right place. . . ."[5]

Late in summer, usually in August, numerous visitors also came to the island to pick blackcap raspberries, which were very abundant. The island was only five miles from Fish Creek, and that village was a popular departure point for excursion parties.[6]

Life was not all picnics and berries for the Williams family, however. Road conditions were often poor, and once Green Bay froze over, residents took to the ice with horses and sleighs. Travel on the ice was much faster and more direct than overland routes, and the villages were connected by regular paths across the ice. Also, the railroad reached Marinette-Menominee long before getting to Sturgeon Bay, and there was a great deal of traffic across the ice from Door County to the twin cities, though such travel was not without its perils.

On 9 January 1875, one of the Williams sons set out with a companion from the lighthouse for Eagle Harbor in a sleigh. When about two miles out on the bay ice, they came upon a crack which seemed to be about a foot wide. They got out and led their horse across the crack before discovering that the crack had recently been much wider and that only a thin coating of ice covered the water. The horse broke through the ice, and the two men narrowly escaped going into the water as well. The day was extremely cold, and the men might easily have frozen to death had they gotten wet. As it was, they lost their horse and had to walk the rest of the way to Eagle Harbor.

Two years later, Williams, his daughter, and her girl friend had an equally perilous adventure. They were returning from Menominee late on a January afternoon when, about halfway home, they came upon a large crack in the ice. Williams got out to find a safe crossing, leaving the horse and cutter with the women. He found a place to cross and led the way while they followed with the horse. Just as they were about to cross, Williams shouted at his daughter to stop, but the wind drowned out his calls, and, at that moment, one of the cutter's runners struck a large piece of ice; the cutter lurched and threw the women out onto the ice. The horse bolted, leaped over the crack and headed for home at full speed pulling the cutter. Williams set out after the horse, leaving the women to follow as best they could. He found the horse near Chambers Island with the lines snagged in the ice about two hours later. Williams then turned back in the dark to locate his daughter and her friend. Everyone was finally reunited, but they arrived home after 9 PM.[7]

Williams wrote a note to the editor of the *Door County Advocate* in June 1878 asking that he be sent the "small bill" he owed for receiving the paper. He said he would pay the bill as soon as he got his pension money, which he expected any day. He also told the editor not to continue sending the paper since he didn't want it any more. Six months later the editor printed the letter, noting that Williams was the lighthouse keeper on Chambers Island and was also a pensioner. Williams evidently had not yet received his pension, for the long-suffering editor concluded the article with these words:

> At any rate the balance due us on Lewis S. Williams' subscription remains unsettled. Lewis S. Williams, please liquidate and we will forgive you.[8]

No record exists of how the matter ended, though Williams presumably paid his bill. The editor continued to mention the keeper in the paper.

Activities at Chambers Island continued to be routine, with no major problems through the years. Then, in February 1889, the *Advocate* carried a report that Williams would be transferred to a new lighthouse proposed at Gladstone, Michigan. Instead, in August 1889, Lewis S. Williams, aged 69, sent in his resignation as keeper of the Chambers Island Light that he had tended for twenty-one years. On 18 September 1889, the Board transferred Peter Knudsen from Escanaba to Chambers Island, and Williams and his wife moved to Sturgeon Bay where they planned to live. However, they seem not to have found living there satisfactory; a year later Williams applied for admission to the veteran's home near Waupaca, Wisconsin. There was no retirement program at that time for elderly keepers, and it may have been economics that caused him to move to the veteran's home.[9]

Peter Knudsen, Martin's brother and one of three lighthouse brothers, became second assistant at Pilot Island in 1875. Two years later he became keeper at Poverty Island Light, and he returned to Pilot Island as keeper for five years in 1883. In July 1888, the Board transferred him to the Peninsula Point Light, south of Escanaba, Michigan, before moving him to Chambers Island in 1889. The original builders of the station had done an excellent job; through the years only the entry "minor repairs" appears in the Board's annual report of repairs and modifications at the station. However, that changed in 1890, when a work crew spent most of October at the station. In addition to minor repairs to the dwelling and tower, the men moved the boathouse closer to the shore and installed new boatways. The old landing crib was removed, a new crib was built, and the old one was then placed at the outer end of the new one. The crew also replaced the wooden sidewalks around the tower and dwelling.

Until this time, the keeper's water supply consisted of water carried in buckets from Green Bay or rainwater collected in the basement cistern. Now the men drove a well down forty-five feet and erected a tower thirty-seven feet high and sixteen feet square at the base over it to support a windmill; they also installed a tank of 2,250 gallons capacity to supply water for fire protection and domestic use. Windmills were common on farms in the county and would probably have been useful at other stations, but the Board installed them only at Chambers Island and at the Canal Station Lights. Materials for a two-story barn were delivered, but it was too late in the year to start work on it.

Peter Knudsen's stay at Chambers Island was relatively short. In March 1891, only eighteen months after his appointment, he resigned as keeper and left to go into business at Newport on the Lake Michigan side of the peninsula, south of Northport.

The Board transferred Charles E. Young, first assistant at Pilot Island, to Chambers Island, and promoted him to keeper to replace Peter Knudsen. Young was 22, a Washington Island native, and a bachelor who spent winters with his parents in Washington Harbor. His father Jacob Young was keeper of the light at Cedar River, Michigan, at the time. Young lived alone in the dwelling, but he enjoyed taking the station sailboat to visit his many friends in Sturgeon Bay, Fish Creek, and Sister Bay. A seemingly unrelated event occurred in May 1892 when Mary Knudsen arrived to visit her brothers from Pomeroy, Iowa, where their parents lived. She planned to visit for a year, staying first with Martin and his family on Pilot Island and then with Peter and his family at Newport.

Martin and Peter Knudsen were good friends of Charles Young, and Martin wintered on Washington Island near the Youngs. Thus, it was inevitable that Mary Knudsen would meet Charles Young, which she did in the summer of 1892. Less than a year later on 28 March 1893 the two young people were married at

Peter Knudsen's home in Newport. After the ceremony, the newlyweds returned to Chambers Island to get ready for the coming navigational season.

The following September Mary's parents Peder and Maria Knudsen came to meet their new son-in-law. They had moved several years earlier from Washington Island to Pomeroy, Iowa, a community of several hundred inhabitants. A tornado had struck the village during the summer, badly damaging or demolishing nearly every building. The Knudsen home had been destroyed during the storm, and a piece of wood with a nail in it had struck Maria in the head; she survived, though the nail penetrated her scalp. Knudsen had tornado insurance on the house, and his payment left him well off compared to many other residents. After visiting their children and grandchildren in Door County, the senior Knudsens returned to Iowa.[10]

The light at Chambers Island had always been extinguished when Green Bay froze over, and the Youngs closed the station in early December 1894 and returned to Washington Island for the winter. However, they soon received orders to keep the station open until further orders; the Toledo and Ann Arbor Railroad had decided to try to keep their car ferries sailing all winter from Frankfort, Michigan, to Menominee, Michigan, either through the Sturgeon Bay ship canal or through Deaths Door. Lumber was the chief cargo. Keepers at Pilot Island, Dunlap Reef, and Menominee also received orders to remain open, and the car ferries did not stop running until February that year. However, though they were able to make the passage, the voyage was too slow and costly to be financially successful.[11]

This was to be Young's last winter at Chambers Island; he was transferred to the Ahnapee (Algoma) Pierhead Light in September 1895 after an uneventful summer. Charles immediately went to his new assignment, but Mary stayed behind in Ephriam until spring. She was pregnant and gave birth to a son on December 13, the first of five children. Young was transferred from Ahnapee to Menominee in 1899, then to Plum Island in 1905. He moved to Racine two years later and served there until he retired in 1932.

The new Chambers Island keeper was Soren Christianson, a native of Norway who previously had served at the Point Betsie Light across Lake Michigan. He was born in July 1852 and had immigrated to America in 1872 with his parents, who settled in Chicago. Christianson was 43 and his wife Hannah was 21 when they arrived at his new assignment; she was also Norwegian. Four months before her husband's transfer, Hannah gave birth to a daughter named Grace.[12]

Many changes occurred during Christianson's five-year tenure at the station. In late summer 1896, a work crew came to the light to make extensive improvements. They rebuilt the boathouse and moved it still closer to the shore. The old landing cribs were replaced and new boatways constructed. The men put in a 1,600-foot wire fence along the property line enclosing the reservation; the site was between 30 and 40 acres in size, but it was a peninsula and the fence ran across the peninsula, not all the way around the property. The crew built a woodshed measuring fourteen feet by twenty feet south of the dwelling and laid the usual wooden sidewalk leading to it. The original well had become unreliable, and the crew drove a new well in front of the dwelling and secured an ample supple of pure water. They added a platform, a well house four feet square, and a sidewalk to the dwelling.

The following summer a crew took down the windmill and tank over the old well and built a summer kitchen measuring twelve feet by sixteen feet with a chimney south of the dwelling. Seventy-five feet west of the dwelling, they also erected a brick oil house measuring seven feet by nine feet that could hold as many as ninety five-gallon cans of kerosene. The keeper had a longer walk to get fuel for the burner, but it was no longer stored in the dwelling's basement, which made for a much safer situation. All the outbuildings were buff colored with red roofs, except the oil house, which had a metal roof.

During 1898, equipment to make a change in the lighting apparatus arrived at the station, but the lampist was unavailable to install it. Another new arrival at the station in 1898 was a son, Horace, born in July. The lampist arrived in June 1899 with a new 4th Order Fresnel lens that was made in 1892 by F. Barbier and Company, Paris, France. The lampist also installed a new mercury float pedestal made by the same manufacturer. The lens revolved on the mercury float and was controlled by a clockwork and weights made by Henry Le Paute of Paris, France, another company which built Fresnel lenses and accessories.

The keeper had to wind the clockwork every five hours to keep the lens revolving. This meant that the keeper had to climb up the tower stairs and into the lantern several times a night in order to rewind the clockwork, even if the burner did not require attention. On 15 July 1899, the characteristic of the light was changed from fixed white with a flash every sixty seconds to fixed white with a flash every thirty seconds.[13]

The *Advocate* noted in October 1898 that Christianson had visited a local doctor, but no other information appeared. This may have been a prelude to a story that appeared in late June 1900 reporting that the keeper was ill with what his doctors had diagnosed as cancer of the stomach and that it was feared that the end was very near. He was suffering excruciating pain and was having difficulty taking nourishment. He was not relieved from duty until mid-August, however, when he and his wife and two children went by boat to Menominee and then took the train to Chicago, where his mother still lived. Christianson went into a hospital on arrival, but he returned to his family home and died on 16 September 1900.[14]

To replace Christianson, the Board transferred Joseph Napeizinski from Rawley Point Light near Two Rivers, Wisconsin and promoted him to keeper. Each keeper since Williams had requested an assistant to share the duties of tending the revolving light, but their pleas had fallen on deaf ears. That changed in November 1903 when the Board appointed George W. Drew to be the assistant at Chambers Island.

The landing at the station continued to be a problem, as it had been from the start; it was damaged by storms in 1905 and 1906, In 1906, a crew came and built a new wooden boathouse measuring sixteen feet by thirty-six feet on the shore, as well as a boat landing 115 feet long with a 21-foot crib set at right angles to it at the end. Both of the landing and the crib were 10 feet wide. The men also installed boatways that were 87 feet long. The slope of the shoreline was very gentle, and, despite the length of the landing, the water depth outside the crib was only six feet; it remained impossible to land at the station when strong winds blew from the northeast, north, or northwest. Except for replacement of wooden sidewalks with the cement sidewalks that still remain, the station's buildings were complete in 1906, and the station remained as it was until the Coast Guard closed it in the 1955.

In 1906 the Board transferred Napeizinski back to the Rawley Point Light as keeper. After serving there for five years, he was moved a few miles south to the Manitowoc Breakwater Light where he served until he retired in 1941.[15] Jens J. Rollefson, a red-bearded Norwegian bachelor, replaced Napeizinski as keeper at Chambers Island. Three years later, in 1909, Sam Hanson replaced George Drew as assistant. The 37-year-old Hanson was a native of Ephriam and had grown up on his parents' farm; he had been a fisherman and mailman before entering the lighthouse service. When he received his appointment, he and his wife had three children, a baby daughter Sadie and two sons — Clifford, age 5, and Edgar, a year younger. A second daughter, Doris, was born in 1912. The family had a home in Sister Bay and remained there while Rollefson and Hanson manned the light.

Tragedy struck them in 1915 when Mrs. Hanson died. After that the children stayed with their father in summer and in Sister Bay while school was in session. However, as they grew older, the boys stayed ashore and worked during vacations. Earlier in his life Rollefson had been a schoolteacher, and he taught Doris how to write and read, and to do math using dominos. The men did the cooking, but the girls helped with the dishes, made beds, and did other household chores. The lighthouse tender brought kerosene, coal, and other supplies for the station, but the men bought their own food in Fish Creek — cases of Campbell soup, bushels of potatoes, and (since there was no refrigeration) cases of canned milk and salted and preserved meat. The men made their own bread and caught fish; they had no carrots, onions, or lettuce, and, because Hanson had once fallen sick after eating bananas, he would not let the children eat them. Cherry trees behind the dwelling provided fruit for the children, but the apple trees did not produce ripe fruit until after girls had gone back to school. As always, there were strawberries and raspberries to enjoy during the summer.

The girls slept in the big bedroom upstairs and, instead of counting sheep, counted the flashes of light illuminating the trees to get to sleep. Animals were no longer kept in the station barn, so the girls used the second floor as a playhouse. Hanson bought the children their school clothes in Marinette-Menominee, which had more stores and a greater selection than did Sister Bay. On Saturday night the girls took baths and their then father braided their hair.

Tragedy struck the Hanson family again in 1921. Edgar began experiencing abdominal pain while at the lighthouse in late April. Everyone thought it was an upset stomach, but instead of getting better, he got worse. His father took him to Sturgeon Bay where he died from a ruptured appendix as he was being taken into the hospital on May 2. Sadly this was not the end of the Hansons' disasters. The next spring Clifford Hanson joined his father and Rollefson in preparing the station for the navigation season. On 10 April 1922, he went across the ice to Fish Creek for the mail; warm weather had weakened the ice, and he fell through and drowned. Peter Coughlin witnessed the accident from the tower at Eagle Bluff, but could not summon help in time to save Clifford because a fallen tree limb had knocked out his telephone line.

The deaths of his two sons in less than a year sent Hanson into deep depression. The Lighthouse Bureau transferred him to Cana Island in January 1923, and his daughters went with him, but Hanson resigned from the service in July and went back to Sister Bay. Two years later, he re-entered the service and was sent to the Ludington, Michigan North Pierhead Light. Doris Hanson returned to Sister Bay in 1928 and was married in 1929. Her father continued in the lighthouse service for a time, but never recovered from the deaths of his wife and his two sons. [16]

The Lighthouse Bureau transferred Claude Chapman to the Chambers Island Light from the Sturgeon Bay Canal Light Station in 1925 and promoted him to keeper; Chapman's wife and two children joined him at the light. Perhaps the most important event of Chapman's tenure occurred in 1932; in that year the crew of the *Hyacinth* installed a telephone in the lighthouse. That ended the isolation of the station, though electricity was never provided there. Claude Chapman returned to the canal station on 1 July 1933 as keeper, only to die five months later in a tragic hunting accident. To replace Chapman on Chambers Island, the Bureau transferred

Alfred Cornell from the Green Island Light which had been automated. Cornell retired in 1942; he was the last civilian keeper at Chambers Island.

After the Coast Guard assumed responsibility for the station, three men were usually stationed at Chambers Island. In the 1950s, the Coast Guard was looking to save money and embarked on a program of automating its remaining manned stations. They closed the Chambers Island Station in 1955, shuttered the buildings, removed the landing pier and boatways, and automated the light which had earlier been electrified. Three years later the lantern was removed from the deck of the tower, and the Fresnel lens was sold at a surplus property auction to Harold Warp of Chicago. The Chambers Island lens is now on display at Warp's Pioneer Village museum in Minden, Nebraska, hundreds of miles from the waters of Green Bay that it once illuminated.

After its vacation, the lighthouse dwelling was rented to Mr. Edwin Fitzgerald, who owned the adjacent property to the south and used it occasionally during summers. The Coast Guard built an open steel tower next to the oil house, inside a thirty-foot-square cyclone fence. The light atop the tower exhibits a white flashing light, but its range is only twelve miles. Anxious to reduce its holdings and responsibilities even further, the Coast Guard deeded the land and buildings to the Town of Gibraltar for park purposes on 10 March 1976, reserving only the land within the fence around the steel tower. The park was opened to the public the following year; Joel and Mary Blahnik and their family act as caretakers, living in the dwelling during the summer. They have restored the interior and set up exhibits on the history of the light. Although the lantern is gone, visitors can climb the tower stairs and stand on the lantern deck to look out over the waters of Green Bay, just as Williams and his successors did.

DUNLAP REEF LIGHT HOUSE, STURGEON BAY, WIS.

Dunlap Reef rear range light, 1914; the view is looking south toward the old Sturgeon Bay railroad bridge. Photo courtesy of the Milwaukee Public Library/ Wisconsin Marine Historical Society.

Chapter 9
Dunlap Reef Range Lights

Much older Door County lights still remain in place to remind visitors of their role in history, but only fast-fading memories remain of the Dunlap Reef Range Lights in Sturgeon Bay. For the past seventy years the bay's waters have concealed the site of the range lights, giving no hint of their location or existence. Even the charts mariners use give no indication of where the lights were for over forty years, for nothing remains on Dunlap Reef.

Dunlap Reef or the "middle ground" is a rocky shoal in Sturgeon Bay harbor that emerges in times of low water east of the navigation channel and north of the abandoned railroad bridge. As Sturgeon Bay developed into a center of commerce, even before the completion of the ship canal, mariners requested that aids to navigation be installed to guide them in the bay and to warn them of the location of the reef. In March 1873 Joseph Harris, Sr. and Representative Philetus Sawyer convinced the Lighthouse Board to place buoys at each end of the shoal.

The buoys were sufficient for a time, but with the impending completion of the ship canal and the expected increase in ship traffic, demands arose for more prominent markings on the reef. In 1880 the Lighthouse Board decided to place range lights on the reef not only to mark the area, but also to guide mariners into the channel. Before work could begin, however, the Board had to obtain title to the proposed site from the State of Wisconsin. Once title was transferred to the federal government in April 1881, construction of two wooden cribs was started, using heavy timbers purchased from a local sawmill. The front crib was approximately sixteen feet square and the rear one about twenty-four feet by thirty-six feet. When completed, the cribs were put in position and filled with limestone to anchor them to the reef. On the front crib, located on the northern end of the reef, a Lighthouse Board crew built a four-sided wooden tower and placed an octagonal cast-iron lantern on it. On the larger rear crib, some 680 feet to the south, the crew built a two-story keeper's dwelling. A square wooden tower surmounted by a second octagonal cast-iron lantern was built into the gable on the front of the house. The front tower measured sixteen feet from base to lantern top, while the rear tower was thirty-eight feet high from its base to the top of the lantern. The district lampist installed a lens lantern in the front light and a 5th Order Fresnel lens in the rear light.[1]

Henry C. Graham, who had been appointed keeper a month earlier, exhibited the range lights for the first time on the night of 15 October 1881. Each evening he had to climb the tower in his dwelling to light the kerosene lamp in the lens, then climb down the tower, launch his rowboat, and row 680 feet to the front range light. There he had to dock his boat, climb the tower, light the kerosene lamp in the lens lantern, climb down, and row back home. In the morning the routine was repeated as the lights were extinguished for the day and prepared for the next night. Because of the fixed nature of the lights and the capacity of the fuel tanks, he rarely had to make additional trips during the night, but like a postman's rounds, the task had to be done evening and morning during the navigation season regardless of weather conditions.

Like many of his fellow keepers, Graham was a Civil War veteran. He and his family lived in Egg Harbor, and he resigned his position as county circuit court clerk to accept the appointment as keeper. He moved into the dwelling with his wife and three sons. They spent the first winter in the new house but found the situation too confining and spent subsequent winters ashore. Only several feet separated the walls of the dwelling from the fence that had been built on the outer edge of the crib.

The range lights were at first very popular with maritime interests. Both the front and rear range lights displayed a fixed white light, and, while the rear range light was visible in all directions, the front range light had a restricted arc of visibility. Sailors soon began to complain, however, that it was very difficult to pick out the front range light from city lights in the background as they sailed into Sturgeon Bay, and Graham asked the Lighthouse Board in 1882 to replace the white light in the front range light with a red one. The newspaper thought this was a good idea and that it undoubtedly would be carried out; and so it was, but not until 1907, twenty-five years later.[2]

In 1883 a Lighthouse Board work crew built a new crib twelve feet by twenty-two feet with a slip six feet wide in it for hauling out the keeper's rowboat. It was sunk on the south side of the rear range light, giving Graham and his family a little more room as well as providing a place for his boat. Even with the addition, Graham reported that he difficulty during a storm in later November; spray covered the building and walks with a coating of ice that made it almost impossible to move around outside. When it came time to launch his boat in the evening, he found it half full of ice, and, because of the high winds, waves, and precipitation, he was afraid he would not be able to reach the front crib to light the lantern for the night, though he succeeded in doing so after a great deal of trouble and effort. The editor of the *Advocate* chided the Lighthouse Board for refusing to build an elevated walkway to connect the range lights; he thought the cost would have been but a trifle compared with the safety and convenience afforded the keeper,[3] but the Lighthouse Board apparently had no intention of building a walkway across the gap, perhaps due to the problem of protecting such a span from shifting ice in the winter, but also because such a walkway would have been a hazard to navigation.

Life at Dunlap Reef developed from the beginning into a pattern different from that at the other lighthouses in Door County. Other than tending the lights, there was not a great deal of work for the keeper to do; there were no grounds to keep up, no range to keep clear, no garden to tend, and no outbuildings to maintain. Lighthouse Board personnel repaired any damage to the cribs. It even was possible to live ashore rather than in the dwelling. Indeed, Graham was able in April 1884 to return to his previous job during the day for several weeks while continuing to tend the range lights at night when the circuit court clerk dislocated his ankle so badly that he could not leave his home.[4]

Henry Graham became seriously ill during the winter of 1885. He recovered from his illness, but Graham, the first of only three keepers at Dunlap Reef, had had enough. He resigned effective 4 August 1885 after four years of service. Before resigning, he had bought a farm in Minnesota, and the Grahams left Door County in September for their new home in Minnesota rather than returning to Egg Harbor.[5]

The Lighthouse Board appointed Joseph Harris, Jr. to replace Graham. After leaving the Baileys Harbor Range Lights in 1881, Harris and his family had spent one year at the Green Island Light and had then gone to the Grosse Point Light in Evanston, Illinois, one of the most choice assignments in the district. However, Harris and his wife were anxious to return to Sturgeon Bay, and, when Graham's intention to resign became known, Harris requested a transfer to Dunlap Reef. Harris may well have been aware that tending the range lights in Sturgeon Bay was a much less taxing job than tending range lights at Baileys Harbor. Less than a month after his arrival back in Sturgeon Bay, an advertisement in the *Advocate* announced the opening of a new boatworks known as "Joseph Harris, Jr. Builder and Designer of Canoes, Sailing Boats, and Rowing Boats." His boatworks originally was located in an old blacksmith shop that he repaired and remodeled.[6]

Harris had complained about the lack of space for his family at Green Island, especially for the children. The Dunlap Reef Station was even smaller, but a solution was in the offing; in 1876

Dunlap Reef rear range light and dwelling, date unknown. The view is looking approximately northwest toward the Sawyer side of Sturgeon Bay. Photo courtesy of Orville Schopf.

Joseph Harris, Sr. had built Door County's first brick residence in Bay View, now the west side of Sturgeon Bay. The nine-room structure was built of cream-colored brick and was surrounded by spacious grounds. In November 1885, the senior Harris left Sturgeon Bay for a post in Washington, DC as Senator Sawyer's secretary and was not expected to return until the following August. His daughter Grace planned to spend the winter with friends in Appleton. So, rather than have the residence empty, Joseph Harris, Jr. and his family moved into his father's home. Harris lived much of the rest of the time he spent in Sturgeon Bay in his father's residence, though he did spend periods of time at the light, and he acquired the house when his father died in 1889.[7]

During his first winter back in Sturgeon Bay, Harris finished two boats, one of which he sold to William Sanderson, keeper of the Cana Island Light and father of Clifford Sanderson. Harris's operations soon outgrew the former blacksmith shop, and, in August 1886, he built a building measuring twenty-two feet by forty feet on the shore of the bay in Bay View. His son Edward joined him in his business during the winters as an assistant. Harris designed and built for his own use at Dunlap Reef a special type of rowboat having great stability, and the design so impressed lighthouse officials that they ordered a substantial number of them from Harris for use at lighthouses around the country. He also built a number of sailboats for the local market, as well as two yawls for Lighthouse Board tugs. In 1901, US Representative E.S. Minor asked Harris to build him a forty-five-foot gasoline yacht, but Harris was unable to construct it because his building was too small. He did, however, draw the plans for the yacht, and he built several smaller launches, including one for his brother in 1910. Clearly Joseph Harris, Jr. was one of Sturgeon Bay's ablest and best-known boat builders.[8]

One of the continuing problems at Dunlap Reef was getting to the front range light in bad weather. The Lighthouse Board never built an elevated walkway between the range lights, but in 1888 they made changes in the lighting apparatus to make the task easier. The lampist removed the kerosene burner and installed both a gas burner for illumination and a sun valve that turned on the gas supply when darkness approached, the gas then being ignited by a pilot light. The front range light was illuminated with the gas apparatus on 15 November 1888; from then on Harris had to visit the front range light only once a week to check the gas supply. The crew that assisted the lampist also built a new crib measuring fourteen feet by twenty-four feet that was roofed over and enclosed; it provided a covered boat slip and woodshed at the rear range light.[9]

In late March 1890, Harris received word that the US Senate had confirmed his appointment as Sturgeon Bay Postmaster, a higher-paying job than lighthouse keeper. He ended his 15-year career as a lighthouse keeper on 19 April 1890. Postmaster positions were patronage appointments, and after President Harrison's defeat in 1892, Harris lost his postmastership, but he continued to build boats. Harris was elected mayor of Sturgeon Bay in 1901, and he was reelected the following year, though this was his last public position, as he declined to run for reelection in 1903.

Boats continued to emerge from the Harris boatworks until 1911 when he closed the operation due to ill health and moved to St. Cloud, Florida. There, according to the *Advocate*, "success did not appear to follow him," but exactly what took place was not mentioned. In February 1916, he was taken to a veteran's hospital near Nashville, Tennessee, and he died there on 23 March 1916. He was buried in Tennessee, but his remains eventually were returned to Sturgeon Bay to be interred on 25 May 1916 in the Harris family plot in Bayside Cemetery.[10]

To replace Harris, the Lighthouse Board transferred Clifford Sanderson to Dunlap Reef. Sanderson had begun his lighthouse career in 1884 as assistant to his father, William, at Cana Island. In November 1889, the Lighthouse Board had transferred him to the Cedar River Michigan Light, and now, six months later, he took over the Dunlap Reef Range Lights on 21 April 1890. Sanderson was 32 and a bachelor at the time, and at first he lived in the lighthouse dwelling. After his father retired and his parents returned to their home in Sturgeon Bay from Cana Island, Clifford lived ashore with them for long periods of time until his marriage to Hedwig Oertling of Milwaukee in February 1913.

A major change in the appearance of the Dunlap Reef Range Lights occurred shortly after Sanderson's appointment. In July 1890 a Board crew painted the tower of the front range light, changing its color from white to red. The Board hoped that this would make it easier for mariners to use during the day because the red front tower would show up better against the white front of the rear light. The next year a work crew replaced the deck of the rear crib and rebuilt the fence at the edge of the crib. Also, the boat slide at the station was rebuilt and lowered, and other minor repairs were made.[11]

When the bay froze over in winter, navigation ceased and the keeper extinguished the lights, but that practice changed in the mid-1890s when the Ann Arbor Railroad purchased a number of powerful, steel-hulled car ferries that could break through the ice if it were not too thick. They began trying to operate year round between Menominee, Michigan on the west shore of Green Bay and Frankfort, Michigan, since this enabled the railroad to avoid the expense of sending their rail cars through Chicago. Depending on ice conditions, the ferries went either through the Sturgeon Bay ship canal or through Deaths Door to the north, though sometimes, particularly in the early years, the ice became so thick that no trips took place. However, as long as the ferries ran, the navigation lights had to continue in operation, and the keepers along Sturgeon Bay could no longer count on a long winter holiday.

The cyclic nature of the water level in Lake Michigan (and therefore in Sturgeon Bay) became particularly evident at Dunlap Reef beginning in 1893. At that time the bay's waters and the US economy both declined dramatically. Sanderson reported in August 1894 that the waters around the range lights had fallen fourteen inches since the same time the previous year. By August, the level had fallen two feet from 1893, and at that point the water in the bay was as low as it had been in 1864, though it had not been so apparent then because the boats sailing on the bay were smaller and drew less water than in 1895. In March, 1896, there was no need for an elevated walkway between the range lights because the reef was so high and dry that Sanderson did not even get his feet wet as he walked between the front and rear range lights.[12]

In 1902, improved 5th Order lamps were installed in both range lights at Dunlap Reef. Five years later, the characteristics of the front and rear range lights were changed from fixed white to fixed red, twenty-five years after Keeper Henry Graham had recommended the change. The authorities hoped that this would keep sailors from confusing the range lights with the lights of Sturgeon Bay in the background. No more changes were made after that, and life settled into a familiar routine for Sanderson, as it had for earlier keepers.

Sanderson lived on shore, though in bad weather he could stay in the dwelling and tend the lamps in the evening and morning. In 1913 he married and bought a home, but he and his wife had no children.[13]

The brick or stone lighthouses built on shore were very sturdy and resistant to deterioration, but wooden range lights on their stone-filled wooden cribs were another story altogether. In 1922 the lighthouse authorities recommended that the Dunlap Reef Range Lights be abandoned on the grounds that they were inadequate, obsolete, and (most worrisome of all) in an advanced state of decay. They recommended that the range lights be replaced by new automatic acetylene gas buoys. Two years later the Lighthouse Bureau accepted the recommendation and discontinued the Dunlap Reef Range Lights.

On 29 April 1924, they transferred Clifford Sanderson to Cana Island to replace Oscar Knudson.[14] Later the lantern and tower were removed from Dunlap Reef, and the dwelling was removed from the crib and moved to 411 South 4th Avenue in Sturgeon Bay, where it is still to be seen, indistinguishable from its neighbors and several blocks from the waters of Sturgeon Bay. The front tower was taken down, the cribs were disassembled, and the anchoring rocks removed, eliminating all evidence of the existence of the Dunlap Reef Range Lights.

Chapter 10
Sturgeon Bay Canal Lights

The Sturgeon Bay Canal Station still bustles with activity as the Coast Guardsmen go about their duties, but they no long function as light keepers; both the Pierhead Light with its fog signal and the towering coast light have been automated. Gone too are the great fleets of sailing ships and steam-powered ferries, freighters and passenger vessels. They have been replaced by pleasure boats and smaller lake freighters. Modern bulk carriers are too large to use the ship canal and must go through Deaths Door on their way to the shipyards in Sturgeon Bay just as sailors had to do before the canal was built.

Construction of the Sturgeon Bay ship canal occasioned the building of the lights. The canal itself was largely the result of the vision and drive of one man — Joseph Harris, Sr. — who played a key role in the history of the Door County lights. Within a short time of his arrival in Sturgeon Bay in 1855, Joseph Harris, Sr., editor of *Door County Advocate* and political operative, became convinced that a canal from the head of Sturgeon Bay, southeast of the city, through the sandy ridges to Lake Michigan would make the city of Sturgeon Bay into a thriving lake port while reducing the distance and danger for mariners sailing from Green Bay ports to ports around the Great Lakes. After long and tangled negotiations, dredges of the Sturgeon Bay and Lake Michigan Canal and Harbor Company began digging the canal in July 1872. The canal did not open for full navigation for another ten years, but small craft and vessels without cargo began using the canal in 1880.

Soon after work commenced, Commodore Alexander Murray stopped in Sturgeon Bay while on an inspection tour of lighthouses on the Great Lakes to see how the canal was progressing and to determine when and where new aids to navigation would be required. The issue of navigational aids was complicated by the fact that the canal was privately owned and the owners collected tolls for its use, but both the canal owners and mariners using the canal wanted a lighthouse at the lakeshore entrance to the canal, and they also argued in favor of a breakwater to be built by the government that would both create a harbor of refuge there and also protect the canal entrance and offer shelter to vessels using the waterway. Despite possible complications, Commodore Murray stated that he would report favorably to the Lighthouse Board on the lighthouse question. Lighthouse Board officials visited the canal to check on the progress of the work, and businessmen and mariners from towns along Green Bay sent petitions to Congress asking for lighthouses at the lake entrance to the canal and at the mouth of Sturgeon Bay. The Corps of Engineers began building a breakwater at the lake end of the canal which consisted of a north pier and a south pier. The two piers were 850 feet apart on the shoreline, and each extended out into Lake Michigan about 1,100 feet. They converged offshore to form an entrance about 335 feet wide, and extending in parallel off the end of each pier was a separate pier approximately 150 feet long.[1]

The depth of the water in the canal in 1880 was between ten and eleven feet; this was sufficient for small vessels and for larger ones without heavy cargo, but dredging further deepened the canal. In 1881, when it had the Dunlap Reef Range Lights built, the Lighthouse Board also decided to place a pierhead light on the end of the detached portion of the north pier, and in October of that year, carpenters working at Clay Banks, south of the canal, constructed the wooden frame for the Pierhead Light. A Lighthouse Board crew brought the timber and material for the proposed light to the harbor by barge, and Charles Dobson, who had just supervised construction of the Dunlap Reef Range Lights, took charge of the pierhead project. By late November his men had completed the lighthouse, a bridge connecting the inner and outer portions of the pier, and an elevated walkway from the tower to the shore on which the keeper could walk out to service the light.

North Pier Head light and fog signal, Sturgeon Bay canal light station, about 1940. Photo courtesy of US Coast Guard.

The lantern arrived, but bad weather prevented its installation, and work was suspended for the year. Dobson and his crew came back to Sturgeon Bay from Detroit in mid-March 1882 to complete the work.[2]

The tower was a white, open-frame structure surmounted by a lantern room. A 6th Order Fresnel lens exhibited a fixed red light over an arc of 270 degrees, with a focal plane twenty-nine feet above the pier and thirty-five feet above lake level. The light was designed to be visible in clear weather for a distance of twelve miles. Rear Admiral John Rogers, president of the Lighthouse Board, announced that it would be displayed for the first time on 15 May 1882. Before Dobson left for Chicago, he told local officials that the Board planned to ask Congress for $40,000 to build a lighthouse on the north shore of the canal and that they also needed money to build a dwelling for the keeper of the pierhead light. In addition, he told them that he would return to supervise construction as soon as a valid title could be obtained for the Sherwood Point Light.[3]

On 27 April 1882, the *Advocate* carried the news that A.W. Hall, Milwaukee's port collector, had nominated Rufus M. Wright of Fish Creek to be keeper of the North Pierhead Light, noting that:

> The appointment will no doubt prove a surprise to many, although it is a good one.[4]

The reason it was a surprise was that though Wright was a veteran, he was something of a political maverick in that he had left the Republican Party in the late 1870s to become a Greenback supporter, much to the surprise and dismay of the county's party faithful. At that time, being a Union Civil War veteran and a Republican seemed to be the two most important qualifications for appointment as a lighthouse keeper, and before the days of the Civil Service, the correct political affiliation was critical.[5]

The Lighthouse Board accepted the port collector's recommendation (as it normally did), and Wright became the first keeper of the new light. He was born in 1832 in Oneida County, New York, and married Elizabeth Hoyt in 1857 with whom he had a son. Three years later Wright, either divorced or widowed, came west by himself and enlisted when the Civil War broke out. At the end of his tour of duty, he came to Door County, but in the spring of 1864, he reenlisted in the 12th Wisconsin Infantry. Wright returned to Sturgeon Bay at the end of the war and was elected county judge several years later; while serving as judge, he was also elected town clerk of Sturgeon Bay. At that time, Wright was a faithful Republican and was reelected year after year. In 1871, he married Mrs. Ellen Bunten and the couple had four children. In 1879 he resigned from office and moved to the Fish Creek area where he became a farmer and left the Republican Party.

By this time Joseph Harris, Sr. had become Senator Philetus Sawyer's personal secretary and Sawyer's source of recommendations regarding political appointments, including keepers. In March 1883, E.S. Minor — a faithful Republican politician and well-known Sturgeon Bay businessman — sent Sawyer a letter marked "private and confidential" complaining that Harris was using his position either to punish his personal enemies or to reward his own very small circle of friends at the expense of the Republican Party in Door County. Probably to Minor's surprise and consternation, instead of responding to the letter himself, Sawyer asked Harris to answer it.

Harris wrote Minor defending his actions and also revealing the political nature of the appointment process for lighthouse keepers. Harris claimed that Wright's appointment rescued his wife and four children from suffering, even starvation, thus keeping them off county and town support. Second, according to Harris, the Republican Party was no more injured by getting Wright back into its ranks than it was when it took back Minor's friend Chris

Leonard and nominated him for the state assembly. Wright was a veteran, and he had served the party actively for years before being lured away by the Greenback infection. Minor had not objected to allowing Leonard back into the party and Wright's case was the same. Then Harris got to the crux of the matter. Minor wanted his friend Eli Thompson appointed keeper at the Pierhead Light, but Harris knew the position was not suitable for Thompson and his family because there was no keeper's dwelling at the station. Thompson was unwilling to leave his family in Sturgeon Bay and literally camp out at the new light, while Wright was willing to endure the conditions and leave his family on their Fish Creek farm.

To resolve the problem, Harris established a somewhat complicated arrangement with port collector Hall, who technically made the actual nomination of keepers to the Lighthouse Board. When the Sherwood Point Light was built and Henry Stanley had transferred from the Eagle Bluff Light to the Sherwood Point Light, if Thompson wanted to go to the Pierhead Light, Wright would go to Eagle Bluff; if Watson changed his mind and Stanley was not transferred, Thompson was to have his choice of either Sherwood Point or the Pierhead Light.

Harris told Minor that Wright understood the situation and would be ready to give up the Pierhead Light to Thompson whenever the change was made. By the time the Sherwood Point Light was built, a dwelling would undoubtedly also have been built at the canal, ready for Thompson's occupancy.

> No attempt was made to appoint Wright until Thompson was secure in getting a light. Collector Hall understands that 3 lights were to be built at Sturgeon Bay, one was for H.C. Graham [Dunlap Reef] one for Eli Thompson and one for Wright and I don't see that any injustice was done Eli because at

> the time of Wrights appointment Eli was Town Treasurer and is now County Treasurer and I understand from him that he was satisfied with the arrangement I had made.[6]

Keeper Wright exhibited the North Pierhead Light on 15 May 1882 for the first time. No provision for a dwelling had been made, and Wright lived aboard a canal company dredge that moved about in the canal and harbor. The harbor was an isolated spot, surrounded by unsettled land and with no road connecting it to Sturgeon Bay, four miles to the west. The waterway itself was the only route. Several days after Wright arrived at his post, a raging forest fire frightened his wife and family and threatened to burn his farm home near Fish Creek. Fortunately a heavy rain extinguished the fire.

In September 1882, Joseph Harris assured the *Advocate* that a permanent structure at the lake entrance of the canal would be built for the keeper the following spring, but the usually accurate Harris was incorrect. The canal company transferred 1.12 acres of land to the Federal Government for a station on the north side of the canal at the lake shore, but not until 1884; until that time, the government owned the breakwater piers and the Pierhead Light, but no property on shore. The piece of land (which was almost square) included a site that was reserved for a lifesaving station, which led to some confusion until the entire station passed to the Coast Guard in 1939.[7]

Once the canal opened, marine interests suddenly became aware of the fog that often blanketed the area of the canal, a natural phenomenon that until then had largely gone unnoticed; westerly winds that had been warmed as they passed over land frequently collided with air cooled by Lake Michigan to produce heavy fog banks that made it difficult for mariners to find the canal and harbor of refuge. Indeed, it proved hard enough for some captains to find the entrance to the harbor in clear weather. Twice in May 1883, ships hit the breakwater. In one incident, the elevated walk to the Pierhead Light was slightly damaged, but in the other, the schooner *Olga,* ran her jib boom into the lantern at about midnight, shattering three panes of glass and damaging the lens and lamp. Wright was ashore at the time and so was not injured; the next morning he rigged up a temporary light until permanent repairs could be made.[8] Sturgeon Bay maritime interests and canal company officials spearheaded a drive to secure a fog signal along with a coast light at the canal. They circulated petitions addressed to the Lighthouse Board at almost every port on the western shore of Lake Michigan and secured hundreds of signatures. In July 1883, the Board agreed to erect steam fog whistles at the canal similar to those in use at Milwaukee. The Board let a contract for the boilers, machinery, and building, and arranged for their delivery to Sturgeon Bay, though it was too late to begin work that season.

The lighthouse tender *Warrington* arrived from Detroit at the harbor of refuge on 20 May 1884 with superintendent Robert Miller, a crew of men, and the materials for the fog signal. The fog signal actually consisted of two separate buildings and sets of machinery, so that if one of the fog signals caught fire and was damaged there would still be a backup signal. When the planning began, the government had no site for the signal on land, and the engineers decided to locate the fog signal on the detached north pier, just inshore from the light tower. Each of the buildings was seventeen feet wide, thirty-two feet long, and twelve feet high. The wooden frames of the buildings were covered with corrugated iron, and corrugated iron roofs topped the structures, which were thought to be almost fireproof. The spaces between the studs were filled with a mortar made of lime and sawdust, and the interiors were lined with sheet-iron. Steam was generated in brick-enclosed metal boilers to power ten-inch whistles which could be heard, under favorable conditions, at a distance of eight to twelve miles. On 24 July 1884, the first whistle was successfully tested, but a shortage of bricks prevented completion of the other signal's boiler until the following year. The Lighthouse Board gave formal notice that Number 1 fog whistle at the North Pierhead Light would go into operation on 15 August 1884. The whistle sounded for five seconds followed by a thirty-five second interval of silence before sounding again.[9]

In recognition of the added responsibilities, the Lighthouse Board appointed Charles Oliver Chapman as Wright's first assistant. Chapman was born in Illinois on 10 April 1855. He moved to Baileys Harbor in 1873 and got a job as a helper on a stationary steam engine at a grist mill, and he later took the government exams and received his papers as a steamboat engineer. He moved to Sturgeon Bay and married Addie Davis on 10 April 1878; she was born in North Garland, Maine on 23 March 1861 and had moved to Sturgeon Bay in 1872. In Sturgeon Bay, Chapman became an engineer on several local tugs and was appointed first assistant keeper and engineer of the fog signal in July 1884. Chapman was too young to be a Civil War veteran, and the appointment recognized his steam-engineering experience, which was highly relevant to the job, given the complicated nature of the machinery at the fog signal. Chapman left his family in Sturgeon Bay and moved in with Wright at a boarding house that the canal company had built for its workers near the lake entrance to the canal. His appointment at the pierhead fog signal marked the beginning of a career in the lighthouse service that lasted until his death twenty-six years later.[10]

Once the fog signal went into operation, Sturgeon Bay residents suddenly became very aware of how often fog shrouded the entrance to the canal. From mid-August until the close of navigation in late December, the fog signal operated two or three days a week, and for several weeks it sounded every day. The fog signal was a valuable aid to mariners, but the *Advocate* noted that some nervous people compared "its melancholy wail to the call of a cow for her missing calf." A lady from Sevastopol who was visiting friends in Sturgeon Bay after being ill for several months became so upset when the fog whistle began blowing that she immediately left Sturgeon Bay for home. However, other residents found the sound of the fog signal reassuring.[11]

The Lighthouse Board had secured land from the canal company for a keeper's dwelling in 1884, but Congress did not appropriate funds for construction; construction had been slated for 1885, but no money was available. In May 1885, a work crew did come to the station after the schooner *Olga* again hit and damaged the Pierhead Light. During a severe storm in September, waves broke three windows and tore three shutters off the fog signal — the windows were sixteen feet above lake level and four feet back from the edge of the pier. In the same storm, driftwood broke several stanchions of the elevated walkway, and waves swept away three cords of kindling wood that had been piled outside the fog signal buildings.[12]

Congress finally appropriated $3,300 for a keeper's dwelling in 1886, and on 13 May 1886, the Lighthouse Board signed a contract with Francis Capel of Lakeside, Ohio to build the house. Leathem and Smith of Sturgeon Bay furnished the lumber for a two-story dwelling, and construction began in June and finished in October. A crew built a fence to enclose the station, laid wooden sidewalks around the dwelling and to the out-buildings, and tore down the old canal company boarding house located on the station. Thus, more than four years after completion of the Pierhead Light, the station finally had a keeper's dwelling, though Wright never moved into the new structure; the Lighthouse Board removed him as keeper on 2 October 1886.[13]

No reason for Wright's removal is given in the official record. According to the *Advocate*, Wright:

> was one of the most painstaking and efficient men in the service of the government. His removal will be regretted by the public.[14]

However, Wright's behavior became erratic if not bizarre after he left the light, and perhaps he had begun to act this way before he lost the keeper's position. Wright went back to his family in Fish Creek after his removal and soon began talking about moving to California to live permanently. He had two sisters living at Wright's Station, Santa Clara County, California, who urged him to join them. Wright went to California six weeks after leaving the light, leaving his wife and family alone in Fish Creek. Letters to friends indicate that he was enjoying California and suggested that he probably would not return to Wisconsin; however, in April 1888, sixteen months after he had left, he returned to Fish Creek. He remained with his family for a few months and told friends he expected to remove to Washington Territory, but instead he took a job teaching school on Washington Island. Between school terms in 1889, Wright visited Mr. and Mrs. William B. Lawrence of Sturgeon Bay. He missed breakfast on May 1, and, when Mrs. Lawrence called him for lunch, she found him gasping for breath on the bed. A doctor pronounced him dead of a burst blood vessel. After a service at the Congregation Church in Sturgeon Bay, he was buried in Bayside Cemetery.[15]

There was a great deal of construction activity at the Canal Station during 1886; in addition to putting up a keeper's dwelling, carpenters were building the long-awaited lifesaving station. In 1882, Harris once again used his influence to help local interests by persuading Senator Sawyer to introduce a bill calling for the Secretary of the Treasury to establish lifesaving stations at the entrance to the Sturgeon Bay ship canal and at Baileys Harbor. The bill passed, but no money became available until 1885. When the canal company transferred the land for the light station, an area measuring 100 feet square on the north bank of the canal at the lake was set aside for the lifesaving station. Apparently through a misunderstanding, the Life Saving Service took a plot measuring 100 feet by 200 feet; however, no trouble arose since there was still plenty of room for a lighthouse and both services were under the direction of the Secretary of the Treasury. During the spring and summer the two-story lifesaving station was built with its eight-foot slide for launching lifeboats; that building is the present US Coast Guard Station, though it has been remodeled and moved over the years. In late July 1886, the lifesaving station at the canal went into operation as Captain William Nequette finished selecting his seven-man crew of life savers.[16]

With completion of the livesaving station and the keeper's dwelling, in addition to various buildings owned by the canal company in the immediate vicinity, a population boom occurred. The lifesaving crew had to be readily available in case of an emergency, and many of the men built homes nearby, as did several canal workers and officials and at least one assistant keeper. By the spring of 1887, some forty persons resided in the area, and a school, a store, and more homes were built later, though after the turn of the century, the existence of a good road to Sturgeon Bay caused the community at the east end of the ship canal to all but disappear.

The Lighthouse Board promoted Charles O. Chapman from 1st assistant to keeper to replace Wright. Herbert Davis assisted Chapman, and most people thought he would be appointed first assistant keeper, but the Board appointed Robert Graham to the position. It seems that Eli Thompson was no longer interested in becoming a keeper. Graham was a Sturgeon Bay native who had moved to Egg Harbor two years previously to begin a fishing business. His appointment was a surprise to many, since he had not told anyone he was seeking the appointment. When navigation closed for 1886, Graham returned to Egg Harbor where he and his brother continued fishing. During the winter, Graham and James

Larson built a large iceboat to freight fish from Fish Creek to Menominee, Michigan; given the right conditions — favorable winds and good ice — they could make the trip in less than an hour. Unfortunately, an early spring thaw that year caused the ice to deteriorate before many trips were made.[17]

During 1887 a Lighthouse Board crew drove a well twenty-five feet deep near the dwelling to supply water for cooking and drinking. Water for the fog signals came directly from the lake. The Board also decided to change the 6th Order lens at the pierhead to a 4th Order upon delivery of a lens that they had ordered from France. Assistant Graham never had the opportunity to see if his iceboat would be a commercial success; the Board transferred him to the Grosse Point Light in Evanston, Illinois. Graham and his family left for Grosse Point in late October 1887, but he resigned his position as assistant keeper there in January 1889 to become second engineer at the Evanston water works.[18] The Board transferred William P. Rooney, acting first assistant at Pilot Island, to replace Graham. Apparently Rooney was unsatisfactory, as he never was promoted to permanent status and left the service in October 1888. On 21 November 1888 the Board appointed Henry Gattie second assistant at the canal station, an appointment that marked the beginning of a long and successful career as a keeper.

Several improvements were made during the 1890 season. Board crews built a boathouse measuring twelve feet by eighteen feet on the canal bank where the keepers could store and moor their boats and also filled in the grounds around the dwelling with dirt to cover the drifting sand at the mouth of the canal. They planted grass to hold the dirt in place. Heavy use of the fog signals began to cause equipment failures, despite the best efforts of Chapman and Gattie. One new whistle was installed in April, the second one was replaced in December. More and more vessels were using the canal, which shortened their voyages and allowed them to avoid the dangerous passage through Deaths Door to the north, but as traffic increased, so too did complaints that the North Pierhead Light was of not powerful enough and was placed too low. This is understandable, since it was originally designed to be a harbor light. Responding to the complaints, the Lighthouse Board recommended in 1890 that a new coast light, both taller and more powerful, be built on the shore near the keeper's dwelling. Cost of construction was estimated at $20,000, but, while the Congressional Committee on Commerce reported favorably on the recommendation, no further action was taken at that time.[19]

Before the winter of 1891–92, the light and fog signal had closed no later than January 1 and often earlier if ice had closed navigation before that date. The light then usually reopened in March or April when navigation resumed for the season. However, development of more powerful steel-hulled ships, especially the railroad car ferries, changed all that. At the time, the ferries usually docked in Kewaunee, south of Sturgeon Bay, but in January 1892 Chapman received orders to keep the station at the canal open. Many other Door County keepers were allowed to continue to extinguish their lights for the winter, but, from 1892 on, the lights at the canal operated all year long.

Fire was always a danger at the fog signal houses because of the wood-fired boilers, and both fog whistles were silenced in March 1892 when a fire broke out under the firebox of fog signal Number 1, followed two weeks later by an even more serious fire in fog signal Number 2. Number 1 was repaired a few weeks later, but the signals were not fully operational until January 1893 when a work crew from Detroit thoroughly overhauled them. The editor of the *Advocate* reported at that time that the work had been done so thoroughly that it was unlikely another fire would ever occur, but another fire did break out in September 1894 which required another visit from a district work crew.[20]

In February 1893, Congress approved the Lighthouse Board's recommendation to build a coast light at the canal, but again failed to appropriate money for its construction, though they did provide $103,000 to purchase the privately owned Sturgeon Bay ship canal from the Sturgeon Bay and Lake Michigan Ship Canal and Harbor Company. Government ownership meant an end to tolls and the advent of free passage for shipping, and traffic through the canal increased substantially. The US Army Corps of Engineers took over operation of the canal, and the Board again recommended building a coast light there in 1894. As part of routine maintenance work in 1894, a Board crew put hand railings on both sides of the elevated walk for its entire length, apparently for the first time, and the bridge connecting the elevated walk with the fog signal and light pier was rebuilt; also fog signal Number 1 received a new smokestack, and the wooden sidewalks around the keeper's dwelling were replaced.[21]

Keeper Chapman received additional responsibilities in 1896. The Corps of Engineers had assumed charge of three navigational lights the canal company had erected before they sold the canal to the government and operated the lights since 1893. The Corps now asked the Lighthouse Board to operate the lights, and the Board agreed on 6 April 1896.[22] Thus, Chapman and his assistants (in recognition of the increased workload, the Lighthouse Board authorized appointment of a second assistant) had to light the North Pierhead Light and the three canal lights each evening and also extinguish them and prepare them to be relit every morning. They also had to maintain and operate the fog signals day or night whenever visibility was restricted. Two weeks after the keepers received their new responsibilities, the Board transferred Henry Gattie and promoted him to keeper at the Baileys Harbor Range Lights, though this seems to have been an unrelated action.

Gattie's replacement at the ship canal was Charles Bavry, who had been born 8 May 1872 in Milwaukee but had come to

Door County shortly after his birth. He had been with the Corps of Engineers at the canal for two years previous to his appointment, and his appointment as first assistant keeper there was the opening chapter in a 30-year lighthouse career. The Board also appointed Michael Reagan, former owner and master of the schooner *Mary Ludwig*, as second assistant keeper, though Reagan quit in early August 1897, and the Board appointed Walter Lockhart to replace him.[23]

In March 1895, Congress approved $20,000 for construction of the coast light at the canal, but this was just another step in a long process that caused great impatience among those who used the canal. A crew made test borings in 1896 to determine whether a tower could be erected north of the keeper's dwelling, and lighthouse engineers decided to experiment with the design of the light. They planned a hollow steel tower eight feet in diameter surmounted by a watchroom and lantern; eight buttresses sixteen feet high provided the only support to the tower, as originally designed. The plan was so unusual that the Lighthouse Board built a brass working model of the light for their display at the US Exposition Building at Omaha, Nebraska. Another unusual feature of the proposed light was the use of curved glass from France in the lantern, thus preventing reflections from flat surfaces as the light flashed. Contracts were let for the various parts of the light during the summer of 1897.

On 13 May 1898, five years after Congress approved the light and three years after they appropriated the money, the lighthouse supply steamer *Amaranth* docked in Sturgeon Bay with construction materials for the station. Supervised by Mr. Todd, the construction crew began preparing the site. They first built the foundation for the tower, a block of concrete twenty-nine feet square and eight feet deep, in which they inserted anchor bolts two inches in diameter and seven feet six inches long. Next, they placed a cast-iron foundation disk on top of the concrete and bolted

Sturgeon Bay canal light station, 1898. Notice that there are not yet guy wires on the canal light at the left. Photo from the Annual Report of the Lighthouse Board, 1898.

it to the block. The area around the foundation was graded, and crushed rock was laid down to prevent erosion of the sand. Workers then began to erect the tower itself, which had ½-inch steel outer shell eight feet in diameter and a ⅜-inch steel inner shell, with a cast-iron spiral staircase built between them. Inside the inner shell was a space two feet in diameter in which hung the clock weights for the light. The tower was supported by eight buttresses, each of which was sixteen feet high and extended six feet out from the tower. On top of the tower, which was seventy-eight feet high, the workmen assembled a watchroom which was twelve feet in diameter and seven feet high. The lantern, measuring seventeen feet nine inches to the top of the ventilator ball by eight feet seven inches in diameter, was erected on top of that, and the lighting apparatus was installed. The lens was a third Order Fresnel lens, the same size as at Cana Island, built by Henri Le Paute of Paris, France. The eight-paneled lens rotated to produce a flashing light. The tower and watchroom were painted brown, while the lantern was black. On 3 October 1898, Todd accepted the light as complete, and the contractors received their final payments.[24]

Though it was not yet officially in operation, Chapman, with the approval of his superiors, exhibited the new light in mid-October 1898. It was immediately apparent that the Lighthouse engineers had made a serious blunder in the design of the light. They had not taken into account the winds in the area, and the winds caused the tower to vibrate so strongly that it affected the clock mechanism that rotated the lens, making the light flash at irregular intervals. After some study, Lighthouse officials decided to install guy wires to try to eliminate the vibration. In early December 1898, four cement blocks, each six feet square and with a large eye bolt, were sunk at the base of the tower, and steel guy wires with turnbuckles were strung from the tower to the eye bolts in the anchor blocks. The work was completed at the end of December; two weeks later the *Advocate* reported that the light-

Sturgeon Bay canal light, 1899; notice the braces and the cables designed to stabilize the tower against vibrations. Photo from the Annual Report of the Lighthouse Board, 1898.

house was "a construction failure." The heat of the sun on one side of the tower would cause the steel wire on that side to expand while wire in the shade on the other side of the tower contracted in the cold, causing the tower to list, and, when the turnbuckles were loosened to counteract the effect of the contraction and expansion, the wind again produced enough vibration to affect the clock works. The engineers went back to their drawing boards.[25]

However, vibrations or no, the Lighthouse Board gave official notice to mariners that the Sturgeon Bay Canal Light was operational on 17 March 1899. The 3rd Order lens exhibited an light that flashed alternately red and white, with an interval of ten seconds between flashes, and had a focal plane 107 feet above mean lake level. Two weeks later, one of the guy wires snapped with an explosive sound that startled those in the area; the differential between the rates of cooling of the tower and the guys caused the problem, and, though the broken guy was replaced, the vibrations continued. The revolving mechanism of the light worked, but the vibrations caused the clock's mechanism to malfunction. The light was designed to be seen at a distance of 18½ miles in clear weather, but captains soon began reporting that they had seen the flashes from 30, 40, or even more than 50 miles away. In June 1899, the Board appointed George F. Wright (no relation to Rufus Wright), whose parents had owned and operated Idlewild Resort near the Sherwood Point Light, as third assistant keeper.[26]

The new light soon became a source of interest and pleasure to those on land. Many people enjoyed either watching the light flash at night from Sturgeon Bay or actually going to the station to marvel at the height of the light and to watch its flash. However, the drive to the station was long and difficult, since there was no direct route. The *Advocate* soon began calling for a road to be built along the north shore of the canal for the convenience of those going to and from the station, but a major effort at the canal to widen and deepen the waterway took precedence.

The canal was 100 feet wide for its entire length when the government bought it. The project was to widen it to 160 feet at the lake end and to 190 feet at the bay end. Because the soil was sandy, a retaining wall had to be built as soon as the dredges completed their work. Widening the canal forced the engineers to jack up the two-story lifesaving station and move it back fifty feet to its present location, and also to shift the light located on land at the opening of the canal back away from the channel. The lighthouse station's boathouse also was moved back from the canal until the widening project was completed. But no road was built along the canal.[27]

During 1900 there was a great deal of activity at the canal station. A brick oil house with a capacity of 1,590 gallons was built to store oil for all the lights at the station. The 3rd Order light consumed about 1½ gallons of kerosene each night; together the five lights tended by Chapman and his assistants burned about 1500 gallons of kerosene a year. Perhaps the most noticeable change at the station was to paint the lighthouse tower glistening white, which made it one of the most prominent landmarks on the coast. When it was reddish-brown, the tower was easily lost in the background of trees during the day, and mariners complained that the white keeper's residence could often be picked out sooner by approaching vessels than the tower itself, though the tower was much taller. Painted white, the tower was an excellent daytime landmark. The tower continued to vibrate however. In September, the district lampist completely disassembled the illuminating and revolving mechanisms; he replaced everything except the lens itself. At the same time, carpenters installed wainscoting in the watch-room and put a sliding door in the opening from the tower stairs; the previous winter the keepers had had great difficulty staying warm in the watch room while on duty during the long winter nights. Keeping the small coal stove supplied with fuel was probably a more difficult job for the keepers than carrying kerosene up the stairs for the light; the stove burned seven tons of coal the first winter. To increase the light's visibility, the Lighthouse Board replaced the original 6th Order lens on the pierhead with a 5th Order lens, and two years later a new 5th Order lamp was installed in the lens.[28]

Walter Lockhardt, second assistant keeper, resigned his position in January 1902 to accept an appointment as heating plant engineer at a government building in Lapoint, Wisconsin; his new salary was $720 a year, almost twice his keeper's salary. Alphonse Gattie, brother of Henry Gattie, replaced Lockhardt for two years.[29]

The lighthouse engineers decided that attaching the steel guy wires to the watchroom rather than lower down on the tower might reduce the vibrations which still plagued the light. Workers made the change in 1902, but the problem continued. The crew also erected a windmill with a reserve tank over the station's well; only the Chambers Island Light had a similar windmill.

A survey of the station in 1902 revealed that the original open tower of the North Pierhead Light needed extensive repairs and that the fog signal houses and machinery also needed considerable work. Instead of spending the money to repair the deteriorating structures, the Lighthouse Board decided to build a new fog signal house combined with a light tower, and lighthouse engineers developed plans and specifications and let contracts for the new structure. In May 1903, George F. Wright and recently appointed John Meikle resigned their positions before work began. Wright became the engineer at Sturgeon Bay's east side public school. Alphonse Gattie was promoted to second assistant keeper and Frank Raduenz, from Algoma, was appointed fourth assistant.

The Board working party arrived at the station on 7 May 1903 to disassemble and bring ashore the fog signal houses and equipment. They temporarily moved the old light to the outer end of the pier and began putting in concrete footings and foundations for the new building. They next erected the metal work for the building's tower and deck; ¼-inch steel plate was then riveted to the twenty-four foot by thirty-three foot building. The three-story building had a hipped roof surmounted by a round light tower on its east end. On 18 July 1903 the upper portion of the old lantern and 5th Order lens were taken off the old tower and installed in the new structure. The tower was thirty-nine feet from its base to the top of the ventilator ball. Next the new fog signal boilers, smokestacks, tanks, pumps, and whistle valves were installed. After receiving three coats of paint (red, yellow, and finally white), and with all the equipment fully tested, the new Pierhead Light and fog signal was completed in early September 1903.[30]

The 1902 review of the Canal Station convinced the engineers that attempts to stabilize the coast light tower with guy wires had failed and that a new method of bracing was required. They decided to rebuild the structure almost completely and erected a six-legged steel skeleton tower with open lattice buttresses at the base. The original tower had borne the entire weight of the watchroom, lantern, and tower itself; under the new plan, its concrete base was enlarged and the tower became a cylindrical stair tower supporting the stairway alone. When the crew had finished the steel work on the pierhead, they turned to the erection of the six buttresses, the six legs of the tower, and the bracing between the legs. When complete, the open steel tower solidly supported the weight of the watchroom and lantern, and, once the new structure was finished, there was no noticeable vibration of the tower. A new clock had been ordered, but the old clockwork, troublesome in the past, now operated satisfactorily. Except for the color (which is now red), the pierhead light and the coast light appeared in the fall of 1903 much as they do today.[31]

Alphonse Gattie resigned his appointment as second assistant in 1903 and was replaced by Otto H. Schmiling. The Lighthouse Board transferred first assistant Charles Bavry to the

Pilot Island Light early in 1904 and appointed Carl Witzman to replace him. The last major structural change at the canal station occurred in 1904 when the keeper's dwelling was doubled in size to fourteen rooms. This provided two complete sets of living quarters and a single room for a third keeper, but the Chapman and Schmiling families filled the new dwelling. The Chapman's thirteen-year-old daughter lived at home, but their son Claude was an assistant keeper at the Sheboygan Light, but they had two boarders, a surfman from the lifesaving station and his wife. The Schmilings had two daughters under 2 years of age when they moved in; by 1912, when Schmiling left the canal station, two sons and another daughter had been born, so there must have been some lively times at the station.[32]

The first week of 1905, a severe winter storm with extremely high seas swept Lake Michigan. The waves washed completely over the breakwater piers at the station so that, at times, the water enveloped the new pierhead light building and there was concern that the structure would be swept off the pier and into the harbor. This did not occur, but waves damaged its exposed north and east sides. A work crew repaired the damage and installed a number of vertical steel beams to strengthen the building and prevent further damage in the future. The crew also replaced the elevated wooden walkway that ran from shore to the pierhead with a metal walkway.[33]

Christmas in 1906 was particularly joyful for keeper Chapman and his family. Shortly before Christmas, 20-year-old Claude had been transferred from Sheboygan back to the Canal Station as third assistant, which meant that all the Chapmans were once again together.

Life for keepers at the Canal Station settled into a familiar routine in the following years. Only minor repairs needed to be made at the station, and the lights and fog signal performed with

Sturgeon Bay canal light station and life-saving station (on the right), after 1903, since the new support structures on the light are in place. Photo courtesy of the Milwaukee Public Library/Wisconsin Marine Historical Society.

no significant problems under the faithful care of Chapman and his assistants. On 5 April 1909, Claude Chapman married Agnes Quam of Sturgeon Bay. However, in the fall of 1909, Charles Chapman became ill with what his doctor in Sturgeon Bay diagnosed as stomach cancer. February 1910 was the last time the well-known keeper in his familiar lighthouse keeper's uniform was able to visit his doctor's office on his own. He lingered until 26 May 1910, when he died at his canal home after a twenty-six year career as a keeper; he had spent his entire career at the canal station. Friends, family, and members of the local Masonic Lodge, Fraternal Order of Eagles, and Marine Engineers Beneficial Association attended the funeral, which was held at the station. Due to the difficulty of getting there, the mourners chartered the steamer *Sailor Boy* to bring them to the station from Sturgeon Bay. After the service, they accompanied the body back to Sturgeon Bay aboard the *Sailor Boy* and then to Bayside Cemetery for burial.[34]

To replace Chapman, Lighthouse officials transferred Charles Bavry (who had left the Canal Station for Pilot Island in 1904) from his assignment at Holland, Michigan, back to the Canal Station. Carl Witzman, first assistant, was transferred and Otto Schmiling was promoted to first assistant. Claude Chapman was promoted to second assistant, and Charles Kunter became third assistant. Two years later, when Schmiling was transferred, Chapman was promoted to first assistant, a position he held until 1925 when he became keeper of the Chambers Island Light. Kunter resigned in 1912, and the Lighthouse Bureau transferred John T. Trucker from Pilot Island Light. Trucker was willing to go from first assistant at Pilot Island to third assistant at the canal station so that his son Walter could go to school more easily. The Truckers remained at the Canal Station until 5 November 1916, when John was transferred to the Grosse Point Light in Evanston, Illinois.[35]

Charles Bavry remained as keeper at the Canal Station until 1922, when he was transferred to the Grand Haven Light south of

Muskegon, Michigan. In July 1926, he returned to the canal station where he had begun his career in the lighthouse service. On Saturday 19 March 1927, he climbed down from the watchroom in the tower at midnight, having completed his watch. He suffered a massive heart attack and died shortly after going to bed. At his funeral the following Wednesday, the six pallbearers were his fellow keepers: Claude Chapman and John Hahn from the canal station; C.W. Sanderson from Cana Island; William Cochems from Sherwood Point; Captain Alfred Hansen from the *Peshtigo Reef Lightship*; and Assistant Hanson from the *Eleven Foot Shoal Lightship*.[36]

The Lighthouse Bureau transferred Conrad Stram to the canal station from his assignment as the captain of the *Lansing Shoal Lightship*, where he had served since being shifted in 1918 from Cana Island. In 1931, the Bureau moved Theodore Grosskopf from Cana Island to the canal station; he remained there as first assistant for two years until his promotion to keeper of the Lansing Shoal Light. Grosskopf later moved to the Wind Point Light in Racine, where he replaced Henry Bevry. Stram remained at the canal station until 1 July 1933 when the Bureau transferred him to Sherwood Point upon the retirement of William Cochems. To replace Stram at the canal, lighthouse officials transferred Claude Chapman from the Chambers Island Light.

Claude Chapman's tenure at the canal station ended in tragedy less than five months later. On 4 November 1933, the government dredge *Kewaunee* and tug *Marinette* were moored in the harbor at the canal mouth, and the tug's captain, Palmer La Plante, went duck hunting that morning. Chapman went out to the *Kewaunee* to see the dredge's engineer. At 12:30 PM, as Captain La Plante was unloading his shotgun after the hunt, it discharged striking Chapman in the back at close range and killing him instantly. The coroner investigated the incident and declared the shooting accidental. On Wednesday 8 November 1933, Claude Chapman was buried near his parents in Bayside Cemetery.[37]

No new keeper was appointed until 1 April 1934. At that time the Lighthouse Bureau transferred John Trucker from Grosse Point back to the canal station, which he had left in 1916. At Grosse Point he had been appointed first assistant in 1917. When Oscar Knudson, former keeper at Cana Island, retired in 1930, Trucker had been appointed keeper at Grosse Point. Trucker was of slight stature, only five feet six inches tall, and a quiet private man. The *Bible* was often his companion while on watch at night, and he read it from beginning to end more than seven times. Like many keepers, he was very skilled at building things and making repairs, and he was also very adept at woodcarving. Trucker's son Walter lost his job during the Depression, and Walter, his wife, and two daughters moved in with his parents at the keeper's dwelling at the canal station in 1935.

Trucker's 5-year-old granddaughter Marilou often went with him when he climbed the tower stairs to wind the light's clock every night. While he wound the mechanism and polished the lens, he allowed her to go outside on the gallery to enjoy the view of the lake and surrounding countryside. She also sometimes went with him in the station boat as he lit the lights in the canal. During Door County's famous February blizzard of 1936, the road to the station was blocked and Marilou and her sister could not go to school. Their grandfather turned his carving skills to larger objects, fashioning several animals out of snow, including a horse and a dog large enough for the girls to sit on and imagine they were riding over the snow-covered landscape at the station. Marilou has vivid memories of the red snow that drifted by her bedroom window as the large white flakes were turned red by the alternating red rays of the coast light.

John Trucker (1881–1962) was keeper at the Sturgeon Bay canal light from 1934–1945.
Photo Courtesy of Marylou Trucker Sanders.

The two-story watch tower constructed by the Coast Guard at the very end of the canal also played a role in the young girls' lives. A coast guardsman kept watch there on activities on the lake and canal, and his duties included ringing out the hour and half hour on a large brass bell. He also sometimes rang the bell if the girls wandered too far down the beach or swam into deep water, alerting them that they had overstepped their boundaries. After living with the senior Truckers for three years, Walter found a new job, and the girls and their parents left the station, though they continued to return to the Canal Station during summer vacations until their grandfather retired.[38]

In 1939 the Coast Guard took over the operation of all of the country's lighthouses. Trucker elected to remain a civilian keeper until 1940. At that time he was given a rating of first class boatswain's mate, and he became a chief boatswain's mate in 1944. John Trucker was the last civilian keeper at the canal station. He retired in 1945 and spent his retirement years in Sturgeon Bay before dying on 18 January 1962 at age 80. He was replaced by John Hahn who had started his career as a civilian at Cana Island, but was then a chief boatswain's mate in the Coast Guard. Hahn was transferred 2½ years later, and Coast Guard personnel took over the operation of the canal station.[39]

The coast light and pierhead lights have been electrified and automated, and the steam fog signals have been removed from the North Pierhead Light structure, but the lights of the canal station still guide mariners to the Sturgeon Bay ship canal, and, in foggy weather, the electric fog signal still sounds for those on the lake. Alone among the Door County lights, the canal station is still manned by Coast Guard personnel.

Chapter 11
Sherwood Point Light

The Sherwood Point Light is at the end of a county road that follows a point as it hooks around Sawyer Harbor for several miles. When the lighthouse was built, there were few buildings near it, but today there are many driveways leading off to cottages and homes along the shore. There is no sign to direct you, but about halfway down the point, a road slightly larger than a driveway leads off to the left; at the end of it you arrive at the neatly mowed lawn of Sherwood Point Light. Several of the outbuildings are gone along with the beautiful keeper's gardens, but the signature lighthouse-shaped birdhouse and the familiar cement sideways remain just as they were when the keepers tended them. The dwelling and grounds are maintained by the Coast Guard, so it may be hard for casual visitors to realize that no keeper will emerge from the dwelling to greet them or to climb the tower to polish the lens in the lantern.

Like other preglacial valleys in Door County, Sturgeon Bay trends generally northwest to southeast. Sherwood Point lies on the northwest side of the body of water called Sturgeon Bay and curves around to the south to form Sawyer Harbor. As the city of Sturgeon Bay grew as a commercial center and port in the 1870s, it became clear that a lighthouse to mark the mouth of the bay was needed. The only light in the vicinity at that time was at Green Island, some fourteen miles to the north. In 1879, 160 vessels totaling 32,071 tons entered Sturgeon Bay, and, according to its promoters, the impending completion of the Sturgeon Bay ship canal promised to increase that traffic dramatically. They were right; in 1882, 3,050 vessels totaling 493,781 tons passed through the canal and bay.[1]

Even before the ship canal was completed, the Sturgeon Bay and Lake Michigan Ship Canal and Harbor Company reached an agreement with the Lighthouse Board that the government would construct and maintain a lighthouse at a location known as the "Wolf's Head" on Sherwood Point, provided that the company secured title to the proposed lighthouse site and conveyed it to the government. As early as March 1880, the Sherwood Point site had been selected. One of the chief figures in working out the agreement with the Lighthouse Board was Jesse Spalding, Chicago's port collector, the official who made recommendations regarding all keeper appointments in the district, and who was also president of the Canal Company.[2]

On 3 March 1881, Congress appropriated $12,000 to build a lighthouse at Sherwood Point, but the project could not proceed because the Canal Company had not secured clear title to the site. Peter Sherwood was the original owner of the point bearing his name; he died in 1867 leaving his wife Clarissa Sherwood as his sole heir. The company had not been able to locate Mrs. Sherwood, but they discovered that she had sold off the property, including the lighthouse site, to several different individuals. Eventually, Elias Haines came to own the site, though no satisfactory record of his title could be established and, in any event, the company and Haines could not agree on a price. The impasse was broken in March 1882, when legislation by the State of Wisconsin allowed the company to condemn the lighthouse site in return for paying an amount to be established by three court-appointed commissioners who were to estimate its value. Door County Circuit Court Judge George H. Meyers appointed Sturgeon Bay North Pierhead Light keeper Rufus M. Wright along with J.C. Pinney, and George Walker to undertake the process the appraisal.

The company expected the commissioners to finish their work quickly to allow construction of the lighthouse to begin, but the summer of 1882 came and went with no progress. In September of 1882, Joseph Harris, Sr. wrote from Washington, DC, predicting that construction would commence in a short time; plans for the lighthouse had already been prepared, and the building materials were ready to be shipped from the lighthouse depot in Detroit as soon as the matter of the title was settled. Harris doubted that the lighthouse could be constructed before the close of navigation, but he was sure that no time would be lost once construction began.[3] In fact, as early as February 1883, without a single brick having been laid, there was speculation that Henry Stanley would be transferred to Sherwood Point and that Emmanuel Davidson would be transferred to Eagle Bluff from Pilot Island.[4] Stanley eventually came to Sherwood Point, but Davidson was transferred to the light at Grand Haven, Michigan.

Finally, on 17 July 1883, Judge Meyers decreed that Elias Haines was the owner in fee simple of the lighthouse site, and the Sturgeon Bay & Lake Michigan Ship Canal and Harbor Company became the owner of the property in return for payment of $125.00, the value determined by the commissioners. The site consisted of 1.1 acres of land on the Green Bay (north) side of Sherwood Point as well as a long narrow strip across the point to Sawyer Harbor on the south side of the point for a landing and access to the lighthouse site. Once in possession of the property, the Canal Company transferred title to the Federal Government.[5]

The court did not act until July 1883, but the outcome was apparent before that date, and the lighthouse authorities gave the go-ahead to begin construction. The *Warrington* docked in Sturgeon Bay on May 9, having come from the Lighthouse Board Depot in Detroit, Michigan. The *Warrington* carried 40,000 bricks and other construction materials needed for the lighthouse including the lantern. Since Detroit was the source of the bricks, they were red rather than cream-colored, and Sherwood Point became the only lighthouse in Door County built of red brick; all the others were built of local limestone or of cream-colored Milwaukee brick. The captain of the *Warrington* secured a lighter to transfer the material to shore because Sawyer Harbor was too shallow for the steamer to enter and the shore at the lighthouse site was too steep and exposed for them to land materials there.

A crew of twenty men supervised by veteran builder Charles Dobson landed the supplies about half a mile from the actual site, cut a road through the woods from the landing, and cleared about an acre of trees at the site. Dobson then hired local teamsters to bring the construction materials from the landing, Clerk Doak to supply sand for the mortar from the excavation at the ship canal, and Edward Thomas, a local well-driller, to drill a well for the lighthouse. Considerable blasting was done to excavate the cellar from the limestone bedrock, and then the rubble was blasted again to provide rock for the foundation of the tower and dwelling. By 30 June 1883, only six weeks after supplies were landed at Sawyer Harbor, masons had laid a brick drain sixty feet long from the cellar to the edge of the bluff on Green Bay, had completed the stone foundation, and had begun laying the tower and dwelling brick. Thomas had drilled a well forty-two feet deep, lined it with iron pipe, and provided a hand pump.[6]

By the end of July the masons had completed work on the 1½-story dwelling and thirty-five foot attached square brick tower. By late August the dwelling was ready for occupancy, but the lantern's 4th Order Fresnel lens was not yet operational. On 20 September 1883, the Lighthouse Board officially transferred Henry Stanley from Eagle Bluff Light, where he had served since 1868 when the station opened, to Sherwood Point Light. Stanley did not actually turn Eagle Bluff over to his successor, William Duclon, until September 30, though Dobson had declared the new station complete two days before and left with his crew left to make repairs at the Cana Island Light.

Stanley officially exhibited the new light on 10 October 1883. In clear weather the light was designed to be visible for fifteen miles, with a focal plane that was sixty-one feet above the waters of Green Bay. Sherwood Point used a kerosene lamp, but the lens mechanism was much more complicated than the one at Eagle Bluff, where the light was a fixed white light that had no moving parts and all Stanley had to do was make certain the lamp stayed lit. At Sherwood Point the characteristic of the light was fixed white with an alternating red flash; a complex clock-work mechanism and revolving table in the lantern produced a fixed white light for 44½ seconds, followed by a 5½ second eclipse, then a 4½ second red flash, and a 5½ second eclipse before the cycle was repeated. The split-second timing meant that proper functioning of the clockworks was vital to the light's operation. Unfortunately, problems with the light soon developed which would plague the keepers for years.[7]

In a review of the records of the day, three themes stand out in the history of Henry Stanley's twelve years at Sherwood Point. First was the difficulty he had in getting the lighting apparatus to function, a problem that remained unresolved during his tenure. Second was his wife's poor health; hardly a year went by that Katherine did not suffer some serious illness, and she was often incapacitated for months at a time. In spite of her illnesses, the third theme was the seemingly endless stream of friends who came to visit the couple, along with an ever-increasing number of tourists, some of whom also became friends. Idlewild, a well-known resort, was close at hand, as were several campgrounds, and it was an easy ride from Sturgeon Bay for visitors staying there.

Shortly after they moved in, the Stanleys purchased a fine new buggy from a Sturgeon Bay merchant with which they made frequent trips to Sturgeon Bay, a distance of about nine miles by land, and Stanley later bought a sailboat that they also used to journey to Sturgeon Bay. The ease of transportation allowed Mrs. Stanley to become active in practicing her faith at St. Joseph's Catholic Church.

On 20 December 1883, the bay was frozen over, and Stanley extinguished his light for the season. Three days later Dr. F.L. Lewis, husband of their late daughter Elizabeth (see chapter on Eagle Bluff), came to the lighthouse to care for Mrs. Stanley, who had fallen seriously ill. Dr. Lewis left five days later after spending Christmas with the Stanleys. Father Blume of St. Joseph's Church called at the lighthouse after learning of the serious nature of Mrs. Stanley's illness, and Dr. Hendricks, a local doctor, visited the station five weeks later to attend to Mrs. Stanley, but with inconclusive results.

On January 27, Henry left the station to take Katherine to Dr. Lewis in Fort Howard and stayed with his wife for several weeks before returning to Sherwood Point in late February. He exhibited the light for the season on April 24 by himself, since Katherine did not come back until May 7, after almost 3½ months away. In July, Dr. Lewis and his new wife spent a week with the Stanleys, a visit that combined a vacation with business, since Mrs. Stanley became ill once again. Apparently her condition did not improve; on August 29 three of Dr. Lewis's friends and colleagues, two from Green Bay and one from Chicago, came to Sherwood Point and took Mrs. Stanley back with them to Green Bay where "a difficult and dangerous surgical operation was performed on her in a successful manner."[8]

Mrs. Stanley returned to the light on September 17, but she required further surgery on October 12 and did not return again until November 15. The *Advocate* reported in mid-December that

> Mrs. Henry Stanley is rapidly recovering from her terrible illness, and her friends expect to see her abroad again before many weeks elapse. She has had a long siege of sickness while the pain she has had to endure much of the time has been agonizing.[9]

Katherine had recovered sufficiently by February 1885 to visit occasionally with friends when her husband drove to Sturgeon Bay. Unfortunately there was no hint of what her health problem was, and it should be remembered that she was not this ill continually.

On 22 May 1884, a month after Stanley displayed the light for the season, the *Warrington* stopped to resupply the station and brought a machinist to overhaul the failing machinery for the light. The machinist put things in working order, but the mechanism gave out again shortly after he left. Stanley hired a clockmaker from Sturgeon Bay who was able to restore it to working condition, and on June 24 the lighthouse inspector made an official visit accompanied by the district lampist, who inspected the lamp and found everything in good order. However, only five days later, the clockworks broke down yet again and had to be overhauled by the local clockmaker. It broke down once more in July. That time, however, after being repaired, the mechanism continued to operate until the end of the navigation season in December.

On 24 August 1884, Stanley recorded in his log an event with great significance for the future — Miss Minnie Hesh, Mrs. Stanley's 21-year-old niece, arrived at Sherwood Point from Brooklyn, New York. After Minnie's parents died, her aunt and uncle invited the young lady to live with them at the lighthouse. Minnie had accompanied her aunt while she was in Green Bay due to illness that fall. In addition, she helped her uncle perform routine duties around the station and was particularly helpful when the clockwork mechanism broke down and the light had to be operated by hand. Shortly after she arrived, Minnie began to make many of the entries in her uncle's log. Officially, entries in the station's log were the responsibility of the keeper, but the inspector did not object to the situation. Except for several differences in spelling and Minnie's occasional references to "Auntie" instead of "Mrs. Stanley," her entries were almost indistinguishable from her uncle's.

Minnie was similar in age to their late daughter and fit easily into the station's routine and into the life of her new family.

Entries in the log record large numbers of visitors that came to Sherwood Point. By the late 1800s, Door County was already a popular vacation spot. After the completion of the ship canal, regular steamship connections to Milwaukee and Chicago, as well as to other Lake Michigan ports, made it possible for vacationers to travel easily, cheaply, and quickly to Sturgeon Bay, Fish Creek, Ephraim, Sister Bay, and Washington Harbor.

As mentioned above, one of the popular spots in the Sturgeon Bay area was the Idlewild Resort Hotel run by Mr. and Mrs. Wright and located only a short distance from the light station on Sherwood Point. Adjoining the hotel was a large campground which was the scene of camp meetings during the summer. Walking over to pay a call on the Stanleys was a popular pastime for those at Idlewild, and visitors staying in Sturgeon Bay often came by boat to spend the day at Idlewild and to visit the lighthouse. For example, for one day in August 1887, the log contains the names of thirty visitors who came from Waupun, Oconto, and Fort Howard, Wisconsin; from Chicago, Illinois; from Omaha, Nebraska; from St. George, New Brunswick; from New York City; and from Louisville, Kentucky.

A second group of visitors was the many friends the Stanleys had developed over their years in Door County. Their friends apparently found it very easy to pay a call on the popular couple and their niece.

A third group were relatives of the Stanleys. Mrs. Stanley's brother and his wife spent several months with them, as did an uncle of Mr. Stanley, and other family members came for shorter periods of time. Henry's job kept him at his post, so relatives traveled by train to Chicago or Milwaukee and then by boat to

Sturgeon Bay. The Stanleys also continued to maintain both a close personal and a professional relationship with Dr. Lewis and his family. They had no grandchildren of their own, and the Stanleys were pleased when Robert and Helen Lewis came to visit, referring to them as their grandchildren. The tradition of an early spring surprise party that had been so popular at Eagle Bluff was also instituted at Sherwood Point. On 18 March 1885, twenty-one people in two sleighs made the five-mile trip over the ice from Sturgeon Bay, and such a happy time was had by all that the guests did not start back until nearly three in the morning. On the way home, the lead sleigh ran out of the track and tipped over in deep snow, burying the occupants in a drift. However, those in the second sleigh dug them out, and the partygoers returned without further incident, arriving in Sturgeon Bay after four in the morning.[10]

In summer, small sailboats and launches replaced sleighs as the means of transportation. Stanley himself had an eighteen-foot sloop built for the family's use. But, despite all the company and Katherine's illnesses, Henry still had his job as light keeper to perform. In April 1885 a work crew came to build a covered entrance to the dwelling and to lay wooden sidewalks between the buildings at the station. The men also cleared and graded the area around the lighthouse and, together with the Stanleys, planted grass, shade trees, and other shrubbery on the grounds. In September, another work crew built a boathouse at the station dock on Sawyer Harbor.

Unfortunately, the lighting apparatus continued to be troublesome. Responding to Stanley's requests, district lampist Crump came to Sherwood Point in September 1886 to overhaul the machinery that caused the light to revolve. Crump spent a week working in the tower, and the apparatus was apparently in good working order when he left since it operated satisfactorily for the rest of the season. Also in September, Mrs. Stanley left to visit friends in Chicago. Minnie Hesh joined her there after several weeks, and the two women went on to New York City to visit relatives. Mrs. Stanley returned after a three-month absence on 19 December 1886, but Minnie did not return until May 1887 after an absence of more than eight months. During the winter of 1886–87, for the first time since moving to Sherwood Point the Stanleys did not stay at the lighthouse for the winter; instead, they lived in the upper story of Mr. and Mrs. Eli Thompson's new home in Sturgeon Bay. The Thompsons were friends and frequent visitors at the lighthouse; indeed, Thompson had at one point been discussed as a potential keeper at Sherwood Point. While visiting friends that winter in Green Bay, Mrs. Stanley once again fell ill and stayed in Green Bay from late January until early March.

After this illness, the year went quite smoothly for the Stanleys. Minnie returned from her visit to the east coast, large numbers of visitors came to the lighthouse, evenings were spent playing cards at Idlewild, and the light continued to operate. Among their visitors were Mr. and Mrs. Joseph Harris, Jr. from Dunlap Reef, Mrs. William Sanderson and her daughter from Cana Island, and Mrs. Hanson from Green Island. Unfortunately, the clockworks stopped twice during the night of August 2, and Stanley was unable to solve the problem. Beginning in September the log entries repeat themselves monotonously, day after day: "The clock stopped during the night;" "The clock stopped three times last night;" "The clock stopped repeatedly last night." From September 1 to November 1, the clock stopped at least once on roughly half the nights. It became necessary for the Stanleys and Minnie to divide the night into regular watches and to operate the light by hand, if necessary, to prevent it from becoming stationary or even going out. The *Advocate* warned mariners that

> in the event of anything appearing wrong with the light it is due to the fact that the machinery is not in proper working order. This light has been a cause

> of much trouble to Capt. Stanley ever since it was established on account of something being wrong with the machinery.[11]

After repeated requests, the Lighthouse Board notified Stanley that, after the close of navigation, Mr. Crump would again be sent to overhaul the apparatus. The Stanleys moved to Sturgeon Bay after spending Christmas at the lighthouse, but on 21 January 1888 went back to the station so that Henry could assist Mr. Crump as he performed a complete overhaul of the lighting apparatus. Crump left ten days later, and the Stanleys moved back to Sturgeon Bay for the rest of the winter. Despite Mr. Crump's expertise, Stanley feared that the mechanism would not operate satisfactorily when the navigation season opened.

To save money, in 1888 the Lighthouse Board made the keepers responsible for painting and minor maintenance at their stations. Stanley now spent most of April cleaning, painting, and repairing the tower, dwelling, boat, boathouse, woodshed, privy, and fence at Sherwood Point. Fortunately, it seems that Stanley's apprehension about the success of Crump's work was unfounded, as the light worked all season without a problem. In fact, 1888 passed very smoothly for the Stanleys. Katherine's health was good and many visitors continued to pay their respects. Among the visitors was a dear friend, Miss Ula D. Noble, who had been one of the closest friends of Elizabeth (their late daughter) and had often stayed with the Stanleys at Eagle Bluff. Though highly regarded as an excellent teacher, she had left teaching to attend the Chicago School of Pharmacy and then returned to work toward becoming a pharmacist at H.G. Hildebrant's drug store in Sturgeon Bay. Another visitor was Dr. Lewis's wife, who brought their baby son Frank to spend a week at the lighthouse. A three-man working crew arrived at the station on 9 November 1888 to build a brick wall dividing the basement into two separate rooms so that the kerosene and other supplies for the light could be stored apart from other items and goods. That work took the crew two days to complete. Once again, the Stanleys moved into Sturgeon Bay with the closing of navigation on 1 January 1889.

Navigation reopened on 8 April 1889, and Stanley spent his spring cleaning and painting. The clockworks operated without stopping, and the Stanleys enjoyed a good year. A special occasion for them occurred on 22 August 1889 — the marriage of Minnie Hesh and William Cochems. From the time Minnie Hesh had come to live with the Stanleys five years before, she had proved to be a very personable and popular young woman who developed many friends among the area's young people. One of these friends was William Cochems, and their friendship had deepened into love.

Cochems, age 23, was the second son of Mathias Cochems, a prominent and successful Sturgeon Bay businessman. William was born 8 April 1866 in Mishicot, Wisconsin, fifty miles south of Sturgeon Bay, and his parents moved to Sturgeon Bay the same year. Mathias Cochems was a miller, but soon shifted to commerce and operated a large general store in downtown Sturgeon Bay. Stanley recorded in his log:

> August 22 — a wedding occurred at this Station. The event was the marriage of William Cochems of Sturgeon Bay and Miss Minnie Hesh of Sherwood Point our niece.

Stanley exaggerated slightly, since the wedding actually took place on the lawn of the Idlewild Resort. Over a hundred friends and relatives gathered to witness the ceremony performed by a local Congregational minister. After the vows were spoken, the guests moved into Idlewild's large dining room where they enjoyed an elaborate wedding feast followed by a pleasant afternoon on the grounds with the newlyweds. On their return from their wedding trip, the couple moved into their new home on Lawrence Street in

Sturgeon Bay; the Stanleys were welcomed in their stay there the following winter when they left Sherwood Point. In August 1889, Melvin Haines, who along with his wife was a frequent guest of the Stanleys, subdivided a large area of land he owned near the lighthouse into lots for summer cottages. The Stanleys bought land from their friend and eventually built several cottages on their property.[12]

In 1890 the Lighthouse Board decided that a more suitable landing, including a landing crib and stairs, should be built in front of the Station on the bay itself. Up to this time, the lighthouse tender bringing supplies had to steam around Sherwood Point and anchor off the mouth of Sawyer Harbor in deep water before launching a small boat to ferry the supplies more than a mile to the landing and boathouse. Once on land, the supplies had to be transported another half mile through the woods to the lighthouse, a process that took four or five boat trips and as many hours to complete. The only suitable place for a landing on the bay side of the station was privately owned, but, happily, the owner was willing to sell the required triangular quarter-acre of land adjacent to the extreme northeast corner of the station. In August 1890, the Lighthouse Board paid $100 for the property — $25 for the land and $75 for the legal fees. A work crew then built a stone-filled wooden land crib and a stairway down the steep cliff to the crib. The landing and boathouse on Sawyer Harbor were not abandoned, however, because the station's boats could not be kept at the new landing, which was too exposed for a permanent mooring.

The clockworks failed repeatedly in 1890, and Stanley again began to record in his log how many times each night the clock stopped. Minnie was married and no longer living at the lighthouse, so only Henry and Katherine were available to take turns minding the mechanism. After another visit by lampist Crump, the *Advocate* reported that the clockwork could not be made to work satisfactorily and would be replaced by the Lighthouse Board at a cost of $400. The editor commented that Stanley had

> had no end of trouble since entering on his duties down there to make the thing work at all times, it being frequently necessary for him or an assistant to move the machinery by hand. This is not a very desirable job during the fall of year when the nights are twelve or more hours long.[13]

But, unfortunately, the editor was wrong about the replacement of the machinery; it would be another eight years and countless stoppages later before the Lighthouse Board finally acted.

Except for their problems with the clockworks, the Stanleys enjoyed an uneventful 1891, though the Lighthouse Board did build a new woodshed at the station.

The following year, however, a substantial change occurred. In clear weather, the white and red lights from the tower were a significant aid to mariners entering Sturgeon Bay, but in foggy weather the lighthouse was of little help, and so the Lighthouse Board decided to install a fog signal at Sherwood Point. Rather than a horn or siren, which would have been more expensive both to install and to operate, they decided to use a fog bell struck by a mechanically operated hammer. On 23 May 1892, a lighthouse employee arrived to begin construction of a square-based pyramidal tower in front of the lighthouse on the cliff above the water; only five weeks later on July 1, the structure was complete, the bell machinery had been installed, and the signal was ready for use. The rectangular shed presently attached to the fog signal tower was added later to house radio transmission equipment. During foggy weather, the bell, located on the outside of the tower, was struck a single stroke every 12 seconds. A wooden sidewalk was laid between the tower and the dwelling.[14]

Sherwood Point light and fog signal tower, midwinter 1910; note the large bell which was used as the fog signal. Photo Courtesy of Lee Traven.

William and Minnie Cochems regularly visited Sherwood Point, and they often brought their son Stanley, who had been born 18 August 1890. During this period, William Cochems had a number of different jobs. In September 1892, he and Andrew Koch formed a partnership to open a hardware store in Bayview, now the west side of Sturgeon Bay. Koch borrowed money from his father and Cochems got a loan from his uncle John.

After spending the winter in Sturgeon Bay, during which time Katherine was ill for over a month, the Stanleys returned to Sherwood Point in early April 1893. In the decade since they arrived at the new lighthouse, they had spent a great deal of time and effort improving the grounds, and the beauty of the station was one of the attractions for many visitors.

> One of the most beautiful and sequestered spots to be found in this region is in and about the lighthouse premises down at Sherwood Point. Capt. Stanley and his wife, thro' years of unremitting toil, have succeeded in making the place a veritable Eden.[15]

In June 1893 tragedy struck the family of Dr. Lewis. Mrs. Stanley was called to Green Bay because of the death of

> her dear friend, the wife of Dr. Lewis. . . This is the third time the Dr. has been called upon to mourn the death of his wife, the second being the only daughter of Mr. and Mrs. Stanley.[16]

As the Panic of 1893 and the ensuing depression gripped the country, business began to slow in Door County, bringing hard times to William Cochems and his wife. Late in the summer, Koch withdrew from his partnership without repaying his father's note; when it came due, Koch's father tried to collect from Cochems. In

September, Cochems was appointed Postmaster at Sawyer, but sales continued to decline at his hardware store, and, when creditors pressed him for payment, the store was seized by the sheriff, and the matter entered the courts. In May 1894, William Cochems, a victim of the Panic of 1893, finally settled with his creditors for fifty cents on the dollar, ending his business career. Perhaps his father's business was in difficulty too, because Mathias Cochems seems to have made no effort to assist his son. Compounding his problems, Cochems resigned his postmaster's position in July 1894, and Minnie gave birth to a daughter, Alice Louisa, on 6 August 1894.[17]

Fortunately for the new father, his wife's uncle came to his aid. Perhaps because he was now over 70, Stanley persuaded his superiors to allow him to hire a laborer to assist him at the lighthouse. Laborers were not appointed, but rather were simply hired by the keepers. On 27 September 1894 Stanley officially hired William Cochems as a laborer, and he and his family moved to the Sherwood Point Light. Laborers had little or no security, so Stanley next worked to convince the district inspector and, in turn, the Lighthouse Board that the Sherwood Point Station should have an assistant keeper for the first time in its history. He succeeded, and on 11 November 1894 the Board appointed William Cochems acting assistant keeper at a salary of $400 per year. After the difficulties of the recent past, the appointment virtually guaranteed a secure future for the Cochems family.[18]

During the winter of 1895, Henry Stanley became seriously ill for one of a very few times in his life, and there was even concern that he might die. He recovered sufficiently to return to his post in April 1895 when the navigation season opened, but his health remained delicate. On May 7 the Lighthouse Board promoted Cochems to assistant keeper. On October 13, there was a stark entry in the station's log:

> Mr. Henry Stanley Keeper of the Sherwood Point Light Station expired Oct. 13th 1895 at 8:20 AM.

Two days later, a large group of friends gathered at St. Joseph's Catholic Church for Henry Stanley's funeral.[19] His death surprised many who had expected him to outlive his wife, considering her numerous bouts with illness. Henry Stanley had become a lighthouse keeper in 1868 at the age of 45, and he spent the last twenty-seven years of his life tending in succession two Door County lights, Eagle Bluff and Sherwood Point. At both of them he was the first keeper.

Stanley's death posed the problem of who should become the new keeper. In such cases another keeper or experienced assistant usually would be transferred to the vacant post. Eight days after Stanley's death, district inspector Captain Dayton visited Sherwood Point, and William Cochems, supported presumably by his wife and Katherine Stanley, must have made an extremely good impression on the inspector. Cochems was promoted to keeper on 27 October 1895, and at the same time, in an even more surprising action for an agency with a reputation for rigidly following strict procedures, the Board appointed Mrs. Katherine Stanley assistant keeper at Sherwood Point. At the time, there was no pension plan for keepers or assistants, and in some ways this extremely welcome action was more a pension than a wage paid for work done. Minnie actually did more of the assistant's work than her aunt did.[20]

After her husband's death, Katherine Stanley spent winters in Sturgeon Bay with friends and summers at Sherwood Point. She continued to suffer from various illnesses and was hospitalized both in Milwaukee and in Stoughton, Wisconsin for periods of time. While visiting friends in Green Bay, she and a friend were thrown from their carriage through a barbed wire fence; fortunately, though the heavy fur coat she was wearing was ruined, she suffered only cuts and bruises. On 24 June 1898 Mrs. Katherine Stanley resigned her appointment as assistant keeper.

After that she made numerous trips, including one of four months to Brooklyn, New York. However, she spent enough time in Sturgeon Bay to meet a fellow member of St. Joseph's Church, a widower named Frank Barnhardt, whom she married on 10 October 1901. Barnhardt had been born in Silesia in 1833 and had come to America, married in 1856, and settled on a farm near Forestville, south of Sturgeon Bay. He and his wife had twelve children, but in 1897 his wife died, leaving him alone on the home farm for four years. Immediately following the ceremony, the couple took the train to Niagara Falls, New York. The Barnhardts lived in Sturgeon Bay until Katherine died 12 November 1915, twenty years after the death of her first husband. Frank Barnhardt died the following year on November 25. His grave is on one side of Katherine and Henry's is on the other in St. Joseph's Cemetery in Sturgeon Bay.[21]

The daily routine of the new keeper — tending the light and maintaining the buildings and grounds — continued unchanged from the time of Stanley's tenure, as did the erratic behavior of the clockwork apparatus in the lantern. Like the Stanleys, the Cochems received a steady stream of visitors, especially relatives. Even though Mathias Cochems had not helped his son when his hardware store failed, there seems to have been a good relationship between father and son, and William's parents were frequent visitors at Sherwood Point.

William was one of twelve children, and his brothers and sisters also paid calls at the light, though one of these visits ended in tragedy. Thomas Reynolds and William's younger brother Edward skated out to the lighthouse in January 1897. On their way home, using skate sails, they were unable to avoid a thin spot in the ice and plunged through into the water. Edward was able to crawl out of the water onto the ice, but could not save his companion from drowning.[22] William also had aunts and uncles in the area who enjoyed coming to the light.

As time went on and Door County became an increasingly popular tourist destination, lighthouse visitors came from farther and farther away, though the most frequent visitors, the Melvin Haines family, came from right next door. There were two differences between this new tenure and that of the Stanleys, however; the keeper's wife was a healthy young woman, and, since they had sold their home in Sturgeon Bay, the Cochems stayed at Sherwood Point year round for many years rather than leaving in the winter.

A six-man Lighthouse Board crew came to Sherwood Point in November 1897 for a week; they erected a new fifty-foot cedar flag pole, put a new chimney in the dwelling, and also installed a new roof. The district lampist ordered Cochems to ship the entire illuminating apparatus to the district repair depot in Detroit when the season ended 29 December 1897. Workers in Detroit found the apparatus unrepairable and discarded everything except two flash panels. They shipped Cochems an up-to-date, ball-bearing apparatus consisting of the 1880 Fresnel lens formerly in use at the Passage Island Light in Lake Superior along with a new pedestal, revolving table, clock, bearings, and service table. The district lampist came to Sherwood Point on 23 March 1898 to set it up and adjust it, and from then on the light operated without further problems. In May the lampist returned and installed a new 4th Order incandescent oil vapor lamp (IOV).[23]

With Katherine Stanley's resignation as assistant keeper on 24 June 1898, Minnie Cochems was appointed probationary assistant keeper, and her position was made permanent 7 February 1899. The Lighthouse Board was chronically short of funds, so why they appointed an assistant at a station that had opened in 1883 and functioned until 1894 without one is not clear. Perhaps because of the addition of the fog signal, but, for whatever reason, both William and Minnie now had secure government appointments.

Through the years, life was good for the keeper and his family at Sherwood Point. Their lives centered around keeping the light and all that that entailed, including sounding the fog signal when necessary and maintaining the station, but there was also time for other pursuits. Cochems was an avid fisherman and also enjoyed hunting ducks and birds in the largely unpopulated Sherwood Point area. In 1900 he received from the Lighthouse Board a new eighteen foot sailboat built by former keeper Joseph Harris. For a while after the turn of the century, Cochems owned a twenty-five foot gasoline-powered launch that he used to carry passengers between Sherwood Point and Sturgeon Bay. In 1902 a crew finally built a fireproof oil house at the station, and the kerosene was moved out of the front cellar. Two years later a crew replaced the wooden walks at the station with concrete ones.

Stanley and Alicia Cochems grew up at the Sherwood Point. Stanley moved away after his marriage, but Alicia married Phillip Overbeck, the son of a well-known local family, and remained in Door County. After her marriage, the Cochems began spending winters in Sturgeon Bay with the Overbecks.

No major shipwrecks occurred near the station, although in later years, Cochems liked to tell of a boatload of seven "Zionist" men and three women from Marinette and Menominee who went ashore west of the light on the evening of 7 September 1907. A northerly wind blew their sloop up on the rocks.

> We took the whole party, dripping wet from the spray, into the lighthouse to get dry clothing and warm up by the fire. . . . Later they held a prayer meeting and wanted me to join them, but I refused to be "converted."[24]

The next morning a crew from the Sturgeon Bay Life Saving Station released the sloop and took it back to Sturgeon Bay for repairs.

The Cochems bought a car, and, as roads improved, it became easier for them to get into Sturgeon Bay to shop, get groceries, and participate in community activities. Minnie became especially active in Eastern Star and the Ladies Aid Society of Hope Congregational Church. The Cochems took great pride in the appearance of the station, and William several times received commendations from the inspectors for how well-maintained the station was. Of special pride was a sunken flower garden that was dug out by hand. There was also a vegetable garden and several varieties of fruit trees. The gardens were enclosed in whitewashed fences.

A favorite spot for visitors to the lighthouse was the so-called Lover's Leap. The waves had eroded a weaker layer of the limestone cliff on the bay shore in front of the lighthouse, leaving a large slab of rock jutting out over the water. According to tradition, the formation was named for a young Indian couple who leaped into the water below and drowned because they had been forbidden to marry. Visitors could rest in the cool shade under the overhanging rock, and the Sturgeon Bay High School class of 1912 held their class picnic under Lover's Leap on June 20. A few hours later, Cochems was awakened from sleep by what he thought was a large explosion. However, when he went outside the next morning, he discovered that Lover's Leap had collapsed on the rocks below. No one was injured, but had it happened a few hours earlier the results would have been tragic.[25]

Minnie Cochems reached her 65th birthday on 4 August 1928 making her eligible to retire and receive a pension. However, she was in good health and happy with her position, so she continued working. After her birthday, the Cochems' son Stanley came from New York City with his wife and one son to visit at the lighthouse. As Minnie Hesh Cochems was getting out of bed the morning of 17 August 1928, she collapsed and died of an apparent heart attack. A large number of friends and family gathered at the Overbeck's home for her funeral before her burial in Bayside Cemetery, Sturgeon Bay.[26] In tribute to his wife, Cochems placed a marker in their beautiful garden east of the lighthouse with a metal plate inscribed:

In Memory of Minnie Hesh Cochems
Assistant Light-Keeper, 1898-1928

Stanley Cochems served temporarily as his father's assistant, but this was only a short-term arrangement, and Stanley and his family soon left for their home in New York City. Lighthouse Bureau officials were unwilling to continue paying an assistant keeper, but they did allow Cochems to hire a laborer. Cochems had heard from a friend about Alfred and Eunice Schopf who were taking care of a farm and orchard near Egg Harbor, and he hired them. Alfred helped with the painting and other maintenance chores, while Eunice did the housework and cooked meals. On several occasions when the fog bell mechanism broke down, Alfred hit the bell with a hammer to warn mariners. The Schopfs also took care of several nearby cottages that Cochems had inherited from the Stanleys, Cochems paid them for that work himself.[27]

William Cochems decided to retire on 1 July 1933 at age 67, two years after he first became eligible for retirement but three years shy of compulsory retirement age. He and Clifford Sanderson of Cana Island retired at the same time in order to provide openings for keepers at two stations that were being automated. Cochems had the distinction of spending his entire career — almost 39 years — at Sherwood Point. Some other keepers had longer service records, but no other Door County keeper served so long at a single lighthouse. Upon retirement, Cochems made his home for a number of years with his daughter and son-in-law, Mr. and Mrs. Phillip Overbeck. In 1950 he moved to Los Angeles, California to live with his son Stanley. He died in Los Angeles on 4 August 1953 and was buried in Bayside Cemetery, Sturgeon Bay.[28]

The Lighthouse Bureau transferred Conrad Stram from the Sturgeon Bay Canal Light, where he had served for the past six years, to replace William Cochems at Sherwood Point. With his wife Elnora and their two children, Matthew and Hazel, Stram moved into the lighthouse in July. Alfred and Eunice Schopf continued working at the station for the rest of the season, but when Schopf asked Stram about continuing to work for him, Stram responded that he did not know whether he would be allowed to hire a laborer. He said he would not be surprised if an assistant was appointed; he had learned that the fog bell tower was going to have some work done on it so that it could accommodate the control apparatus for the Peshtigo Reef Light ten miles to the northwest. Stram also told Schopf that if he did not get an assistant, he planned to hire Ray Dier, Stram's brother-in-law, since he had been unable to find a job due to the Depression.[29] Stram did in fact hire Dier, but in 1935 an assistant keeper was appointed at Sherwood Point.

In 1935, modern technology began making a major impact at Sherwood Point. Most other Door County lighthouses continued to operate much as they had in the 19th century — most had phones, but electricity was available at only a few — but at Sherwood Point, several innovations helped to update functions of the lighthouse, including the installation of electricity and of running water.

Electricity was necessary because a radio room was established in an addition to the fog signal tower; Sherwood Point was the only station in the county to have a radio broadcasting facility. Four times a day, Stram was to contact the Milwaukee

Breakwater Light and the lighthouse tender *Hollyhock* by radio telephone. He also broadcast daily weather reports at 10:20 AM and 10:20 PM by short wave radio. In addition, the keepers maintained radio watches, monitoring for distress and emergency calls. Also, electric fog horns had replaced the bell in the fog signal tower.

However, technological innovation meant increased duties for some keepers. In 1935, the Lighthouse Bureau installed an acetylene gas system controlled by a sun valve at the Green Island Light, southeast of Marinette-Menominee and fourteen miles northwest of Sherwood Point. Responsibility for maintenance of this station was assigned to the Sherwood Point keepers; they were expected to visit Green Island once a month if the light was operating normally, but they had to go immediately if the light failed. The keepers at Cana Island had similar responsibility for the Eagle Bluff Light and the Baileys Harbor Range Lights, though they travelled by car instead of by boat.

In 1936 even more intricate electronic devices came to Sherwood Point. The dangerous Peshtigo Reef lay two miles out in Green Bay, off the mouth of the Peshtigo River, and ten miles northwest of Sherwood Point. Nineteenth century construction techniques were not advanced enough to build a lighthouse out in the bay, and the Lighthouse Board had stationed the *Peshtigo Reef Lightship* on the reef to warn mariners of the danger. Stram had been captain of the *Peshtigo Reef Lightship* from 1908 until 1913, before he was transferred to Cana Island. In 1935, the lightship was replaced by a light atop a white, conical steel tower seventy-two feet tall standing on a round, concrete crib; it also had a fog signal.

The light was operated by an astronomical clock that took account of the changes in the length of daylight hours during the year; the clock controlled the light at night, but, if the day got too dark or if the light failed to operate, a sun valve activated the emergency acetylene gas system.

The fog signal was controlled remotely from Sherwood Point; rather than pulling a rope to ring a bell in foggy weather as when he was captain of the lightship, Stram transmitted a tone from a tuning fork to a reed of the same calibration in a receiver at the Peshtigo Reef Light. The vibrations tripped a relay which operated the station's fog horn, and a transmitter in the tower broadcast the actual sound of the fog signal back to Sherwood Point so that Stram could be sure it was operating correctly. Once a week, regardless of weather, the keepers at Sherwood Point went to service the Peshtigo Reef Light. In good weather Stram often took visitors with him in the station's launch on the trip to the lighthouse. In 1938, the Lighthouse Bureau bought a new boathouse site on Sawyer Harbor with access to deeper water, since Stram needed a larger boat to make the weekly runs.

Like his predecessors, Stram was a dedicated keeper and took great pride in his job and his station. In 1938 he received the Efficiency Flag — the highest award that could be conferred on a keeper — for being the outstanding lighthouse keeper in the district, and he flew the flag from the station's flag pole throughout 1938. This seems to have been the first time that a Door County lighthouse had won the Efficiency Flag, although many had won superintendent's stars, a lower level of recognition. The award was no fluke, evidenced by the fact that in 1940 Stram received the commandant's efficiency star conferred by the U.S. Coast Guard; that honor required winning the district commander's efficiency star for three previous, consecutive years. Stram shared credit for the awards with his first assistant Anton Jessen and his second assistant E.J. Hennessy.[30]

In 1939 the US Coast Guard absorbed the Lighthouse Bureau. Civilian keepers were allowed either to remain or to join the Coast Guard, and Stram elected at first to remain a civilian. In spring 1940 the Coast Guard added a radio beacon to the other electronic equipment at Sherwood Point. This helped mariners to

Sherwood Point light, about 1940. The fog signal tower is on the extreme left and the addition to it was for radio equipment. Photo courtesy of the US Coast Guard.

establish their positions with much greater precision than previously, while at the same time reducing the need for lighthouses.

In July 1941, Stram, the last civilian keeper at Sherwood Point, entered the Coast Guard as a boatswain's mate; he was promoted to chief boatswain's mate on 1 November 1943. When Stram reached age 64 on 20 February 1944, he was placed on the retired list of the Coast Guard, though he remained on active duty until 16 July 1945, when he officially retired after serving as a keeper, afloat and ashore, for over forty-two years.[31]

After retirement, the Strams continued to live in Sturgeon Bay; they had bought a home at 605 Fifth Avenue. Stram soon became very involved in a number of community activities. He served as alderman and county supervisor from the city's first ward from 1948 until 1955, and for several years he was the deputy clerk of court. Stram was very interested in the history of Door County and helped to revive the Door County Historical Society. He was one of the driving forces in arranging for the society to acquire, restore, and operate the Eagle Bluff Light in Peninsula State Park; that facility allows thousands of visitors each year to share the experience that he and other Door County keepers lived. Stram also was chairman of the Door County Museum committee and was active in Post 72 of the American Legion and in the Independent Order of Odd Fellows. For over thirty years, he served as an elder and trustee of the Moravian Church in Sturgeon Bay. He attended both the morning and a special anniversary service at the church on Sunday 29 January 1961. The next day he did not feel well and checked himself into the Door County Memorial Hospital. He died there on Tuesday 31 January 1961 and was buried next to his wife, who had died in 1957, in Bayside Cemetery in Sturgeon Bay.[32]

The Coast Guard continued to operate the Sherwood Point Light, but, in the 1970s increasing budget pressures, a decline in commercial shipping, improved electronic navigational aids, and increased reliability of automated equipment caused the Coast Guard to automate many of the Great Lakes lights and to redeploy the manpower elsewhere. In September 1983, a hundred years after it began operating, the Coast Guard automated Sherwood Point Light. The station was not only the last Door County light to be automated, it was also the last manned lighthouse on the Great Lakes.

A light still shines out from the tower every night, but the radio beacon and fog horns have been removed from the fog signal tower; their functions are carried out by a light buoy marking Sherwood Point reef about a mile northwest of the station. Stanley, Cochems, and Stram are now long gone, but the proud tradition they established is still carried on. Rather than abandoning Sherwood Point to the elements, the Coast Guard continues to maintain the lighthouse and grounds for the use of its personnel while on leave.

Appendix A
Door County Lighthouse Keepers

POTTOWATOMIE LIGHT

David Corbin	January 1837 - December 1852
Mr. Cass	December 1852 - December 1853
Capt. Allen	December 1853 - July 1855
Jos. LeCuyer, Sr.	July 1855 - July 1857
Simon Allaird	July 1857 - February 1859
Frank Sawyer	February 1859 - August 1861
Martin Trobee	August 1861 - May 1865
Abraham Capers	May 1865 - March 1870
William C. Betts	March 1870 - May 1886
Jesse L. Miner	May 1886 - October 1898
Lewis Hutzler	October 1898 - June 1899
Lawrence Brown	June 1899 - June 1902
Charley Boshka	June 1902 - November 1911
Edward Cornell	November 1911 - 1928
John Fitzgerald	1928 - 1941
Ernest Lockhart	1941 - 1946

PORTE DES MORTS PASSAGE LIGHT - PLUM ISLAND

William Riggins	August 1849 - July 1857
William Shurtteffy	July 1857 - January(?) 1858

PORTE DES MORTS PASSAGE LIGHT - PILOT ISLAND

William Shurtteffy	January(?) 1858 - May 1859
Mathew Garey	May 1859 - March 1861
E.T. Wells	March 1861 - June 1863

John Kenard	June 1863 - January 1864
D.C. Read	January 1864 - October 1864
Jacob Stahl	October 1864 - June 1865
John Kenard	June 1865 - August 1866
Victor Rohn	August 1866 - September 1876
Emmanuel Davidson	October 1876 - March 1883
Peter Knudsen	March 1883 - July 1888
Nelson Knudsen	July 1888 - September 1889
Martin Knudsen	September 1889 - March 1897
Gottfried MS Hansen	March 1897 - February 1902
Charles Bavry	February 1902 - April 1906
Henry Bevry	April 1906 - 1913
Walter Otteson	1913 - 1923
Robert Young	
C.I. Haas	
Clarence Anderson	

BAILEYS HARBOR LIGHT

David Ward	February 1853 - September 1854
Michael Green	September 1854 - March 1855
Newton Bacon	March 1855 - January 1862
William Mitchell	January 1862 - August 1863
William Darling	August 1863 - December 1869

EAGLE BLUFF LIGHT

Henry Stanley	September 1868 - September 1883
William Duclon	September 1883 - December 1918
Peter Coughlin	January 1919 - September 1926

CHAMBERS ISLAND LIGHT

Lewis S. Williams	September 1868 - August 1889
Peter Knudsen	September 1889 - March 1891
Charles E. Young	March 1891 - November 1895
Soren Christianson	September 1895 - August 1900
Joseph Napeizinski	August 1900 - May 1906
Jens J. Rollefson	May 1906 - 1925
Claude Chapman	1925 - 1933
Alfred Cornell	1933 - 1942

BAILEYS HARBOR RANGE LIGHTS

Fabian Trudell	December 1869 - September 1872
Marcus Shaler	September 1872 - April 1875
Joseph Harris, Jr.	April 1875 - May 1881
Hans L. Hanson	May 1881 - July 1882
George Larson	August 1882 - March 1888
John Millidge	March 1888 - May 1896
Henry Gattie	May 1896 - September 1923

CANA ISLAND LIGHT

William Jackson	November 1869 - November 1872
Julius Warren	November 1872 - November 1875
William Sanderson	November 1875 - January 1891
Thomas Brown	January 1891 - April 1913
Conrad Stram	April 1913 - March 1918
Oscar Knudson	March 1918 - March 1924
Clifford Sanderson	April 1924 - July 1933
Ross Wright	July 1933 - June 1941

Dunlap Reef Range Lights

Graham Henry	September 1881 - July 1882
Joseph Harris, Jr.	July 1882 - April 1890
Clifford W. Sanderson	April 1890 - April 1924

Sturgeon Bay Canal Lights

Rufus M. Wright	July 1882 - October 1886
Charles O. Chapman	October 1886 - May 1910
Charles Bavry	November 1910 - 1921
Charles Bavry	July 1926 - March 1927
Conrad Stram	March 1927 - June 1933
Claude Chapman	June 1933 - November 1933
John Trucker	1934 - 1940

Sherwood Point Light

Henry Stanley	September 1883 - October 1895
William Cochems	November 1895 - July 1933
Conrad Stram	July 1933 - 1945

Plum Island Range Lights

Martin Knudsen	March 1897 - August 1899
Hans Hanson	August 1899 - August 1905
Charles E. Young	August 1905 - July 1907
Joseph Boshka	July 1907 - November 1911
Charley Boshka	November 1911 - 1925
Oscar Johnson	1925 - 1933
Clayton Kinkaide	1933 - 1939

Endnotes

Chapter 2: Pottowatomie Light — Rock Island

1. *In the Supreme Court of the United States,* October Term, 1925; Original #19, In Equity, Brief of the Defendant, State of Wisconsin (Judd and Detweiler: Washington, DC, 1925), pp. 158-60.

2. *Statement of Appropriations, Etc., from March 4, 1789 to June 30, 1882,* published 1886, Records Group #26, National Archives.

3. Jackson Kemper, D.D., "Journal of an Episcopalian Missionary's Tour to Green Bay, 1834," *Wisconsin Historical Collections,* Vol. XIV (Madison, WI: Democrat Publishing Co., 1898), pp. 441-42.

4. *Documents for the Construction of the Original 1836 Pottowatomie Light,* RG #26, NA.

5. *Ibid.*

6. *Ibid.*

7. Jesse Miner, "History of the Island of the Pottowatomie, Rock Island," typewritten manuscript, State Historical Society of Wisconsin, Madison, WI. p. 17.

8. J. Whitcomb, Commissioner, General Land Office, to S. Pleasanton, Fifth Auditor, Treasury Department, 9 June 1840, RG #26, NA.

9. Inspector W.D. Wilson to Pleasanton, 24 May 1841, Wisconsin Territorial Papers.

10. Inspector John McReynolds to Pleasanton, 8 July 1845, Wisconsin Territorial Papers.

11. McReynolds to Pleasanton, 20 November 1846, Wisconsin Territorial Papers.

12. McReynolds to Pleasanton, 10 July 1847, Wisconsin Territorial Papers.

13. Hjalmar R. Holand, *Old Peninsula Days,* (Ellison Bay, WI: Wm Caxton Ltd, 1990 reprint of 1925 (1st) edition), p. 70.

14. Miner, pp. 8-9.

15. 1850 U.S. Census, Wisconsin, Door County, Town of Washington.

16. Conan B. Eaton, *Rock Island* (Sturgeon Bay, WI: Bayprint, rev ed, 1979), pp. 16-17.

17. Official List of Keepers, Pottowatomie Light, RG #26, NA.

18. *Description of Buildings, Premises, Equipment, Etc., Pottowatomie Light Station, Rock Island, Lake Michigan, Wisconsin,* 19 September 1909, RG #26, NA; Lighthouses 1859, pp. 80-81, RG #26, NA; *List of Light-Houses, Lighted Beacons, and Floating Lights of the United States,* corrected to January 1859, pp. 80-81, RG #26, NA; 1912 Light List, pp. 194-95, RG #26, NA.

19. Official List; Conan B. Eaton *Washington Island, 1836-1876* (Sturgeon Bay, WI: Bayprint, rev ed, 1980), pp. 24, 33.

20. *Door County Advocate,* 21 September 1882, p. 2.

21. *DCA,* 3 June 1886, p. 2.

22. *DCA,* 5 December 1930, pp. 1, 6; Anne T. Whitney, *Let's Talk About Washington Island, 1850 - 1950* (Chicago: Techni-Graphics/Graphic Dimensions, 1973), pp. 47-48.

23. *DCA,* 23 July 1887, p. 2 and 25 August 1888, p. 2.

24. *DCA,* 29 September 1888, p. 2 and 13 October 1888, p. 3.

25. Whitney, p. 64.

26. *DCA,* 7 December 1889, p. 3.

27. *DCA,* 23 March 1895, p. 8.

28. *DCA,* 30 December 1915, p. 1.

29. *DCA,* 22 July 1899, p. 8; Official List, RG #26, NA.

30. *DCA,* 8 June 1901, p. 3.

31. *Annual Report of the Light-House Board of the United States, 1905* (Washington, DC: Government Printing Office, 1905), p. 118: *Description of Buildings,* RG #26, NA.

32. *DCA,* 23 September 1905, p. 1.

33. Eaton, *Rock Island,* pp. 27 - 30.

34. 1920 US Census, Wis, Door County, Washington Twnshp; *DCA,* 23 October 1953, p. 2.

35. Interview, Kirby Foss, Washington Island, WI, 3 July 1992.

36. Foss.

Chapter 3: Plum Island Lights

1. Robert Shrock, "Geology of Washington Island," *Transactions of the Wisconsin Academy of Sciences, Arts, and Letters,* Vol. 32 (Madison, WI: Wisconsin Academy of Sciences, Arts, and Letters, 1940), pp. 220-21.

2. *In the Supreme Court of the United States,* October Term, 1925; Original #19, In Equity, Brief of the Defendant, State of Wisconsin (Judd and Detweiler: Washington, DC, 1925), pp. 184-85.

3. Wisconsin Brief, p. 183.

4. 1850 U.S. Census, Wisconsin, Door County, Town of Washington; Official List of Keepers, Porte des Morts Passage Light, Records Group #26, National Archives.

5. *Green Bay Advocate,* 5 April 1856.

6. Hjalmar R. Holand, "The Forgotten Lighthouse," *Peninsula Historical Review,* Vol. II, No. 1 (Sturgeon Bay, WI: Door County Advocate, January 1928), p. 68.

7. *Extract from Annual Report,* 9 Eng. 30, June 1891, Vol. 895, p. 804, RG #26, NA.

8. Hjalmar R. Holand, *Old Peninsula Days,* (Ellison Bay, WI: Wm Caxton Ltd, 1990 reprint of 1925 (1st) edition), pp. 106–111.

9. *Door County Advocate,* 1 June 1889, p. 1.

10. *Annual Report of the Light-House Board of the United States, 1890* (Washington, DC: Government Printing Office, 1890), p. 136.

11. *DCA,* 21 September 1895, p. 8.

12. *Annual Report, 1897,* pp. 135-36; *DCA,* 8 August 1896, p. 8 and 22 August 1896, p. 8.

13. *DCA,* 24 April 1897, p. 1.

14. *DCA,* 5 August 1899, p. 1.

15. *DCA,* 30 July 1943, p. 1; Martin Arthur and Evelyn Knudsen, *A Gleam Across the Wave, The Biography of Martin Nicolai Knudsen* (privately printed, 1948), p. 63.

16. *DCA,* 12 October 1923, p. 1.

17. *DCA,* 21 October 1938, p. 1.

18. *DCA,* 13 February 1920, p. 12.

19. *DCA,* 16 October 1925, p. 3 and 7 September 1945, p. 1.

20. Interview, Mrs. Helen Erickson Carlson and Mrs. Joan Erickson Milaeger, Sister Bay, WI, 23 July 1992.

Chapter 4: Pilot Island

1. *Statement of Appropriations, Etc., from March 4, 1789 to June 30, 1882,* published 1886, Records Group #26, National Archives; Porte des Morts Light Station, General Land Office, Department of the Interior, 30 June 1882, RG #26, NA.; Pilot Island Survey, A.R. Flint, 26 October 1883, RG #26, NA.

2. Official List of Light Keepers, Porte des Morts Light, RG #26, NA.

3. Hjalmar R. Holand, *History of Door County, Wisconsin,* Vol. I (Ellison Bay, WI: Wm Caxton Ltd, 1993 reprint of original 1917 edition), p. 257.

4. J.B. Mansfield, *History of the Great Lakes,* Vol. I (Chicago, IL: J.H. Beers and Company, 1899, reprint Freshwater Press, Cleveland, OH, 1972), p. 369.

5. *Door County Advocate,* 11 November 1875, p. 3; Official List, RG #26, NA.

6. *DCA,* 31 March 1911, p. 3; Martin Arthur and Evelyn Knudsen, *A Gleam Across the Wave, The Biography of Martin Nicolai Knudsen* (privately printed, 1948), pp. 3-6, 11, and 13-14.

7. *DCA,* 30 October 1879, p. 3; 13 November 1879, p. 3; and 21 October 1881, p. 3.

8. *DCA,* 4 December 1879, p. 3.

9. Knudsen, pp. 32-34.

10. Interview, Kirby Foss, Washington Island, 3 July 1992.

11. *DCA,* 1 July 1880, p. 3.

12. Knudsen, p. 35.

13. *DCA,* 31 March 1911, p. 3 and 13 January 1922, p. 1.

14. Pilot Island Survey.

15. *DCA,* 17 January 1884, p. 2 and 31 January 1884, p. 2.

16. *DCA,* 3 March 1888, p. 3.

17. *DCA,* 21 July 1888, p. 3; 14 July 1888, p. 3; and 26 December 1891, p. 5.

18. List of Keepers.

19. List of Keepers; Knudsen, pp. 49-49; *DCA,* 7 December 1889, p. 8; 14 December 1889, p. 8; and 11 January 1890, p. 8.

20. Ben Fagg, *DCA,* 6 September 1890, p. 8.

21. Knudsen, pp. 49-50.

22. *DCA,* 21 May 1892, p. 8; Knudsen, p. 52.

23. Anne T. Whitney, *Let's Talk About Washington Island, 1850-1950* (Chicago, IL: Techni-Graphics/Graphic Dimensions, 1973), pp. 52-53.

24. Walter M. and Mary K. Hirthe, *Schooner Days in Door County* (Minneapolis, MN: Voyageur Press, 1986), p. 38.

25. *DCA,* 12 November 1892, p. 5; Knudsen, pp. 58 and 62; Hirthe, pp. 35-36.

26. *DCA,* 24 December 1892, p. 5; 8 April 1893, p. 1; and 19 August 1893, p. 1.

27. *DCA,* 21 October 1938, p. 1.

28. *DCA,* 29 December 1894, p. 4.

29. *DCA,* 3 August 1895, p. 5; 21 September 1895, p. 8; 28 December 1895, p. 5; 1 February 1896, p. 5; 14 March 1896, p. 5; and 13 June 1896, p. 5.

30. *DCA,* 25 December 1931, p. 10; Whitney, p. 49.

31. *DCA,* 25 December 1931, p. 10.

32. List of Keepers.

33. *Annual Report of the Light-House Board of the United States* (Washington, DC: Government Printing Office). 1904, p. 119 and 1905, p. 117.

34. *DCA,* 15 April 1958, p. 2.

35. Interview, Mrs. Marylou Trucker Sanders, Sturgeon Bay, WI, 17 October 1993.

36. *DCA,* 25 October 1915, p. 2.

37. Interview, Mrs. Carolyn Anderson Jessen, Washington Island, WI, 3 July 1992.

38. Interview, Eldron Ellefson, Washington Island, WI, 3 July 1992.

Chapter 5: Baileys Harbor Lights

1. Roy Lukes, *The Ridges Sanctuary, Its History, Geology, Plants and Animals* (Baileys Harbor, WI: The Door Reminder, 1988), pp. 53-56; Hjalmar R. Holand, *History of Door County,* Vol. I (Ellison Bay, WI: Wm Caxton Ltd, 1993 reprint of original 1917 edition), p. 257.

2. Official List of Light Keepers, Baileys Harbor Light, Records Group #26, National Archives; *Door County Democrat,* 10 September 1915, p. 12.

3. Extract from the Annual Report for the 11th District for 1867, RG #26, NA; *Statement of Appropriations, Etc., from March 4, 1789 to June 30, 1882,* published 1886, RG #26, NA; *Questionnaire Govt. Owned Real Estate,* 1 April 1930, RG #26, NA.

4. *Door County Democrat,* 10 September 1915, p. 12.

5. Lukes, p. 24.

6. *Door County Advocate,* 31 March 1870, p. 4.

7. *DCA,* 11 February 1875, p. 3.

8. List of Keepers.

9. *DCA,* 9 March 1876, p. 3 and 27 April 1876, p. 3.

10. *DCA,* 22 August 1878, p. 3.

11. *DCA,* 7 July 1881, p. 3.

12. *DCA,* 19 January 1892, p. 3 and 30 August 1890, p. 5; List of Keepers.

13. *DCA,* 2 November 1882, p. 3 and 14 June 1883, p. 3.

14. *DCA,* 3 July 1884, p. 3.

15. *DCA,* 2 September 1886, p. 3 and 3 March 1887, p. 3.

16. *DCA,* 31 December 1887, p. 2.

17. *DCA,* 24 March 1888, p. 2 and 18 November 1899, p. 8.

18. *DCA,* 7 January 1893, p. 8.

19. *DCA,* 31 August p. 8; *Description of Buildings, Premises, Equipment, Etc., Baileys Harbor Range Lights,* 14 June 1909, RG #26, NA.

20. *DCA,* 9 November 1895, p. 8 and 4 June 1904, p. 8.

21. *DCA,* 5 September 1896, p. 5.

22. *DCA,* 5 September 1896, p. 8.

23. *DCA,* 6 March 1897, p. 8 and 24 April 1897, p. 8.

24. *Description of Buildings.*

25. *DCA,* 13 November 1897, p. 8.

26. *DCA,* 9 December 1899, p. 8.

27. *DCA,* 23 February 1901, p. 8 and 2 March 1901, p. 8.

28. *Description of Buildings.*

29. *DCA,* 30 April 1948, part 3, p. 1.

30. *Revocable Lease Baileys Harbor Lighthouse Dwelling,* 8 June 1937, RG #26, NA.

31. *Revocable Lease Baileys Harbor Light Reservation,* 19 January 1934, RG #26, NA; Lukes, p. 134.

32. Lukes, pp. 92-93 and 111-12.

Chapter 6: Cana Island Light

1. *Door County Advocate,* 3 February 1870, p. 4 and 16 September 1869, p. 4; *Description of the Buildings, Premises, Equipment, Etc. at Cana Island Light Station, Wisconsin,* 12 December 1911, Records Group #26, National Archives; Excerpts from *Annual Report of the Light-House Board of the United States, 1868, 1869, and 1870,* RG #26, NA.

2. *DCA,* 4 January 1872, p. 3.

3. *DCA,* 2 November 1871, p. 3.

4. *DCA,* 11 November 1875, p. 3 and 22 August 1924, p. 3.

5. *DCA,* 16 June 1922, p. 1; Hjalmar Holand, *History of Door County Wisconsin,* Vol. II (Ellison Bay, WI: Wm Caxton Ltd, 1993 reprint of original 1917 edition) p. 232; 1880 U.S. Census, Wisconsin, Door County, Town of Baileys Harbor.

6. *DCA,* 17 April 1877, p. 3.

7. *DCA,* 28 October 1880, p. 3.

8. *DCA,* 22 November 1880, p. 3.

9. *DCA,* 26 July 1883, p. 3.

10. *DCA,* 4 October 1883, p. 2; *Annual Report of the Light-House Board of the United States* (Washington, DC: Government Printing Office, 1884), p. 75.

11. *DCA,* 29 November 1883, p. 2.

12. *DCA,* 10 January 1884, p. 3; 17 January 1884, p. 3; and 24 March 1884, p. 3.

13. *DCA,* 14 July 1888, p. 2; Official List of Light Keepers, Cana Island, RG #26, NA.

14. *DCA,* 3 May 1890, p. 5 and 12 July 1890; p. 5; *Broad Report, 1890,* p. 136.

15. *DCA,* 21 January 1891, p. 5.

16. *DCA,* 9 May 1891, p. 5 and 16 June 1922, p. 1.

17. 1900 US Census, Wisconsin, Door County, Town of Baileys Harbor; List of Keepers; Letter, Clyde Brown, Jr., to author, 19 August 1993.

18. *DCA,* 14 October 1894, p. 5; 21 October 1893, p. 8; 16 December 1893, p. 5; 10 February 1894, p. 5; Walter M. and Mary K. Hirthe, *Schooner Days in Door County* (Minneapolis, MN: Voyageur Press, 1986), pp. 45-47.

19. *DCA,* 23 June 1894, p. 8.

20. *DCA,* 22 August 1896, p. 5.

21. *DCA,* 1 April 1899, p. 8; *Description of Buildings.*

22. *DCA,* 20 May 1899, p. 1.

23. *DCA,* 13 May 1899, p. 1 and 27 May 1899, p. 1.

24. *DCA,* 16 December 1899, p. 8.

25. *DCA,* 22 August 1941, p. 2.

26. Interview, Mrs. Ruby Weiss Cornell, Baileys Harbor, WI, 15 April 1992.

27. Brown, 19 August 1993.

28. Letter of Conrad Stram, 8 April 1908, personal collection Rick Stram.

29. Inspector Stoddard to Conrad Stram, 2 November 1917, Stram collection.

30. Interview, Mrs. Marion Augustine, Baileys Harbor, WI, 22 July 1991.

31. *Ibid.*

32. Cornell, 15 April 1992.

33. Arthur C. and Lucy F. Frederickson, *Ships and Shipwrecks in Door County, Wisconsin,* Vol. 2. (Appleton, WI: Clark Willick, 1963), pp. 55-58.

34. Interview, Mrs. Marion Augustine, Baileys Harbor, WI, 24 July 1992.

35. Arthur C. and Lucy F. Frederickson, *Ships and Shipwrecks in Door County, Wisconsin,* Vol 2. (Appleton, WI: Clark Willick, 1961), pp. 22-23.

36. *DCA,* 21 September 1945, part 3, p. 1 and 25 August 1939, p. 2.

37. *DCA,* 9 January 1942, p. 1.

38. *DCA,* 25 August 1939, p. 2.

39. *DCA,* 21 September 1945, part 3, p. 1.

40. Interview, Barbara Smith, Milwaukee, WI, 9 September 1994.

Chapter 7: Eagle Bluff Light

1. *Statement of Appropriations, Etc. from March 4, 1789 to June 30, 1882,* published 1886, Records Group #26, National Archives; Excerpts from *Annual Report of the Light-House Board of the United States* (Washington, DC: Government Printing Office), 1865 and 1866.

2. *Description of Buildings, Premises, Equipment, Etc., Eagle Bluff Light Station, Wisconsin,* 21 June 1909, RG #26, NA.

3. *Door County Advocate,* 19 October 1895, p. 4 and 13 November 1915, p. 1.

4. 1870 US Census, Wis, Door County, Gibraltar Township; *DCA,* 30 June 1870, p. 3.

5. Francis Badtke, *Eagle Lighthouse* (Sturgeon Bay, WI: Door County Publishing Company, 1964), p. 13.

6. *DCA,* 17 June 1880, p. 3.

7. *DCA,* 8 July 1880, p. 3.

8. *The United States Biographical Dictionary and Portrait Gallery of Eminent and Self-Made Men,* Wisconsin Volume (Chicago, Cincinnati, and New York: American Biographical Publishing Company, 1877), pp. 212-13.

9. *Green Bay Advocate,* 17 November 1881, p. 3; *DCA,* 17 November 1881, p. 2.

10. *DCA,* 18 December 1881, p. 3 and 9 March 1892, p. 3.

11. *DCA,* 10 September 1922, pp. 1 & 7; Craig Jones, *Duclon Genealogy,* manuscript, Sturgeon Bay Public Library, Sturgeon Bay, WI; Edward and Lois Schreiber, eds., *Fish Creek Voices* (Sister Bay, WI: Wm Caxton Limited, 1990), p. 183.

12. Schreiber, p. 184.

13. *DCA,* 17 December 1882, p. 2.

14. Schreiber, p. 184.

15. Arthur C. and Lucy F. Frederickson, *Ships and Shipwrecks in Door County, Wisconsin,* Vol 1. (Appleton, WI: Clark Willick, 1961), p. 8.

16. *DCA,* 15 December 1894, p. 1.

17. Badtke, p. 20; Schreiber, p. 184.

18. *DCA,* 9 January 1893, p. 8.

19. *DCA,* 4 April 1896, p. 5 and 11 April 1896, p. 8.

20. *DCA,* 15 January 1896, p. 8.

21. 1900 U.S. Census, Wisconsin, Door County, Town of Gibraltar; Duclon Genealogy.

22. *Board Reports,* 1893, p. 132; 1898, p. 150; 1899, p. 147; 1900, p. 144; *Description.*

23. Badtke, p. 31; Schreiber, p. 186.

24. *DCA,* 20 September 1922, p. 6 and 10 September 1926, pp. 1 & 7.

25. 1920 U.S. Census, Wisconsin, Door County, Gibraltar Township.

26. *DCA,* 16 April 1926, p. 6.

27. *DCA,* 24 September 1926, p. 3.

28. *DCA,* 12 October 1934, p. 1.

29. Commissioner of Lighthouses to Secretary of Commerce, 2 March 1926, RG #26, NA; Revocable License Eagle Bluff Reservation, 9 May 1936, RG #26, NA.

30. Badtke, pp. 33-47.

Chapter 8: Chambers Island Light

1. *In the Supreme Court of the United States,* October Term 1925; Original #19, In Equity, Brief of The Defendant, State of Wisconsin (Washington, DC: Judd and Detweiler, 1925), pp. 185.

2. Hjalmar R. Holand, *History of Door County, Wisconsin,* Vol. II (Ellison Bay, WI: Wm Caxton Ltd, 1993 reprint of original 1917 edition), pp. 329-30.

3. Copy of deed dated 8 May 1867, Lewis S. and Anna B. Williams to U.S., Chambers Island, RG #26, NA; Col. W.F. Reynolds to Rear Admiral W.B. Shubrick, 7 November 1866, RG #26, NA; *Statement of Appropriations, Etc., from March 4, 1789 to June 30, 1882,* published 1886, RG #26, NA; Excerpts from *Annual Report Light-House Board of the United States* (Washington, DC: Government Printing Office), 1865 and 1866.

4. *Door County Advocate,* 11 June 1868, p. 4 and 8 October 1868, p. 4; *Description of Buildings, Premises, Etc., Chambers Island,* 19 November 1906, RG #26, NA.

5. *DCA,* 10 July 1873, p. 3.

6. *DCA,* 20 August 1885, p. 2.

7. *DCA,* 28 January 1875, p. 3 and 25 January 1877, p. 3.

8. *DCA,* 19 December 1878, p. 3.

9. *DCA,* 2 February 1889, p. 2; 24 August 1889, p. 5; 21 September 1889, p. 5; 27 September 1890, p. 5.

10. *DCA,* 11 March 1893, p. 8 and 30 September 1893, p. 8.

11. *DCA,* 22 December 1894, p. 5 and 2 February 1895, p. 5.

12. 1900 U.S. Census, Wisconsin, Door County, Gibraltar Township.

13. *Description.*

14. *DCA,* 8 October 1898, p. 8; 23 June 1900, p. 1; 18 August 1900, p. 1; 22 September 1900, p. 1.

15. *Description.*

16. Interview, Mrs. Doris Hanson Anderson, Sister Bay, WI, 24 July 1992.

Chapter 9: Dunlap Reef Range Lights

1. *Annual Report of the Light-House Board of the United States* (Washington, DC: Government Printing Office, 1881), p. 63.

2. *Door County Advocate,* 27 April 1882, p. 3.

3. *DCA,* 22 November 1883, p. 3.

4. *DCA,* 14 July 1884, p. 3.

5. *DCA,* 30 July 1885, p. 3.

6. *DCA,* 24 September 1885, p. 3.

7. *DCA,* 25 November 1885, p. 3 and 15 April 1886, p. 3.

8. Carl R. Christianson, *Ship Building and Boat Building in Sturgeon Bay, Wisconsin From the Beginning to 1985* (Sturgeon Bay, WI: The Print Shop, 1989), pp. 8, 10, 11, and 12; *DCA,* 14 September 1910, p. 5 and 2 November 1901, p. 5.

9. *Board Reports,* 1888, p. 123 and 1889, p. 131.

10. *DCA,* 30 March 1916, p. 1 and 25 May 1916, p. 1.

11. *Board Reports,* 1890, p. 136 and 1891, p. 127.

12. *DCA,* 24 August 1895, p. 5; 31 August 1895, p. 5; 18 April 1896, p. 1.

13. *Board Reports,* 1902, p. 177 and 1907, p. 111.

14. *Board Reports,* 1922, p. 76 and 1924, p. 76.

Chapter 10: Sturgeon Bay Canal Lights

1. *Door County Advocate,* 8 August 1872, p. 3; 25 December 1879, p. 3.

2. *DCA,* 8 February 1880, p. 3; 27 October 1881, p. 3; 3 November 1881, p. 3; 1 December 1881, p. 3.

3. *DCA,* 20 March 1882, p. 3 and 14 May 1882, p. 3.

4. *DCA,* 27 April 1882, p. 3.

5. *DCA,* 4 May 1889, p. 3.

6. Joseph Harris, Sr. to E.S. Minor, March 1883, Joseph Harris Papers, Archives, State Historical Society of Wisconsin, Madison, WI.

7. *DCA,* 7 September 1882, p. 3.

8. *DCA,* 14 May 1883, p. 3.

9 *DCA,* 22 May 1884, p. 3; 24 July 1884, p. 3; 14 August 1884, p. 3.

10. *Door County Democrat,* 3 June 1910, p. 5; *DCA,* 27 April 1937, p. 3.

11. *DCA,* 11 September 1884, p. 3.

12. *DCA,* 21 May 1885, p. 3 and 17 September 1885, p. 3.

13. *DCA,* 20 May 1886, p. 3 & 21 October 1886, p. 3; *Annual Report Light-House Board of the United States* (Washington, DC: Government Printing Office, 1887), pp. 80-81.

14. *DCA,* 21 October 1886, p. 3.

15. *DCA,* 11 November 1886, p. 2; 17 February 1887, p. 3; 7 March 1888, p. 3; 26 May 1888, p. 2; 4 May 1889, p. 3.

16. *DCA,* 22 July 1886, p. 2.

17. *DCA,* 25 November 1886, p. 3; 30 December 1886, p. 3; 27 March 1887, p. 3.

18. *DCA,* 1 October 1887, p. 3 and 19 January 1889, p. 3.

19. *Board Report,* 1890, p. 135; *DCA,* 16 April 1890, p. 5.

20. *Board Report,* 1892, p. 134; *DCA,* 26 March 1892, p. 5; 14 January 1893, p. 5; 13 October 1894, p. 5.

21. *Board Report,* 1894, p. 1440.

22. Capt. George A. Zinn, Corps of Engineers, Milwaukee, WI to Comdr. James H. Dayton, U.S. Navy, Inspector 9th Light-House District, Chicago, IL, 16 June 1896, Records Group #26, National Archives.

23. *DCA,* 16 May 1896, p. 5; 25 March 1927, p. 1; 9 August 1897, p. 1.

24. *DCA,* 14 May 1898, p. 1 and 16 July 1898, p. 1.

25. *DCA,* 13 December 1898, p. 1 and 14 January 1899, p. 1.

26. *DCA,* 18 March 1899, p. 1 and 8 April 1899, p. 1.

27. *DCA,* 22 April 1899, p. 5; 29 July 1899, p. 5, 16 June 1900, p. 1.

28. *DCA,* 25 August 1900, p. 1; 29 September 1900, p. 1; 9 January 1900, p. 1; *Board Reports,* 1900, p. 143.

29. *DCA,* 4 January 1902, p. 1 and 1 March 1901, p. 5.

30. *DCA,* 2 May 1903, p. 1; 9 May 1903, p. 1; 11 July 1903, p. 9; 5 September 1903, p. 1; *Board Reports,* 1903, p. 60; 1904, p. 119.

31. *Board Reports,* 1903, p. 60; 1904, p. 119.

32. 1910 U.S. Census, Wisconsin, Door County, Township of Sturgeon Bay.

33. *DCA,* 7 January 1905, p. 1; *Board Reports,* 1905, p. 117.

34. *Door County Democrat,* 3 June 1910, p. 5.

35. Interview, Mrs. Marylou Trucker Sanders, Sturgeon Bay, WI, 17 October 1993.

36. *DCA,* 25 March 1927, p. 1.

37. *DCA,* 10 November 1933, p. 1.

38. Sanders, 17 October 1993.

39. *Ibid.*

Chapter 11: Sherwood Point Light

1. *Door County Advocate,* 25 October 1883, p. 3.

2. *Ibid.*

3. *DCA,* 7 September 1882, p. 3.

4. *DCA,* 15 February 1883, p. 3.

5. Circuit Court, Door County, Sherwood Point, Records Group #26, National Archives.

6. *DCA,* 17 May 1883, p. 3 and 14 June 1883, p. 3; *Annual Report of the Light-House Board of the United States* (Washington, DC: Government Printing Office, 1883), p. 78.

7. *Board Report,* 1884, p. 75; *DCA,* 6 September 1883, p. 3.

8. *DCA,* 4 September 1884, p. 3.

9. *DCA,* 11 December 1884, p. 3.

10. *DCA,* 19 March 1885, p. 3.

11. *DCA,* 17 September 1887, p. 3.

12. *DCA,* 24 August 1889, p. 5.

13. *DCA,* 4 October 1890, p. 5.

14. *Board Report,* 1892, p. 139.

15. *DCA,* 26 August 1893, p. 5.

16. *DCA,* 1 July 1893, p. 8.

17. *DCA,* 9 September 1893, p. 5; 9 December 1893, p. 5; 19 May 1894, p. 3.

18. Official List of Keepers, Sherwood Point, RG #26, NA.

19. *DCA,* 19 October 1895, p. 4.

20. *DCA,* 26 October 1895, p. 5.

21. *DCA,* 13 November 1915, p. 1 and 28 October 1916, p. 1.

22. *DCA,* 16 January 1897, p. 1.

23. *Board Report,* 1898, p. 150.

24. *DCA,* 30 June 1933, pp. 1 & 5.

25. *DCA,* 26 June 1912, p. 1.

26. *DCA,* 24 August 1928, pp. 1 & 4.

27. Interview, Mrs. Eunice Schopf, Sturgeon Bay, WI, 10 May 1992.

28. *DCA,* 30 June 1933, p. 1 & 6 August 1953, p. 2.

29. Conrad Stram to Alfred Schopf, 12 March 1934, personal collection Rick Stram.

30. *DCA,* 4 February 1938, p. 1, 6 November 1940, p. 25; *Milwaukee Journal,* 15 March 1966, p. 1.

31. Ludwig Wedemeyer to D.G.G.O., Cleveland, 9th Naval District, 4 January 1944; S.H. Clark to CO C.G. Station, Sturgeon Bay, WI, 19 January 1944; E. Zoole to C.B.M. Conrad Andrew Stram, 27 June 1945, all from Rick Stram collection.

32. *DCA,* 2 February 1961, p. 1.

Bibliography

Books, Journals, & Manuscripts

Badtke, Francis. *Eagle Lighthouse.* Sturgeon Bay, WI: Door County Publishing Co., 1964.

Christianson, Carl R. *Ship Building and Boat Building in Sturgeon Bay, Wisconsin From the Beginning to 1985.* Sturgeon Bay, WI: The Print Shop, 1989.

Eaton, Conan B. *Rock Island.* 1979 ed. Sturgeon Bay, WI: Bayprint, Inc., 1969.

Washington Island, 1863-1876. 1980 ed. Sturgeon Bay, WI: Bayprint, Inc., 1972.

Frederickson, Arthur C. and Lucy F. *Ships and Shipwrecks in Door County.* Vol. 1. Appleton, WI: Clark Willick, 1961.

Ships and Shipwrecks in Door County. Vol. 2. Appleton, WI: Clark Willick, 1963.

Hirthe, Walter M. and Mary K. *Schooner Days in Door County.* Minneapolis, MN: Voyageur Press, 1968.

Holand, Hjalmar R. "The Forgotten Lighthouse." *Peninsula Historical Review, 1927-30.* Sturgeon Bay, WI: Door County Historical Society, 1930.

History of Door County Wisconsin, 2 Vols. Chicago, IL: S.J. Clarke Publishing Co., 1917; 1993 reprint by Wm Caxton Ltd, Ellison Bay, WI.

Old Peninsula Days. Ellison Bay WI: Wm Caxton Ltd, 1990 reprint of 1925 (1st) edition.

Hyde, Charles K. *The Northern Lights.* Lansing, MI: Two Peninsula Press, 1986.

Jones, Craig. *Duclon Genealogy.* Typewritten manuscript, Sturgeon Bay Public Library, Sturgeon Bay, WI.

Kemper, Jackson. "Journal of an Episcopalian Missionary's Tour to Green Bay." *Wisconsin Historical Collections,* Vol. XIV. Madison, WI: Democrat Publishing Co., 1898.

Knudsen, Martin Arthur and Evelyn. *A Gleam Across the Wave, The Biography of Martin Nicolai Knudsen.* Privately printed, 1948.

Lukes, Roy. *The Ridges Sanctuary, Its History, Geology, Plants and Animals.* Sister Bay, WI: The Door Reminder, 1988.

Mansfield, J. B. *History of the Great Lakes,* Vol. I. Chicago: J. H. Beers and Company, 1899; reprint Freshwater Press, Cleveland, Ohio, 1972.

Miner, Jesse. "History of the Island of the Pottowatomie, Rock Island." Typewritten manuscript, State Historical Society of Wisconsin, Madison, WI.

Shrock, Robert. "Geology of Washington Island." *Transactions of the Wisconsin Academy of Sciences, Arts, and Letters,* Vol. 32. Madison, WI: Academy of Sciences, Arts, and Letters, 1940.

Schreiber, Edward and Lois, eds. *Fish Creek Voices: An Oral History of A Door County Village.* Sister Bay, WI: Wm Caxton Ltd, 1990.

The United States Biographical Dictionary and Portrait Gallery of Eminent and Self-Made Men, Wisconsin Volume. Chicago, Cincinnati, and New York: American Biographical Publishing Co., 1877.

Whitney, Anne T. *Let's Talk About Washington Island, 1850-1950.* Chicago: Techni-Graphics/Graphic Dimensions, 1973.

Government Documents

Annual Report of the Light-House Board of the United States. Washington, DC: Government Printing Office, 1865–1905.

In the Supreme Court of the United States, October Term, 1925. Original #19, In Equity Brief of the Defendant, State of Wisconsin. Washington, DC: Judd and Detweiler, 1925.

Keepers Logs — all or part of the following: Pottowatomie Light, Pilot Island Light, Plum Island Range Lights, Cana Island Light, Baileys Harbor Range Lights, Eagle Bluff Light, and Sherwood Point Light.

National Archives — Records Group # 26.

United States Bureau of the Census. *United States Census 1850, 1870, 1900, 1910, and 1920.* Manuscript copy, State Historical Society of Wisconsin, Madison, WI.

Wisconsin Territorial Papers, 1841-46. State Historical Society of Wisconsin, Madison, WI.

Interviews

Anderson, Mrs. Doris Hanson. Sister Bay, WI. 24 July 1992.

Augustine, Mrs. Marion. Baileys Harbor, WI. 22 July 1991 and 24 July 1992.

Carlson, Mrs. Helen Erickson & Mrs. Joan Erickson Milaeger, Sister Bay, WI. 23 July 1992.

Cornell, Mrs. Ruby Weiss. Baileys Harbor, WI. 15 April 1992.

Ellefson, Mr. Eldron. Washington Island. 3 July 1992.

Foss, Mr. Kirby, Washington Island. 3 July 1992.

Jessen, Mrs. Carolyn Anderson. Washington Island. 3 July 1992.

Sanders, Mrs. Marylou Trucker. Sturgeon Bay, WI. 17 October 1993.

Schopf, Mrs. Eunice, Sturgeon Bay, WI. 10 May 1992.

Smith, Mrs. Barbara. Milwaukee, WI. 9 September 1994.

Letters

Brown, Clyde Jr. to author, 19 August 1993.

Harris, Joseph Sr. to E. S. Minor, March 1883. Joseph Harris Papers, Archives, State Historical Society of Wisconsin, Madison, WI.

Stram, Rick — personal collection of Conrad Stram's letters.

Newspapers

Door County Advocate

Door County Democrat

Green Bay Advocate

Milwaukee Journal